D0325673

10/23
STRAND PRICE
$ 5.00

A TRUST
BETRAYED

A TRUST
BETRAYED

The Untold Story of
Camp Lejeune and the
Poisoning of Generations of
Marines and Their Families

MIKE MAGNER

A MERLOYD LAWRENCE BOOK
DA CAPO PRESS
A Member of the Perseus Books Group

Copyright © 2014 by Mike Magner

All rights reserved. No part of this publication may be reproduced, stored in a retrieval system, or transmitted, in any form or by any means, electronic, mechanical, photocopying, recording, or otherwise, without the prior written permission of the publisher. Printed in the United States of America. For information, address Da Capo Press, 44 Farnsworth Street, 3rd Floor, Boston, MA 02210.

Set in 11.5 point Adobe Caslon Pro by The Perseus Books Group

Library of Congress Cataloging-in-Publication Data

Magner, Mike.
    A trust betrayed : the untold story of Camp Lejeune and the poisoning of generations of marines and their families / Mike Magner.
        pages cm.
    "A Merloyd Lawrence book."
    Includes bibliographical references and index.
    ISBN 978-0-306-82257-5 (hardback) — ISBN 978-0-306-82258-2 (e-book)
    1. Drinking water—Contamination—North Carolina—Camp Lejeune—History.
    2. Groundwater—Pollution—North Carolina—Camp Lejeune—History.
    3. Marines—Health and hygiene—North Carolina—Camp Lejeune—History.
    4. Families of military personnel—Health and hygiene—North Carolina—Camp Lejeune—History. 5. Poisoning—North Carolina—Camp Lejeune—History.
    6. Environmentally induced diseases—North Carolina—Camp Lejeune—History.
    7. Camp Lejeune (N.C.)—History. 8. Camp Lejeune (N.C.)—Environmental conditions. I. Title.

    RA592.N8M34 2014
    363.6'10975623—dc23
                                                                        2013045263
Published as a Merloyd Lawrence Book by Da Capo Press
A Member of the Perseus Books Group
www.dacapopress.com

Da Capo Press books are available at special discounts for bulk purchases in the U.S. by corporations, institutions, and other organizations. For more information, please contact the Special Markets Department at the Perseus Books Group, 2300 Chestnut Street, Suite 200, Philadelphia, PA 19103, or call (800) 810-4145, ext. 5000, or e-mail special.markets@perseusbooks.com.

10 9 8 7 6 5 4 3 2 1

*For the victims of military and industrial pollution,
especially those exposed during service to their country,
only to be treated as collateral damage.*

Contents

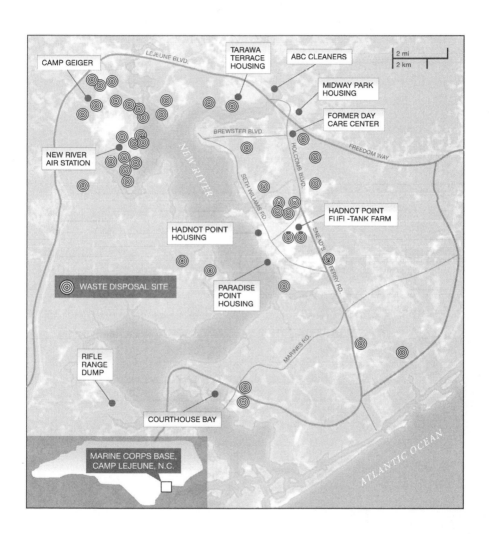

CAMP GEIGER

LEJEUNE BLVD.

TARAWA
TERRACE
HOUSING

ABC CLEANERS

MIDWAY PARK
HOUSING

FORMER DAY
CARE CENTER

BREWSTER BLVD.

FREEDOM WAY

NEW RIVER
AIR STATION

NEW RIVER

SETH WILLIAMS RD.

HOLCOMB BLVD.

HADNOT POINT
HOUSING

HADNOT POINT
FUEL-TANK FARM

SNEAD'S FERRY RD.

WASTE DISPOSAL SITE

PARADISE
POINT
HOUSING

RIFLE
RANGE
DUMP

MARINES RD.

COURTHOUSE BAY

ATLANTIC OCEAN

MARINE CORPS BASE,
CAMP LEJEUNE, N.C.

2 mi
2 km

1

THE MARINE CORPS FAMILY

We take care of our own.
—MARINE CORPS SLOGAN

The ambulance from Fort Belvoir, Virginia, raced around the freshly built Capital Beltway, siren screaming and red lights whirling, on the evening of June 26, 1967, carrying Anne Townsend and her gasping three-month-old son to Bethesda Naval Hospital in Maryland. As Anne cradled her baby on the back bench, the driver remarked that he and his fellow medic liked to stick to the busy freeways so that, if the aging vehicle broke down—which happened frequently, he said without much alarm—they'd be able to get help fairly quickly. "I prayed that this would not be the night," Anne would recall later.[1]

When the van pulled into the driveway of the world's most famous military hospital around 10:30 p.m., the attendants rushed the infant inside and told Anne to go directly to the admissions desk. There she was relieved to see, scrawled on the blackboard:

1

"Townsend baby to pediatric ward." "At least they were expecting us," she thought. After checking in, Anne followed the green line on the floor to pediatrics as she had been instructed, rushing down the hallways anxious to see how the doctors were treating her son. When she arrived at the ward, she was stunned to find four or five attendants in hospital garb casually sitting around near the entry, a few with their feet propped up on the reception desk. Then she spotted her baby in the arms of a nurse, who looked at her colleagues and said matter-of-factly, "Doesn't he need oxygen? He's turning blue."

—◊—

The boy, Christopher Thomas Townsend, was the son of a career Marine who was literally a child of Pearl Harbor. Tom Townsend was ten years old in 1941 when his father, Arthur M. Townsend of Jackson, Michigan, was an officer on the USS *St. Louis*, a light cruiser based at the headquarters of the Pacific fleet in Hawaii. A 1924 graduate of the United States Naval Academy, Arthur Townsend had served for years at the Navy base in San Diego— where Tom was born on New Year's Day in 1931—before being transferred to Hawaii in 1938. The family—Arthur and his wife, Nietta, along with Tom and his older brother, Jack—lived in the beach community of Kailua, on the north side of the island less than ten miles from Honolulu.

Life on the island was about as close as a boy could get to paradise. Tom would often wander along the beach scavenging for limpets, a type of sea snail considered a delicacy in the Pacific. An abandoned pool filled by waves from the surf served as his personal swimming hole. Once as he was lounging in the pool and eating limpets, a young woman came along and struck up a conversation. She invited Tom to her home for cake and cookies; the "home" turned out to be a palatial mansion called Shangri La, and his hostess turned out to be Doris Duke, a tobacco-fortune heiress who at the time was known as "the richest girl in the world."

The *St. Louis* went to sea in November 1941—Tom learned later that his father's ship had been part of a mission to the Dutch East Indies to help the Dutch and British navies coordinate their defenses against Japanese expansion in the region. The cruiser returned to Pearl Harbor on December 4, and two days later, on Saturday night, Arthur Townsend and his wife went to a dance to celebrate their reunion, leaving Tom and his brother at home.

Tom woke up before the rest of the family the next morning and, as he usually did on Sundays, went outside to find the *Advertiser* so he could read the funnies. Before he even looked for the newspaper, though, his eyes were diverted toward the southern skies, which were filled with buzzing planes and clouds of smoke. Tom's neighborhood was on a hill near the Punchbowl Crater (where a military cemetery sits today), and when he moved to a spot at the edge of a cliff, he could see the city of Honolulu and, to the right, behind the hills, the Navy base in Pearl Harbor. "I watched a couple of dogfights and saw antiaircraft fire," Townsend later recalled. "Then I saw a big explosion, with thick black smoke and red and yellow flames. I assume that's when the *Arizona* got hit."

The boy ran to a water tank further up the hill, in a field surrounded by a thick hedge that kept Tom and his friends from running off the edge of a cliff when they played football there. Looking down over the hedge toward the port at Honolulu, he "noticed the Coast Guard ship, the *Roger B. Taney*, firing at aircraft," Townsend said. "Then all of a sudden a Zero came from the north, went down in the crater and came up and was machine-gunning the Coast Guard ship in the harbor. It flew right past me maybe fifty feet away. I looked right at the pilot, and he was firing his guns that shoot out of the wing. . . . I knew it was a Zero because I'd read about them, and it had the big red circle on the sides and the wings."

Tom starting picking up the brass remains of shell casings that had dropped from the plane. They were hot, so he quickly scooped them into his baseball cap and ran home. His parents were still asleep, so Tom pounded on the door, burst into the bedroom, and dumped the warm metal on his father's chest, exclaiming, "Here you go, Dad. The Japanese are bombing Pearl Harbor!" Arthur Townsend shot out of bed and scrambled into his uniform, then went out and sped away in his refurbished 1930 Model-A Ford, headed to his ship.

For a brief time, the *St. Louis* was a sitting duck at the dock. Repairs had just been made on one of the ship's boilers, so a big section of the hull was open to provide access for the work crew. Arthur Townsend was the damage-control officer, a lieutenant colonel at the time, and he immediately took charge of having the ship welded back together. In short order the *St. Louis* was moving toward the harbor opening, at twice its usual speed, while planes roared overhead, bullets whizzed past, and explosions echoed across the water. It rammed right through a cable it encountered in the harbor and barely skirted the reef where ships must make a hard turn on their way out to sea. A Japanese submarine sent two torpedoes toward the *St. Louis*, but the bombs struck the reef and exploded away from the ship. Gunners fired a few rounds back at the sub while the cruiser headed out, on its way to rendezvous with the aircraft carriers that were still safely in the Pacific under the command of Admiral William Halsey Jr.

Nietta Townsend had been the head nurse at Mercy Hospital in Jackson, Michigan, when she met her future husband, so she spent most of December 7 caring for the wounded at the Pearl Harbor hospital. Jack Townsend was in the high-school ROTC program, so he was put on guard duty at one of the water or power facilities on the island while martial law was in effect after the Japanese attack. That meant Tom, twenty-four days shy of his eleventh birthday, was left alone that evening, sitting in a dark house under a mandatory blackout, listening to the reports of war on a San Francisco radio station. Occasionally he would slip outside to listen to the sounds of gunfire that continued through the night, and at one point the lights suddenly went on at the main power station down at Honolulu—Tom thought it was probably an act of sabotage by local Japanese.

The *St. Louis* spent a couple of weeks in the Pacific after the war began, transporting troops and briefly assisting in a fight with the Japanese occupying the Aleutian Islands near Alaska. The cruiser was back at Pearl Harbor right before Christmas, just in time for Arthur to help his family get to the mainland along with thousands of other Americans being moved out of harm's way. (Before he went home, Arthur found his Model A still parked near the dock, riddled with bullets. He vowed revenge against the Japanese for damaging his prized possession, and it was a promise he would keep in the years ahead.)

On Christmas Eve the Townsends were told they were to report the next morning to the SS *Lurline*, a luxury liner that had been pressed into service to transport civilians and some of the wounded sailors from Hawaii to San Francisco. "So we packed our bags," Tom Townsend remembered. "I was given a Christmas present and put it in my suitcase. My brother and I were put in a cabin and my mom was with the nurses. At the pier they were loading the wounded below. I didn't see them but knew what was going on. My mom had told me it had been horrible—there were so many burned in oil and fuel fires."

There were probably a thousand children on the liner with their families. The ship's huge ballroom was converted into a kind of playground, with dozens of Monopoly games going on all at once. The adults on board were too nervous to be entertained; the ship's constant zigzagging was a reminder that there were Japanese submarines lurking below the surface that could attack at any moment. The *St. Louis* had been assigned to be part of the convoy; for Nietta, knowing her husband was on duty nearby helped ease the anxiety.

The *Lurline* arrived in San Francisco on the afternoon of December 31. The cold temperature was a shock to Tom, who was still dressed in his Hawaiian shirt, shorts, and tennis shoes. A Red Cross volunteer gave him some long pants and a sweater. The Townsends reunited with Arthur, who found his family a room in a hotel on Market Street, not far from the piers. The boys settled in, and while Arthur and Nietta went out to dinner, they locked the door to the room, turned out the lights, and tossed water balloons from the window into the street below, which was filled with revelers for New Year's Eve.

Arthur Townsend was granted leave to relocate his family, which wanted to head for warmer climes. They decided to move to Sarasota, Florida, but didn't stay there long. Arthur went to war in the South Pacific, and Nietta moved to California so she could be with him whenever he returned to the base in San Francisco. Tom and Jack went to Michigan to live with an uncle near Jackson and go to school there. Jack joined the Navy after finishing high school, while Tom decided to move back with his mother and start high school in Berkeley.

Arthur saw plenty of action during the war in the Pacific, leading a squadron of destroyer-like ships that had been converted to mine-layers and participating in assaults on islands occupied by the Japanese. At Okinawa, nearly all of the squadron's twelve ships were hit by Kamikaze pilots; some had four or five planes crash into their decks and hulls. By the war's end, Arthur was unharmed physically, but he was mentally exhausted. Put in charge of cleaning up mines, he forced some of the captured members of the Imperial Japanese Navy to do the job, saying he wouldn't put any more American lives at risk. He positioned his ship nearby with its guns pointed at the Japanese and told them if they did anything amiss he would blow them out of the water. Because his actions were considered too harsh, Arthur Townsend was told he could not attend the Japanese surrender in Tokyo Bay on September 2, 1945; instead, he would have to return immediately to the United States. He ended up spending a year at Bethesda Naval Hospital suffering from combat fatigue. After his release in 1946, he eventually retired. He was awarded the Legion of Merit for his service during the war.

Tom Townsend graduated from high school in 1948 and immediately took the entrance exam for the Naval Academy in Annapolis, Maryland. He didn't do well enough for admission, so he decided to enlist in the US Marine Corps. His first stop was Parris Island in South Carolina for boot camp. Afterward, he landed an appointment at a Naval Academy prep school in Rhode Island, and in 1950, he ended up getting into Annapolis after all. "That was a hellish year," Townsend said. "I was not a good midshipman." He was now older than most of the students in the class above him, but that didn't stop them from treating him with the usual disdain for a plebe—it probably made things worse. "I didn't do well being harassed by the young punks," Townsend said. "I had all kinds of problems. . . . I was belligerent." His grades suffered, too, and by the end of the year Townsend was told he could either repeat as a freshman or leave the academy. After a trip to Europe to reflect on his life, Townsend decided to return to Jackson and use the academic credits he had earned to try to obtain a degree at the University of Michigan. Then he would return to the Marines.

Townsend carried a heavy load of classes at Michigan and also worked as a waiter and cleanup man at a fraternity house in return for his room and board. His schedule left little time for anything but studying and working. In his senior year in 1954, he had a blind date with a student at Michigan State Normal College (now Eastern Michigan University). Anne Taubitz had grown up in Greenbush on the shore of Lake Huron. Her parents ran a country store in the tiny crossroads town, and when Anne took Tom up to meet them, her father, a former Marine, instantly welcomed him into the family. Tom was going back into the Corps right after graduation from Michigan, this time commissioned as a second lieutenant. He went for his six months of training at the Marine Corps base in Quantico, Virginia, and then he returned to Greenbush on December 28, 1954, to marry Anne.

Townsend's first assignment in the Corps was the artillery regiment of the 1st Battalion, 10th Marines, at Camp Lejeune, North Carolina, in January 1955. One of five lieutenants in the battery, he was designated as a forward observer on the firing range. During his first day at the base, Townsend was getting a rundown from the first sergeant at the range station when he heard some loud banging from the locker area. The sergeant scampered over and opened one of the lockers to reveal a young Marine stuffed inside. The grunt was ordered to keep quiet, the door was slammed shut again, and the unofficial punishment was continued for whatever breach had been committed—Townsend didn't ask for details. He eventually became good friends with the burly sergeant, often inviting him to home-cooked meals that Anne would prepare at their small apartment in the Tarawa Terrace housing complex on the base.

The year at Camp Lejeune flew by, especially after Anne became pregnant with their first child, Mark, who was born in late 1955. The following year Townsend was sent to Parris Island, where he was assigned to the rifle range, a post he held for more than two years. Then he received a dream transfer, to the Marine Corps Air Station at Kaneohe Bay, Hawaii, in July 1958. For Tom it was like coming home; for Anne it was a chance to enjoy a relaxed family life in a heavenly beach community. She also was schooled by her husband in "the social protocol of rank," she would write later, "and adapted to wearing gloves while balancing a drink, nibbling an hors d'oeuvre and clutching an evening bag—while being mindful of the cocktail hat rule (is the party before 6 PM or after?)."

After three happy years in Hawaii, where Tom was an executive officer in the artillery unit of the 3rd Battalion, 12th Marines, the Townsends moved to the Sandia Base in Albuquerque, New Mexico, the center of the US military's nuclear weapons operations. Tom was a training officer and one of the few field Marines at the joint facilities shared with the Army and Air Force. For entertainment in the desert wasteland, Townsend would sometimes dress as a commando and harass the Army units training in the sands, calling in his friend, who was the only Marine pilot at the base, to buzz the troops, which were amassed in large units with dozens of heavy weapons. Once when he was out scouting for action, Townsend strayed near the fence surrounding the nuclear weapons site at Kirkland Air Force Base and was immediately seized by Air Force guards. With no identification, wearing camouflage fatigues and black paint on his face, Townsend was seen as a serious threat, and the guards roughed him up against the fence while demanding an explanation of what he was doing. It was only after Townsend convinced them to call his commanding officer that the guards let him go. His days as a faux commando ended.

The Townsends' second child, Aimee, arrived at the Sandia base hospital in 1962. Two years later, Tom was shipped to Okinawa, Japan, to take over as logistics officer at the division headquarters

there for the 3rd Marines. The Vietnam War was starting to esca-
late, and he ended up being sent to Da Nang for the last few
months of his thirteen-month tour overseas.

In August 1965, Townsend was sent back to Camp Lejeune to
be a logistics officer, training Marines in the art of establishing
field operations and keeping things running even under the duress
of war. His wife and two children were thrilled to have Tom with
them again. Their new home was a three-bedroom "cracker box,"
but it was located in the special area called Paradise Point that was
reserved for officers and their families. The following summer,
when Tom was promoted to major, they moved to even larger
quarters near the Officers' Club—"the best housing we would oc-
cupy in our more than twenty years in the Marine Corps," Anne
later recalled. Mark and Aimee loved hanging out at the club's
swimming pool and had many friends on the base—life was good
at Camp Lejeune.

Within a few weeks of their move into the "double-decker" that
was designated as Quarters 2509, Anne discovered she was pregnant again, "an unexpected but most welcome condition," she said.
Christopher Thomas Townsend was born on March 16, 1967, a
small baby at five pounds, ten ounces, who needed assistance to
start breathing. When he was brought to his mother's room two
days later, Anne noticed he had a high-pitched cry unlike any she
had ever heard from a newborn, and he seemed to have problems
feeding. But the doctor insisted all was well, and mother and son
went home to Paradise Point on March 20.

Despite the reassurances from the medical staff at the base hospital, Anne had lingering concerns about Christopher's health. He
was a passive baby and didn't retain formula well, often vomiting
after his feedings. At three and a half weeks, the baby's color suddenly turned dusky while he was in his seat, but it returned to normal within a few minutes after Anne picked him up and moved

him around. It was a frightening moment that Anne described to a pair of visiting nurses who came to check on the boy a few days later, but they looked at his records and said there was no reason for concern.

The worries about Christopher subsided somewhat as the family prepared for Tom's latest TDY, or temporary duty. On April 26 he was to head to Vieques, Puerto Rico, to take command at Camp Garcia, a Navy training base on an island just off the Puerto Rican mainland. The TDY was expected to last four to six months, which left Anne, still recovering from Christopher's birth, with the unenviable task of looking after three children, including a newborn, all on her own.

Still, there was some comfort in remembering the drumbeat about "the Marine Corps family" that Anne had been hearing since she married into it thirteen years earlier. "During the early years there was one underlying message—do what's expected and the Corps will take care of you," Anne wrote later as she looked back on her family's time in the Corps. "There was solace in this dictum because the husbands—our reason for being where we were—were most frequently gone. Never fear, even if your partner was 'in the field' for several weeks, or TDY for several months, you were safe—looked after by the Corps. The husbands and fathers— the Marines—relied on this tacit understanding, knowing that their loved ones were, if need arose, looked after by a cadre of support personnel. This knowledge allowed them to concentrate solely on the mission at hand." The slogan of the service, *Semper Fidelis*—Latin for "Always Faithful"—seemed to extend to the spouses and children of Marines, who shared the same bonds as the enlisted men and women, officers, and veterans.

Tom left for Vieques at 5 a.m. on April 26, the same day Christopher was scheduled for his six-week checkup at the Camp Lejeune hospital. Eleven-year-old Mark would be in school, but five-year-old Aimee had a cold and would have to stay home alone for a couple of hours while Anne took Christopher for his 9 a.m. appointment. "Knowing I would be gone for 2 hours or less there was no worry—she was a very trustworthy youngster," Anne wrote years later. There was comfort, too, in knowing Aimee was at home on a Marine base, with neighbors always available and ready to assist.

The baby was given his DPT vaccination (combining the vaccines for diphtheria, pertussis, and tetanus) before the doctor conducted the exam, which seemed to take forever. After a long time probing, feeling, and listening to the boy, the doctor turned to Anne and said, "Sit down, Mrs. Townsend, I have something to tell you. Your baby has a serious heart defect and pneumonia. We need to admit him to the hospital today."

"I thought I was prepared for nearly anything, but I certainly was not ready for this," Anne recalled later. A hospital volunteer accompanied mother and son to the lab for blood work, X-rays, and paperwork. Anne called a neighbor across the street to ask her to take care of Aimee while Christopher was being admitted and given initial treatment. It wasn't until late afternoon that Anne left her son at the hospital and in a daze made her way through heavy traffic on the base back to Paradise Point: "I prayed the Chrysler station wagon past the intersection, with the MP standing on a barrel [directing traffic], to home," she said.

Unable to bear the thought of her baby being alone in a sterile hospital room, and still in shock from the news that he had very serious health problems, Anne set about cleaning the house, doing the laundry, and struggling to make a meat loaf for dinner. Adding to the stress was her inability to reach Tom on that Wednesday evening. That would have to wait until the next afternoon, because personal communications to Vieques were limited to Tuesdays and Thursdays between 2 and 4 p.m. via ham radio.

Anne was able to visit Christopher for an hour each day. That routine went on for ten days until the boy was finally sent home, with instructions for the mother to check on him constantly while he was awake. She had to make sure he was sitting up, because it enabled him to breathe more easily. It was also best for him not to cry too much, because it strained his weak lungs, and he was to be kept away from large groups of people to avoid possible infection. There were weekly checkups at the base hospital, and an appointment was scheduled in late May for Christopher to be evaluated at Bethesda Naval Hospital.

Tom was kept up to date twice a week in conversations monitored by the ham radio operator on duty at Camp Lejeune. He desperately wanted to return home to help, but the Marine commanders at Lejeune and in Washington said it would not be possible because they were so short of officers as a result of the steady buildup in Vietnam. So Tom contacted his parents in Florida and persuaded them to go up to North Carolina. They would take care of Mark and Aimee when Anne took Christopher to Bethesda.

The day before their appointment, Anne and Christopher flew from New Bern, North Carolina, to Washington, DC. They were met at the airport by friends from Tom's tour in Hawaii, Dave and Betty Beach, who had agreed to put them up for a few days at their home in Springfield, Virginia. The next morning, May 26, Betty drove Anne and Christopher to Bethesda, where the boy was admitted to the naval hospital for four days of tests and observation. Anne was told to come daily to feed and help care for the baby, because there was a shortage of support staff at the hospital due to the war.

When Christopher was released on May 30, the doctors told Anne that he had a heart malformation and other birth defects that could not be treated with surgery. The Townsends flew back to North Carolina, arriving at Camp Lejeune in the late afternoon.

But by 8 p.m. they, with Tom's father, were headed to the base hospital—Christopher had come down with a fever and diarrhea, probably from an infection acquired at Bethesda. Later that evening he was admitted to the pediatric ward. Anne and her father-in-law returned home, only to find Christopher's grandmother being cared for by a neighbor. The elder Mrs. Townsend had broken down from the stress of the long wait, fearing that her youngest grandson might never be coming home. "It was invaluable to have their support, but a terrible strain on them," Anne said. "There was a strong sense of frustration because nothing could be done but wait."

Christopher was released from the hospital a few days later. His grandparents returned to Florida, and Anne and her children did their best to maintain some kind of normalcy. School ended, and Mark spent a lot of time riding his bicycle around the base and swimming at the Officers' Club pool. Anne and Aimee took frequent walks with Christopher in his carriage, always avoiding the crowds at the commissary and the PX. The baby had to go for weekly checkups at the base hospital, but always at times when few other children were scheduled for treatment, so that his exposure to infections could be limited. Hanging over all of this, though, was the gloom they all felt because of Tom's absence. Anne was beginning to think that the pledge of "the Marine Corps family" was only a myth.

"One very frustrating element ran through this very trying period," she said. "This was the lack of consideration by the Marine Corps hierarchy. It was evident that they would not allow Tom to return home (base personnel was at half-strength because of the demands of Vietnam), but most upsetting was that no one contacted me regarding our ongoing problem."

Tom was also extremely frustrated. His pleas for leave to return home seemed to fall on deaf ears. "I never heard from anybody in my command," he said. "I had a boss at Camp Lejeune. But everybody just kept their mouth shut."

Finally, after he was told that Anne needed to take Christopher back to Bethesda for a follow-up exam on June 26, Tom took matters into his own hands. A few days before the appointment, he knew there was a plane coming into Vieques from Lejeune with supplies and staff, so he went to the airfield, waited for the plane to empty, and climbed on board for the return trip. "The captain said, 'Where are you going?' I said, 'My child is dying at home,'" Townsend recalled. "He said, 'You don't have orders.' I said, 'I'm going—see you later.' They never said anything about it."

Tom did not tell Anne that he went AWOL; she assumed he had finally been granted a leave. The long drive to Bethesda—Mark and Aimee were left in the care of neighbors—gave them a chance to catch up for the first real time in two months. They started looking ahead to Tom's return from Puerto Rico, by which time they were hoping against hope that Christopher might be on a path toward better health. At Bethesda their spirits were lifted a little, too, when Christopher's evaluation went well. The doctor declared that he was pleased with the boy's progress.

Tom and Anne took Christopher with them back to the Beaches' home in Virginia, where they settled down to enjoy a summer evening cookout. Christopher was put down for a nap around 7 p.m. while the men started grilling the steaks outside. But in a short time Anne heard a distressing cry from the baby's room. When she picked him up to try to comfort him, Christopher suddenly stopped crying and went limp in her arms. Betty Beach, a former nurse, tried putting him in a position that might allow him to breathe more easily, but he remained comatose.

Dave Beach grabbed his car keys and rushed Tom, Anne, and

Christopher to the nearby Springfield fire station, where the boy was immediately administered oxygen. He didn't revive, however, so the ambulance team rushed the baby, Tom, and Anne to the emergency room at the Fort Belvoir military hospital, with Dave Beach following in his car. At the hospital, Anne called the doctor at Bethesda Naval Hospital, who ordered the Fort Belvoir medics to bring the boy there immediately. Dave Beach took Tom Townsend back to Springfield while Anne held Christopher in the ambulance. It raced around the Beltway, arriving in Bethesda around 10:30 p.m.

After checking in, Anne got to the pediatric ward just in time to hear the nurse holding her baby tell a group of laid-back attendants that the boy was turning blue. "Immediately all hands hit the deck," Anne said. "One corpsman quickly escorted me from the area into a glass-enclosed office near the ward entrance and told me to remain there until the doctor could talk to me." Ninety minutes later, with the Fort Belvoir ambulance crew waiting impatiently outside, Anne was told that Christopher was breathing but asleep. She should return to Springfield to get some rest herself.

The ambulance crew returned to the Fort Belvoir hospital around 1:30 a.m. Tom picked up Anne, and they tried to sleep at the Beaches' house, but it was impossible. Their restless night ended at 5 a.m. when the phone rang. Christopher had died. It was June 27, 1967, a mere three and a half months since he had been born at the Camp Lejeune hospital.

Two days later, Christopher was buried at Arlington National Cemetery following a late-morning service attended only by a Catholic chaplain, Tom and Anne Townsend, Dave and Betty Beach, and another family friend. The Townsends' drive back to North Carolina later that day was filled with sadness. For Anne, the feeling was already beginning to grow that she was somehow responsible for her son's death. There seemed to be no other explanation that made any sense to her. For his part, Tom was bitter about his family being left to suffer through the tragedy on its own, without any support from the base commanders and staff. "I felt like the Marine Corps had dropped me off the edge of a cliff," he said.

Tom's grief over Christopher's death changed somewhat after he read an autopsy report that listed the scores of health problems in his tiny body. "In retrospect, God gave us a gift for a few months and took him away," Townsend said. "He would have been screwed up for the rest of his life."

Townsend returned to Vieques in early July and was told he would be relieved of his command there by the end of the month; he had been selected for a program at Wright-Patterson Air Force Base in Dayton, Ohio, where officers from each branch of the military service were being trained in computer literacy.

In Dayton, the entire family was deeply depressed. After the good life at Paradise Point, their housing at Wright-Patterson, converted from old World War II barracks, seemed dingy and drab. The computer school was very demanding, leaving Tom little time for his family, and the stress levels were so high that Tom and Anne had to meet several times with the base chaplain for counseling. Tom was so distraught that he told the Marine Corps brass that he felt another tour in Vietnam, even at the height of the war, would be better for his mental health than staying in Ohio, though he didn't tell Anne this. His request was granted, and he was transferred to Camp Pendleton in California in November 1967 to await orders to ship to Vietnam. After some more training at Fort Sill in Oklahoma, Townsend's orders arrived in the fall of 1968; he left for Da Nang in October and remained there until November 1969.

Townsend ended up his career in the Marines with a posting at Quantico, the sprawling base in Virginia south of Washington, DC, and retired from the Corps in 1974. He and Anne rarely spoke about Christopher, but their memories of their third child never left them. It would be more than twenty-five years before they would finally learn the likely cause of his death.

2

LEJEUNE

... all that is highest in military efficiency and soldierly virtue.
—MARINE BIRTHDAY MESSAGE, JOHN A. LEJEUNE

For a military base that dryly bills itself as "The Home of Marine Expeditionary Forces in Readiness" with "the world's most complete amphibious training program," Marine Corps Base Camp Lejeune on the coast of North Carolina is a fairly resplendent place.

Camp Lejeune is framed by the city of Jacksonville to the northwest, the New River to the southwest, and eleven miles of Atlantic Ocean beaches to the southeast. Only about 10 percent of its 152,000 acres in Onslow County has been developed, yet there are typically more than 100,000 enlisted and civilian personnel on board. The rest of the base—some 220 square miles—is covered with pine and hardwood forests and thousands of acres of marshes, ponds, and streams thriving in a mostly warm coastal environment.

The site is part of what ecologists call the Onslow Bight region, which is described in a Defense Department handbook on biodiversity as "a rich mosaic of saltwater marshes, wetlands, longleaf pine savannas, and other coastal ecosystems" supporting a number of threatened species, including the red-cockaded woodpecker. Some might simply call it a swamp, but it is a splendidly diverse and productive one. The wetlands include many bogs, called *pocosins*—lush with evergreen shrubs—that are unique to coastal North Carolina. The base as a whole is home to a variety of threatened plants, birds, and animals, such as the coastal goldenrod and the Venus flytrap, Wilson's plover and the American oystercatcher, the Eastern cougar and the Eastern diamondback rattlesnake.[1]

Edward Lindley, now a semiretired attorney and treasurer of the Vietnam Veterans of America chapter in San Diego, lived at Camp Lejeune for nine months in 1967 after he was drafted out of high school in upstate New York. He signed up for the Marine Corps to avoid going into the Army. "I figured if you're gonna do it, do it right," he said. (Lindley also wanted to help out a buddy in the Corps—in those days, if a Marine recruited someone to enlist, they were rewarded with an extra thirty days of leave.)

Lindley found Lejeune a pleasant place to be stationed. "Mowed grass, long driveways, . . . two-story brick barracks . . . it was a really nice, even a pretty, base," he said. He was part of the communications unit—in true military fashion, his training included learning Morse Code, "which I never ever used in the Marine Corps"—and on a typical day at Camp Lejeune he would grab a book, jump in a jeep, and drive to Onslow Beach, where he would spend the day reading while maintaining radio contact with his command. "I did that for nine months," he said, until the time came for his thirteen-month tour in Vietnam. There he saw plenty of action ("words cannot describe an 'up close and personal' airstrike by an F-4," he said) while supplying and transporting and occasionally evacuating troops, before he was sent back to Camp Lejeune in December 1968. He resisted all the offers to reenlist, including the promise of a promotion and a $5,000 bonus (enough to buy a new Corvette in the late 1960s). Instead he took early leave to attend college and never looked back.

Just about every former Marine from the eastern United States has memories of Camp Lejeune, many of them shaped by their marital status at the time they were stationed there. "A lot of brown-baggers [married Marines who live off-base] love it because the housing, schools and other facilities are really good," said a 1981 article about Camp Lejeune in the Marine magazine *The Leatherneck*. "Many of the single Marines knock it because they live in squad bays and feel that it's a long swoop to decent liberty. . . . Marines who have been stationed there are not wishy-washy about their feelings. They either love it or they don't."[2]

During the civil rights era, there were some ugly days at Camp Lejeune, although it was the site of the first training base for black Marines, a satellite facility called Camp Johnson that was built in 1942. In 1969, there were dozens of assaults and robberies with racial overtones. Some black Marines took matters into their own hands in midsummer that year by disrupting a party for a battalion that was shipping out the next morning for the Mediterranean. A white Marine died of head injuries, and two others were stabbed in the melee that broke out. Ultimately, charges were filed against forty-four men. More than a dozen of them were later convicted of violent crimes, including a black Marine who was sentenced to nine years of hard labor for manslaughter.[3]

—⁂—

Camp Lejeune was established in 1941 as an advance-force training base. It was named for General John A. Lejeune, who in 1915 had reshaped the mission of the Marine Corps to "be the first to set foot on hostile soil in order to seize, fortify, and hold a port from which, as a base, the Army would prosecute the campaign." It wasn't always so easy to define the United States Marine Corps. From the moment the Second Continental Congress established the Marines on November 10, 1775, the mission of the Corps was a work in progress, largely determined by the military needs at the time. The first assignment was to obtain gunpowder for the Continental Army by invading New Providence Island in the Bahamas, where it was believed the British had six hundred barrels in storage. The Marines landed at the island on March 3, 1776, and seized a British fort, but then proceeded to bed down for the night, giving the British time to load most of the barrels on a ship and send them off to Florida. The next morning, the Americans found only a couple dozen casks of powder and a few guns to carry home.[4]

The Marines began to distinguish themselves early in the nineteenth century, first on "the shores of Tripoli" in the First Barbary War of 1801–1805—one of only two military triumphs commemorated in the well-known "Marines' Hymn" still sung today at bases around the world. President Thomas Jefferson had refused the tribute and ransom demands of pirates from the Barbary States—Algiers, Tunis, Morocco, and Tripoli on the North African coast—and his Navy fleet had managed to take control of the Mediterranean with the aid of ships from five European nations. But after the USS *Philadelphia* grounded while patrolling the coast of Tripoli in 1803, and its crew of more than three hundred, including forty-three Marines, was taken hostage, a small group of Marines joined forces with about five hundred mercenaries from Greece in April 1805 and marched across the desert to capture the coastal city of Derna, nearly five hundred nautical miles east of the port of Tripoli. It was the first battle fought by the United States in a foreign land. The Americans were preparing to advance toward Tripoli when they learned that a peace agreement had been forged by the United States. It stipulated payment of a $60,000 ransom for the return of the captives from the *Philadelphia*. The commander of the force, William Eaton, returned to the United States as an early Marine Corps hero, though it was not the end to the war with Tripoli he had envisioned.[5]

The Marines settled in during the War of 1812 to become a fierce fighting force within the Navy. They gained a reputation as some of the finest marksmen in the world, as many Marines had learned to shoot with great accuracy at long distances in the backwoods of America. Congress officially put the Marines under Navy command in 1834 with passage of a law that also made clear that the Army had no authority over Navy personnel. In fact, it elevated the status of the Marines to that of the Army, with equal pay, a similar command structure, and the same four-year enlistments.[6]

In 1845, Texas became a state, and a war with Mexico was looming, so President James K. Polk decided it was a good time to expand the United States to the coast of California. Over the next two years, units of the Army, the Navy, and the Marines overcame Mexican forces in cities from Sonoma and San Francisco (then Yerba Buena) down to Los Angeles and San Diego. Meanwhile, the Army and the Marines fought their way through Mexico. They converged on Mexico City on September 13, 1847, to take on the remaining army of Antonio López de Santa Anna. After numerous bloody battles that day, Santa Anna abandoned the capital. Early on September 14, Marines stormed Chapultepec Castle, which stood on a hill that was considered a sacred site by the ancient Aztecs because it was where the "Halls of Montezuma" had once been. The war with Mexico ended, the last pieces of the continental United States were in place, and the Marine Corps had one of its most famous moments to sing about for centuries.[7]

The Marines played a minor role in the Civil War, and for the remainder of the nineteenth century the Corps spent much of its time keeping sea lanes open and securing trouble spots, such as Nicaragua and the Fiji Islands. The Spanish-American War in 1898 marked a major turning point for the Marines, who conducted their first amphibious landing at Guantánamo Bay on their way to helping Cuba win its independence. As the twentieth century dawned, Marine Corps leaders pointed to the Guantánamo operation as the blueprint for the service's future core mission.[8]

Japan's 1905 triumph in its war with Russia heightened concerns about the defense of American interests in the Pacific, as it would take days for Navy ships stationed on the West Coast to reach far-flung destinations such as the Philippines. President Theodore Roosevelt convinced Congress to add fourteen battleships and cruisers to the Navy fleet and increase its manpower from 25,000 to 44,500, but proposals to build naval bases in China, Korea, and the Caribbean were rejected when the Army made a case that defending Manila and its vital harbor in the Philippines should take priority.[9]

Concerned that the Army was getting the upper hand in managing America's role as a superpower, a group of Marine officers formed an association in 1911 to oppose any efforts to reduce the Corps' traditional missions and to argue for an important new one, known as the "advanced base force." The concept had begun to germinate in the Navy years earlier, when military leaders in Washington realized that a lack of bases left US possessions in both the Pacific and the Caribbean vulnerable to attack. Defenses could be strengthened if a force such as the Marines was capable of moving quickly to establish temporary bases wherever they were needed and then defending those advanced bases against enemy assaults.[10]

The idea was institutionalized in 1910, when the Marine Corps established an Advanced Base School at New London, Connecticut. But progress was slow, and in 1913, frustrated supporters of the Marines in Congress held a hearing to inquire as to why it was taking so long to organize and train an advanced base force. It was only after a twenty-five-year career officer named John A. Lejeune was appointed a top aide to Marine Corps Commandant George Barnett in 1915 that the new mission started to gain traction.

Born on the Louisiana bayou in 1867, Lejeune was the descendant of French Canadians who fled British rule and migrated to the South. His father was a Confederate officer in the Civil War who wanted his son to go to the US Military Academy. There were no openings at West Point, but his congressman found Lejeune a vacancy at the US Naval Academy, so he left Louisiana State University in 1884 and headed to Annapolis, Maryland.

The young naval cadet barely survived his first year after graduating from Annapolis in 1888. Lejeune was serving on the USS *Vandalia* as it was anchored in the Samoan harbor of Apia when a typhoon struck in March 1889. The waves were so powerful that the sloop was nearly swept out of the harbor; instead, it skidded along the water, dragging its anchor, until it grounded on a reef. Lejeune, twenty-two at the time, climbed into the rigging. He watched in horror as many of his fellow sailors tried to swim to shore and became swamped in the waves. But he and some of his other comrades hung there for hours, looking death in the face, until another Navy ship, the *Trenton*, pulled up alongside the crippled *Vandalia* and rescued those who remained on board.[11]

A year after the near disaster, on July 1, 1890, Lejeune was commissioned as a second lieutenant in the Marine Corps. "A stocky man of average height, with a square leathery face and jug ears," according to one Marine Corps historian, Lejeune climbed the ranks quickly, leading several missions that helped secure America's dominance at the start of the twentieth century. He became a top aide to Barnett, the Marine Corps commandant, at the

beginning of 1915—the height of a redefining period for the Marine Corps. With its recent victory in the Spanish-American War,
the United States had broadened its reach around the globe to include the Philippines, Guam, and the Hawaiian Islands in the Pacific; Puerto Rico in the Caribbean; and the all-important strip of
land where the Panama Canal was built to connect the Atlantic
and Pacific oceans. The Army and the Navy were engaged in in-
tense battles over which service could best protect American interests abroad, and the Marine Corps needed to carve out a clear role
for itself, lest it be left behind in the race for expansion funds and
overseas missions.[12]

Barnett and Lejeune had earlier been impressed with plans laid
out by a young officer from Kansas, Captain Earl Ellis, who had
developed plans for a war against Japan. A core element of these
plans was a strategy for seizing islands as advanced bases that could
serve as stepping-stones toward Japan in the Pacific. Lejeune
drafted Ellis to help plan exercises, and in early 1914, the first ad-
vanced-force brigade, from Philadelphia, joined a regiment that
Lejeune had organized to test out the concept at Culebra Island in
Puerto Rico. The exercise didn't go perfectly, but the results were
promising enough that in 1915 Lejeune went to Philadelphia to
announce, on behalf of the commandant, that the advanced-base
concept would be the heart of the Marine Corps' mission.

Planning for the new mission was put on hold for the American
entry into World War I in 1917, when US troops, including several regiments of Marines, were dispatched to Europe to help drive
the Germans back to their homeland. Brigadier General John Lejeune arrived in France in 1918 to lead the 4th Marine Brigade
that had fought at Belleau Wood, and he later took charge of the
combined Marine and Army division that broke the German lines.
He was the first Marine officer to hold an Army divisional command. Lejeune became known as "the greatest of all leathernecks"

while earning the Distinguished Service Medal, the Badge of the Legion of Honor, and the Croix de Guerre for his wartime valor.[13]

Lejeune later offered a poignant description of military heroism:

> In war, if a man is to keep his sanity, he must come to regard death as being just as normal as life and hold himself always in readiness, mentally and spiritually, to answer the call of the grim reaper whenever fate decrees that his hour has struck. . . . While war is terribly destructive, monstrously cruel, and horrible beyond expression, it nevertheless causes the divine spark in men to glow, to kindle, and to burst into a living flame, and enables them to attain heights of devotion to duty, sheer heroism, and sublime unselfishness that in all probability they would never have reached in the prosecution of peaceful pursuits.[14]

After World War I, Lejeune returned to his role as assistant to the commandant, but he and Barnett faced a new problem: with the world at peace, Congress slashed funding for the Marine Corps and reduced the size of the force from more than 75,000 at the height of the war to less than 30,000 in 1919. Barnett became so frantic in his efforts to preserve and promote the Corps that he began to annoy both Secretary of the Navy Josephus Daniels and the chairman of the Naval Affairs Committee in Congress, Representative Thomas Butler of Pennsylvania. The two pressured Barnett to resign in 1920—two years before his term as commandant was to expire—and Lejeune was tapped to succeed him.[15]

Lejeune seized the opportunity to lay the foundation for the mission he had defined for the Corps five years earlier. He immediately reorganized the advanced base force at Philadelphia as the East Coast Expeditionary Force and began staging maneuvers for military brass, key politicians, and even the general public. An astute politician himself, Lejeune knew there was no substitute for popular support in persuading national leaders to bolster the Corps. He had Marines volunteer for reenactments of Civil War battles, organized a Marine Corps League, and even had Marines help guard the mail from 1921 to 1926, just to show off their reliability and trustworthiness.[16]

At the same time, Lejeune was planning for a future war in the Pacific, as increasingly industrialized Japan showed signs of wanting to expand its empire beyond Korea, Taiwan, and parts of China. The US Navy's so-called Orange Plan for a Pacific theater of operations was built around an amphibious campaign conducted by the Marines. Lejeune had an ace in the hole to help advance his plans for the new Marine Corps mission: he reminded military and political leaders that although the United States had agreed, along with Japan and Britain, not to build new naval bases in the Pacific for ten years after the end of World War I, there were no limits on the development of mobile forces within the Navy. In 1924, the commandant sent the new East Coast Expeditionary Force of 3,300 Marines to the Caribbean for a massive exercise at Culebra Island. It quickly became clear that there was still much work to do on the maneuvers. During a landing at night, the Marines hit the wrong beach and failed to get all their supplies onshore. Another exercise was conducted in Hawaii in 1925, this time coordinated with the Army, and more lessons were learned about the need for better landing craft, improved communications, and adequate training.[17]

Lejeune retired as commandant in 1929 to become superintendent of the Virginia Military Institute, but his mission had been accomplished. The stage was set for the Marines to play a pivotal role in the war with Japan that would begin a dozen years later. A final document defining the Marine Corps' responsibilities that was issued before he stepped down said the Corps would conduct "land operations in support of the fleet for the initial seizure and defense of advanced bases."[18]

By 1940, with war clouds hovering over the planet, the Marine Corps had adopted an official manual outlining the strategy and tactics for amphibious landings by an advanced force, and exercises were being conducted regularly in the Hawaiian Islands and the Caribbean. But the Marines were learning that they still needed not only better landing craft, better weapons, and better communications, but also a training base where the operations could come together. The Marine Corps commandant that year, Major General Thomas Holcomb, ordered one of his top aides, Major John McQueen, to "select a pilot . . . get a plane . . . and find us a training center." After about a month of surveillance over the Atlantic and Gulf coasts from Virginia to Texas, the pair was most impressed by the miles of undeveloped beach near the mouth of the New River in North Carolina.[19]

It didn't hurt that members of Congress from North Carolina were anxious to spur development of a new port that had recently been built with federal funds nearby at Morehead City. The Marine Corps received $14 million for a base called Marine Barracks New River, and by the summer of 1941, Marines were practicing landings on the North Carolina beaches that would prepare them for epic battles at Guadalcanal, Iwo Jima, Okinawa, and elsewhere in the Pacific Theater of World War II. After the death of John A. Lejeune in 1942, the name was changed to Marine Corps Base Camp Lejeune.[20]

The base at first had only a summer cottage that served as headquarters, a warehouse placed in a converted tobacco barn, and a tent city for the Marines. But the forests, swamps, and hot weather at Camp Lejeune were ideal training grounds for troops who would be landing on tropical islands in the Pacific during the war. In fact, a Marine who fought at Guadalcanal was quoted as saying, "If this place had more snakes, it would be just like New River."[21]

After the war, the base benefited from a consolidation of the Marines into three divisions, one headquartered at Okinawa, Japan, and two on the mainland: the 1st Marine Division at Camp Pendleton in California and the 2nd Marine Division at Camp Lejeune, which became known as "The Home of Marine Expeditionary Forces in Readiness." Lejeune became the largest Marine base on the East Coast. Eventually it became a fully equipped base, with schools, commercial strips, movie theaters, a golf course, stocked fish ponds, and recreational beaches reserved for Marine Corps personnel. And for its core mission, the base grew quickly in the postwar era into a massive complex, with an airfield, three urban-terrain battlefields, forty-eight landing zones along the beaches, eighty firing ranges, and enough housing and support buildings to accommodate 180,000 people at any one time. The base also includes an adjacent training facility called Camp Geiger where more than 24,000 Marines go through infantry school each year. "Entrenched into the Marine warrior ethos is 'every Marine is a Rifleman,' and it is at Camp Geiger where Marines learn and develop their war-fighting skills before they attend their secondary schools to learn their military occupational skill," according to the Camp Lejeune website.[22]

—m—

A major challenge in developing this enormous base was providing adequate supplies of potable, nonbrackish water to a constantly changing population, particularly in the hot summer months when demand was highest and rainfall was lowest.

As construction was starting at the base in 1941, the Marine Corps asked David G. Thompson, a scientist for the US Geological Survey (USGS), to scope out the best way to provide water at an installation initially projected to house no more than 6,000 Marines at a time. Thompson looked first at the New River and its many tributaries, but he quickly determined that the water was too salty unless it was withdrawn above the tidal flow, perhaps miles upstream. An intake point would also be difficult to pin down because, when the river was running low, the tides pushed farther inland.

Beneath the base are seven different aquifers, including three with primarily fresh water. Thompson's sampling found—and later USGS studies confirmed—that water in the deepest freshwater aquifers was still very salty and would require substantial treatment. The best option would be the shallow aquifer known as the Castle Hayne, which ran just below the sandy soils at the surface to depths ranging from 150 to 400 feet underground. The shallow aquifer would have to be managed carefully, though; geological studies had shown that overpumping could cause incursions from brackish streams at the surface and from saltwater aquifers below. Also, geologists warned, during the dry summer months, the Castle Hayne aquifer was slow to recharge, so more wells would be needed than in a perfect artesian field.[23]

The Marine Corps tapped into the Castle Hayne when the base opened and over the years built more than 100 wells and 8 treatment plants that pumped potable water through 1,500 miles of pipes to more than 7,000 buildings, including those in the major housing complexes at Tarawa Terrace and Paradise Point. The base pumps anywhere from 4 million to 8 million gallons of water each day from the aquifer depending on the season and the population being served, which ranges from under 100,000 to as many as 180,000 people on any given day.[24]

For the first four decades of Camp Lejeune's operations, from the 1940s through the 1970s, the water treatment processes used there were essentially the same ones found in most cities across the country: filters removed particles, softeners reduced minerals, and chlorination killed microbes. There were no state or federal regulations for chemical contaminants until the late 1970s, after Congress passed the Safe Drinking Water Act in 1974 and the Environmental Protection Agency (EPA) started developing limits for various industrial pollutants that were turning up in drinking water around the nation. It was, after all, the chemical age in the decades following World War II. About all that was known about the thousands of new products brought to the market by new compounds and processes was that they greatly improved the quality of life for millions of people. As for the waste that these advancements produced, an "out of sight, out of mind" mentality prevailed across America. The pollution wasn't just from steel mills and paper mills and auto plants and other factories spewing emissions into the air and water and dumping hazardous waste on the land. Every owner of a car or truck with a tailpipe contributed to the smog that was choking America's cities by the 1970s, and every home equipped with a modern washing machine was sending to local waterways detergents that sucked up the oxygen in the water and harmed fish and wildlife.

Two of the most prevalent industrial pollutants in the postwar era were actually sister compounds, trichloroethylene (commonly called TCE) and tetrachloroethylene (also known as perchloroethylene, or PCE). Their use had exploded since their development as "the safety solvents" in the 1930s. PCE was used mainly as a cleaning agent, particularly in laundry operations, while TCE, a common degreaser, cleaning solvent, and paint thinner, was used in many industrial and commercial processes. The military was a major purchaser of TCE, using large quantities of the liquid solvent to remove grit and grime from planes, tanks, other vehicles, and weapons. And during the early decades of solvent use, it was

widely believed that dumping TCE and PCE on the ground had little or no environmental impact, as the chemicals would simply va-
porize or become assimilated into the soil.

Until studies in the late 1970s and early 1980s began raising
concerns about health effects from exposure to the solvents, there
were no limits on their presence in drinking water. Manufacturers
did not even provide guidelines for disposal. "There was no reason
for industry or the military to focus in on TCE, PCE, or other chlorinated solvents prior to the later 1970s," said a 2009 consultant's
report to the US Department of Justice on waste-disposal practices
at Camp Lejeune. "There were no prior reports of TCE or PCE
groundwater contamination. TCE and PCE were not regulated constituents. TCE was not considered a health risk."[25]

The same was true for benzene, which is today known as a
highly toxic chemical found in gasoline and diesel fuel. But until
the mid-1980s, there were no safety limits for benzene in drinking water; the compound was considered to be ubiquitous in the
environment.

Dumping chemicals and other toxic wastes was common practice at military bases across the country in the decades after World
War II. Before he came to Camp Lejeune as an environmental
worker in 1979, Danny Sharpe spent time at the Cherry Point
Marine Corps Air Station in New Bern, North Carolina, just
north of Camp Lejeune. He remembered a clearing in the woods
at that base that had two unlined pits, each about thirty feet long
by thirty feet wide and about twelve feet deep, where workers
dumped chemical and other wastes on an almost daily basis. The
smell was horrendous, he said.[26]

The same thing was happening at Camp Lejeune on a much
larger scale. Julian Wooten, the base's environmental manager in
the 1960s and 1970s, said every form of waste generated at the
base was either dumped directly on the land or into ditches dug by

Marines. Waste oil from vehicles and equipment was also constantly poured on dirt roads to control dust, Wooten said. Sharpe
recalled that at least until the early 1980s, waste oils at the base
were collected in tanks and then spread over the hundreds of miles
of roads that ran through Camp Lejeune.[27]

In addition, throughout Camp Lejeune, wash racks were used to
clean every type of vehicle and aircraft on the base, from tanks and
trucks to jeeps and cars, Sharpe said. Powerful solvents were used to
remove grit and grease from the vehicles, and the oily chemical mix
was washed directly into the storm drains that emptied into streams
and creeks around the site. One former Marine assigned to vehicle
maintenance at Camp Lejeune in the 1960s, Tom McLaughlin,
said fifty-five-gallon drums containing the degreaser TCE were always on hand at the wash-down areas. Workers would pour the
sweet-smelling liquid onto vehicle engines and bodies and then
hose them down, sending the waste into the floor drains.[28]

Then there were all the waste dumps at Camp Lejeune—a
solid-waste landfill, a garbage pit behind the mess hall, a chemical
dump, and scattered sites where drums of pesticides or even chemical weapons were buried. Wooten said he once went to the rifle-
range chemical dump with a bulldozer operator to build a trail and
mark it with signs, but his eyes were severely burned; he decided
he would never go to the site again if he could avoid it.[29]

Rick Shiver, the state environmental regulator for Onslow
County, was asked in 1975 to do an inventory of contaminated
landfills or waste sites in the area. Shiver said Wooten gave him a
grand tour of Camp Lejeune that year and described what was
happening at numerous locations around the base. "I was very surprised to learn of everything they were dumping into their landfills," Shiver said later. "They were not the garden variety landfills."

3

"BABY HEAVEN"

We didn't think anything of it back then,
you know, it was just part of life.
—JOAN LEWIS, WIFE OF MARINE
STATIONED AT CAMP LEJEUNE

Something was terribly wrong with the babies at Camp Lejeune. When it began isn't clear, but evidence suggests it was in the 1960s or earlier, a decade or two after the base opened in 1941. Few realized what was happening, and among those who did, it seems certain that at the time no one understood it.

One of the first to see the frightening effect without knowing the apparent cause was Sally McLaughlin, who had married her childhood sweetheart, Marine Sergeant Tom McLaughlin, in August 1962 and moved with him to Camp Lejeune immediately afterward.[1]

The couple had grown up in New York City, Tom on the West Side near the Hudson River and Sally in the Bronx. They had met in 1957 at a horse farm in Youngsville, New York, about ninety miles north of the city. Tom was just sixteen and enjoying a trail ride when he came across Sally and her best friend, Gail Fox, on their way to Sally's fourteenth birthday party. Tom was invited to come along and struck up a friendship with Sally that they carried with them back to the city. It didn't seem like they were destined to marry—Tom joined the Marines right out of high school in 1959, and the two stopped communicating. But after Tom wrote Sally after the death of her mother in 1962, their attraction rekindled and they quickly married.

Tom was twenty-one and Sally was eighteen when they moved to Camp Lejeune in August 1962. Soon afterward, they had their first child, a daughter named Carrie. They lived in a drab trailer park on the base, but Carrie was a happy and healthy baby, so life was good for the young couple.

Tom McLaughlin was one of sixteen children in his family. "That's what made me want to join the Marines," he joked. "I wanted to sleep alone." He chose the service for another reason, too: once as a boy out on the streets of New York, he was impressed by a group of Marines in their formal uniforms and decided he would wear one someday as well. "I loved the dress blues," he said.

At Lejeune he was a mechanic in the transport division, and one of his jobs was cleaning vehicles with the powerful degreaser, trichloroethylene. "We'd literally slosh it on our engines," he said. "We had 55-gallon drums of the stuff. Every motor pool did that." No one ever gave a thought to whether it was safe to breathe the sweet-smelling vapors from TCE; nor did anyone who lived on the base suspect anything was wrong with the water or with anything else in the environment at the sprawling coastal installation, McLaughlin said.

At the end of his tour at Lejeune in February 1964, McLaughlin reenlisted and was told he could name his preferred assignment. One of the choices was the Marine Corps base at Kaneohe

Bay, Hawaii, which sounded like paradise to a young couple from New York City just starting a family. A little more than a year into the tour, Sally became pregnant again. After delivering a healthy baby girl three years earlier, she had no reason to expect any problems. But the pregnancy turned out to be difficult, with lots of discomfort from a very swollen abdomen.

When she went into labor on February 5, 1966, Sally sensed immediately that it wasn't going to be like her last delivery. "Everybody had a grim face," she recalled years later. "I kept saying, 'We are having a baby. Why the grim faces?' Nobody was rushing. It was all very matter of fact. They told me to cross my legs because 'We are waiting for a doctor.' They knocked me out.

"I remember the doctor waking me and telling me the baby was dead. I could see her on the table, I could see her naked body and the doctor asked if I wanted to see her face and the nurse said, 'No, you don't.' I just kept saying, 'She's cold, why aren't you wrapping her?'"

It turned out the baby—a girl they named Michelle—had anencephaly, a condition in which most of the brain is missing.

Sally immediately began to question herself—"Did I eat enough vegetables, did I get enough sleep, did I take an aspirin? I just know that for years I didn't know what I did wrong," she said later.

The McLaughlins were devastated and totally on their own in their grief, with family and friends thousands of miles away. "Tom and I went alone to Schofield Barracks Post Cemetery [on the base in Hawaii] to have a funeral," Sally told her local newspaper in Massachusetts in 2007. "We had to borrow money from the Navy Relief because with our life insurance, the baby had to survive for five days and we didn't have the money. . . . We didn't notice anything, we were so grief-stricken." In other words, they received no money from their life insurance policy for the burial, because the baby had not survived long enough to be covered.

More than a year later, after Tom completed a tour in Vietnam, the McLaughlins returned to the cemetery to visit Michelle's gravesite. "It wasn't until we went back in 1967, we noticed more rows, but we didn't make any connection," Sally McLaughlin said. Then, she said, "We happened to notice the section she was in was all babies, born and died within days. A red flag went up. Why so many babies within a day or two of being born? . . . It gave the years (from the 1950s through the mid-1960s) and Tom and I said what in the world is going on? Why so many babies? It bothered me for years, bothered me terribly."

Darrell Stasiak and her Marine husband, Paul, encountered an eerily similar situation at Camp Lejeune after they lost a baby there in September 1966. The girl they had named Eileen Marie had actually died in the womb nine or ten days before her mother delivered, the doctors told her later. Paul Stasiak went to Eileen Marie's funeral alone because his wife was still recovering from the stillborn delivery in the hospital. The burial was in a Jacksonville, North Carolina, cemetery just outside Camp Lejeune, Darrell said years later, after reading the story about Sally and Tom McLaughlin in her local newspaper. "There was a plate there at the time, but years later [Paul] wanted to get a marker," she said. "I called down there and they said we could only tell you within ten or twenty feet of where she was buried, because we were burying them two or three to a grave at a time in those days."[2]

The Stasiaks remained at Camp Lejeune until 1968, and Darrell had two miscarriages in that short time. She also started noticing others having similar tragedies in their families. "We were hearing every week of someone taking a baby home to bury it," Darrell said. "It was common. We thought it was because we were so young and there were so many of us."

Many of those infants ended up alongside Eileen Marie

Stasiak in a section of the Jacksonville cemetery that came to be called "Baby Heaven" by residents of Jacksonville and former residents of Camp Lejeune. One of them was Ricky Gagnoni, the first child of Maggie Gagnoni and her Marine husband, who was stationed at Camp Lejeune. Maggie was feeding her one-month-old boy in their base housing on October 30, 1970, when he started bleeding from his mouth. Maggie rushed the baby to the hospital, but he died the following day, on Halloween. Gagnoni never received an explanation for Ricky's death and blamed herself for years afterward.[3]

The unexplained infant deaths and stillbirths continued through the late 1960s and 1970s. Whole families began to have problems. The experience of the Holliday family was typical. "We conceived a child at Camp Lejeune when we were there in January 1973, and in June my husband John was deployed to the Mediterranean on the USS *Guadalcanal*," Louella Holliday said. "I ended up going home to Mississippi while he was away so my parents could help. I had the baby in November at a small country hospital in Canton, Mississippi. (This was a place that still had separate waiting rooms for blacks and whites.)" She described the scene at the hospital following the delivery:

> I didn't expect the baby on the ninth, but he arrived. We had named him John Samuel Holliday Jr. The doctor came in and said my baby died. I was still in the delivery suite and the baby was right there. I said, "I just heard him breathe, just a minute earlier." The doctor said "No, the baby's dead." Then the doctor went out with the baby and came back and said, "You were right, the baby is alive, but you'd better pray for him to die because he's going to be a vegetable if he lives." He was breathing on an average of only two or three times a minute. But after carrying a child, you can't pray for him to be dead.

John Samuel Holliday Jr. did die, about fifteen hours later, on November 10, 1973.

"For all these years I questioned myself," Holliday said forty years later. "I was just plagued. I had no problems, none whatsoever, until I lived at Camp Lejeune." Holliday had moved into the Tarawa Terrace housing complex at Camp Lejeune at the beginning of 1973 when her husband was a Navy corpsman assigned to the base hospital. She described her pregnancy that year as one in which she was "violently sick from the beginning to the end." It was strange, she said, because she had already had two children without any health problems before moving to the base. And her pregnancy wasn't the only problem: the whole family began having difficulties at Camp Lejeune.

"The kids had these weird things happen," Holliday said. "Like my daughter, Angela, when she wasn't even one yet, had such severe nosebleeds that blood came out of her eyes. My son, William, who was four, his face swelled up horribly once and we had to take him to the doctor."

After the death of her baby, Holliday, then twenty-four, continued to suffer from nausea, vomiting, and dizziness, often severe enough to require her to go to the base hospital. The doctors were baffled, she said. They eventually became so frustrated with her case that one of the hospital officials suggested that she visit a psychiatrist.

It wasn't until the family left the base in January 1976 that things began to improve. Her daughter's nosebleeds dropped off to only once or twice a year, Holliday said. But there would be many more health issues in the years to come.

A woman with the ironic name of Mary Freshwater may have had the most ghastly experiences at Camp Lejeune. Freshwater died of leukemia in January 2013 at the age of sixty-eight. Shortly before her death, she told ABC News that she wasn't the only one who had suffered—by then the stories of many others from Camp Lejeune were being publicized. Nevertheless, nothing could have prepared her for the horrifying reality she would face in 1977 and the years to come.[4]

"I was very active with the Officers' Wives Club," Freshwater said in the ABC interview with Cynthia McFadden in June 2012. "We were at a party . . . one night. There were five of us in different stages of pregnancy. Every one of us lost their baby to a birth defect."

Freshwater had had two healthy children before she and her husband moved to Camp Lejeune, but the third child, a son named Russell Alexander Thorpe, lived just one month after he was born on November 30, 1977—with an open spine. "It was really a shocker when he was born that way and then when he died, he died in my arms. He took his last breath," she said. That was just a little after midnight on the last day of the year in 1977, she said.

Doctors told Freshwater she shouldn't be discouraged from getting pregnant again. But her next child, a boy named Charles Warren Thorpe, died the day he was born—without a cranium. Freshwater then had a miscarriage of twins before giving up on expanding her family.

Although these patterns kept emerging, individual families had no way of knowing their full scope. Joan Lewis had a miscarriage in 1970 after living in base housing at Camp Lejeune for several years, and she remembers friends who lost babies during their pregnancies around the same time. "But we didn't think anything of it back then," she told the *Star-News* in her hometown of Wilmington, North Carolina, in 2007. "You know, it was just part of life."[5]

What was more unusual to Lewis was that four of her five children—three conceived at Camp Lejeune and another who lived there from just under the age of one until she was five—had health issues that neither Joan nor her husband, Eddie, had ever experienced before moving to the base. She and Eddie had married when Joan was twenty-one, and they had moved into base housing on Bogenville Drive in the Tarawa Terrace neighborhood in October 1966.

"We lived there a year, then he went to Vietnam, then we went back after he returned in 13 months," Lewis said. "He saw a lot of action, but he came back okay."

All of Lewis's children "had respiratory problems" while living on the base, she said. "In the middle of the night my oldest daughter had to be taken to the hospital when she was three years old, having breathing problems."

The couple's first boy, Eddie Jr., was born in 1971. "He was conceived at the base but born in Wilmington," Lewis said. "His last two vertebrae in the lower back were fused together. He was born like that. He had no shock absorber in the neck either, no curve, and it causes a lot of pain." After Eddie Jr. was born, Lewis said, she had to have a hysterectomy. The doctors had discovered a number of tumors inside her womb.

People who lived at Lejeune as children have memories of highly unusual illnesses. Sandra Carbone remembers a raft of health problems starting at Camp Lejeune after her family moved to the base in 1968 when she was twelve years old.[6]

"During the time we lived at Camp LeJeune, my siblings and I were always getting sick," she wrote years later on a website for Camp Lejeune veterans and their families. "We never liked the taste of the water there either. My mom would have to make Kool-Aid all the time to hide the taste of the water."

When she was thirteen, Carbone recalled, she ended up with a rash on her chest and arms. "The doctors told my parents the rash was a result of my nerves," she later said. "My sister and I were plagued with headaches and stomachaches. I remember the doctors asking my parents if me, or two of my sisters who were in school, if we had a test coming up in school. They thought we were faking it to get out of school and schoolwork. There were even times when the doctors told my parents they did not know what was wrong with us or what we had."

Carbone said the most serious incident occurred when her baby brother, just three months old and born on the base, started crying while she was changing his diaper. "I looked and his ankles were red," she said. "My mom thought I had done something. But I was really careful—I was the oldest and he was the youngest so I had to take care of him. We were very close."

In that incident, she said, her mother "took him to the hospital and the doctor said if we had waited another day he would have died." Carbone added, "He had some type of toxemia [the presence of toxins in the blood], and had developed septic arthritis (an infection of a joint) in both of his ankles. They had to put the IV in his temple because they couldn't get it into his body, it was so swollen." The baby was in the hospital for three weeks.

Civilians who lived on the base also experienced health problems. John Fristoe and his wife moved to Lejeune in 1958 when he was hired as principal of one of the base's two elementary schools. They brought their two daughters, Karen, who was six, and Terry, two.[7]

"I can remember egg smells in the water," daughter Terry Dyer said in an interview years later. "And I remember we were sick all the time as children. We had a lot of eye infections, gunk in our eyes." Later, a baby sister, Johnsie, arrived, but she soon showed signs of being mentally impaired. She stopped talking in early childhood.

Their father had plenty of health problems, too. "Dad used to have nosebleeds all the time," Dyer said. "He would sneeze all the time in the shower."

Suddenly, at the age of forty-five, Fristoe died of a heart attack after living at Camp Lejeune for fifteen years. The doctors never could explain it, Dyer said, but she pointed out that the family had "lived in four different apartment complexes in Tarawa Terrace."

Unexplained illnesses affected other adults as well. In 1976, an eleven-year Marine and staff sergeant at Camp Lejeune, Lupe Alviar Jr., "started tripping, falling, [and] stumbling"—totally out of the blue. He was thirty years old and thought he was in perfect health.

"My legs just went," he told *The Veteran*, a newsletter for Vietnam veterans, in 2004. "I felt fine at the time, had no health problems that I knew of, and I just fell down. I didn't make much of it. I got up, brushed myself off, and carried on."

Then, about a month later, Alviar fell down again. "No warning," he said. "I just suddenly found myself on the ground. So I got up another time, brushed off, and carried on." Alviar thought he might have been affected by exposure in Vietnam to Agent Orange, the highly toxic herbicide containing dioxin that was used to clear jungle foliage. But his first child's birth defects made him think there might be a connection to something that happened at his base in North Carolina.

"My first child was born at Camp Lejeune in 1969," Alviar said. "He was born with an ear missing and his legs were twisted up like a pretzel."

It would not be until the early 1980s that Alviar's insight into the possible origins of his own and his son's health problems would find support.

4

SOLVENTS!

The lab was not a high priority at the base.

—ELIZABETH BETZ, CHEMIST AT CAMP LEJEUNE

The first authenticated warnings about a serious environmental problem at Camp Lejeune came three decades ago, in late 1980 and early 1981, from an Army laboratory assigned to check whether military installations were able to meet new federal standards for drinking water taking effect in 1982.

The looming regulations set new limits on trihalomethanes, or THMs—chemicals such as chloroform that are by-products of the disinfectant process used at water treatment plants and can be harmful to humans; levels deemed safe had been set by health studies. Camp Lejeune officials knew the water tests were coming: in September 1980, the water supply branch chief at the Environmental Protection Agency notified the base commander that the agency now had primary responsibility for enforcing the Safe Drinking Water Act passed by Congress in 1974. All water systems in the state had to meet federal standards for THMs within the next two years.[1]

The following month, in October 1980, the Army Environmental Hygiene Team from Fort McPherson in Georgia arrived at Camp Lejeune to begin testing for THMs. By that time there were eight different water systems, each with its own treatment plants, at the base. The Army technicians started sampling water from the two largest systems, Hadnot Point and New River, which each served more than 10,000 people.

Ten days after the samples were taken, the Army lab's chief of laboratory services, William C. Neal Jr., printed the following in capital letters at the bottom of the results form: "WATER IS HIGHLY CONTAMINATED WITH LOW MOLECULAR WEIGHT HALOGENATED COMPOUNDS." As a result, Neal wrote, there was "STRONG INTERFERENCE" [from these and other chemicals] in the tests for THMs.

Two months later, on January 22, 1981, Neal had a similar assessment of tests done on samples collected a month before. "HEAVY ORGANIC INTERFERENCE," he noted. "YOU NEED TO ANALYZE FOR CHLORINATED ORGANICS."

Neal repeated the same message in February 1981 on a results form for samples taken in January 30 at the Hadnot Point water system. And then on March 9, 1981, came a final, exasperated warning about samples collected at the base on February 26: "WATER HIGHLY CONTAMINATED WITH OTHER CHLORINATED HYDROCARBONS (SOLVENTS!)," he wrote.[2]

Neal could not recall the testing years later, but after he examined them he did not dispute that he had written the memos, and he told an investigator for a Marine Corps panel that his intent was clear. "I was certainly trying to send them a message with the notes I wrote just below the analysis results," Neal said. The Army lab results did not go directly to Camp Lejeune, however. Neal was supposed to send them to the Navy office overseeing environmental management at Camp Lejeune and other bases in the region, and this is what he did. This office was the Naval Facilities Engineering Command, Atlantic Division, or LANTDIV, headquartered in Norfolk, Virginia.[3]

At LANTDIV, Neal's reports should not have been a complete surprise. In October 1980, a contractor to the Navy engineers, Jennings Laboratories, had collected samples from each of the eight water systems at Camp Lejeune, combined them into one composite sample, and tested it for a variety of chemical contaminants. The results, which were sent to LANTDIV on October 31, 1980, showed trace levels of nearly a dozen potentially toxic compounds, including trichloroethylene (TCE), tetrachloroethylene (or perchloroethylene, PCE), and dichloroethylene (DCE). Since the water from each system at Camp Lejeune had been diluted in the composite sample, the results should have raised red flags about the possibility that one or more systems at the base could have significant levels of contamination. Instead, the results were never even sent to Camp Lejeune.[4]

Steve Azar, who was head of water quality at LANTDIV in the 1970s and 1980s, could not recall years later exactly when he received test results showing solvents in the water at Camp Lejeune, but he was adamant about what his response would have been. "I would have certainly advised them to sample each well and determine which wells were contaminated and to shut those individual wells down," he said in an interview in 2004. At the same time, Azar insisted that LANTDIV was not responsible for enforcing environmental standards at Navy bases but only offered guidance to officials at the installations. "Each base decided on its own whether to follow our advice or not," he said. Other LANTDIV officials also told congressional investigators in 2007 that their agency had "played a limited role" in environmental issues at Camp Lejeune.[5]

To date, no evidence has been found that anyone from LANT-
DIV ever clearly warned Camp Lejeune officials that five different
tests from October 1980 to February 1981 showed the possible
presence of harmful contaminants in the base drinking water. In
an interview in 2004 with an investigator for an independent panel
appointed by the Marine Corps, Elizabeth Betz, the chemist at
Camp Lejeune, recalled receiving the test results from the Navy
office but said LANTDIV had provided no explanation to help her
decide what to do. She said she had no background or training
about solvents. She was primarily concerned about THMs, and her
lab was focused on meeting the coming regulations.[6]

The written record and later interviews show that the three
staffers in the small environmental office at Camp Lejeune were
pretty much on their own in the critical task of ensuring that
drinking water at the base was safe, and they were ill-equipped for
the task.

Elizabeth Betz had started working at Camp Lejeune in November 1979. One of her main duties was making sure the waste-
water going into the seventy-one storm-drain outlets on the base
was sampled regularly and did not violate permit limits for grease,
oil, and suspended solids. If any limits were exceeded, Betz would
report the violations to the Environmental Protection Agency,
which could issue fines or order corrective actions. Betz knew
there were a lot of chemical wastes on the base, including pesticides and transformer fluids containing toxic polychlorinated
biphenyls (PCBs), compounds long used as insulators that were
banned by the EPA in 1979 due to their carcinogenic effects. But
Betz was not in charge of disposal practices or policies. The lab
was not a high priority on the base, Betz said. "You have to understand that our lab was small and undermanned," she said. "We
didn't have the proper equipment, and we had other problems at
that time that we were trying to deal with."[7]

Both of her supervisors at the time, Julian Wooten and Danny Sharpe, concurred with that assessment in later interviews. Wooten, who was Camp Lejeune's environmental manager in the 1960s and 1970s, said the base was not equipped to test water for solvents; if it had been, he said, the contamination probably would have been detected much earlier.

Though he was by no means an expert, with only a college degree in ecology, Wooten was very concerned about the water at Camp Lejeune. He said that coffee made with the base's tap water had a bad taste and sometimes even made him ill. By the 1970s, it seemed pretty clear to him that both surface waters and the groundwater at Camp Lejeune were contaminated, but whenever he tried to raise his concerns with base officials, he was ignored.[8]

Danny Sharpe, Wooten's assistant, felt the same way. The lab was part of the base maintenance department, he said. "That is as low as you can go." Sharpe, who was trained in forestry and had previously worked in a soil conservation program at the US Department of Agriculture, recalled receiving the test results from LANTDIV in late 1980 and early 1981, but he had no idea how to interpret them. "Wooten was an ecologist, Betz was a chemist, and I was a forester. We were a natural resource organization that had been put in charge of environmental affairs. . . . We didn't have the knowledge or expertise to understand the problem and we didn't know what action to take," he said. "I received the reports and sent them up the chain of command," he added.[9]

In addition to Hadnot Point and New River, a third water system at Camp Lejeune, this one serving the Rifle Range area, also became a focus of concern in the spring of 1981. One part of the Rifle Range had been used as a chemical dump for years, and a groundwater sample taken near the dumpsite on March 30, 1981, showed high levels of "chlorinated organic materials," according to a memo that LANTDIV sent to the commanding general at Camp

Lejeune on May 8, 1981. The memo pointed out, however, that a second round of tests in April had shown "greatly reduced levels of organic contaminants," and it was unclear why there was such a big discrepancy. The LANTDIV engineering chief, J. R. Bailey, said more tests were planned, but there was no need to stop using the Rifle Range Water Treatment Plant. "Based on the low level of contaminants found relative to the total trihalomethane standard . . . it is not believed that there is an imminent threat to human health presented by consumption of water from the Rifle Range WTP and distribution system," he wrote.[10]

When Betz received the memo about potential contamination at the Rifle Range, she wrote her own memo saying that it appeared to her that the results were flawed, partly because "old acid bottles" had been used to collect the samples in March, and they may not have been properly cleaned. But the fact that LANTDIV sent the results at all was a sign that Navy engineers were beginning to worry about Camp Lejeune's water supplies, if only because state regulators were getting more involved.[11]

A 1982 memo written at LANTDIV and obtained later by congressional investigators said the Navy was aware that North Carolina had assumed responsibility for Safe Drinking Water Act enforcement in March 1980, "and therefore would have the right to sample and test the drinking water at Camp Lejeune for any contaminants regulated under the act." The memo indicated that LANTDIV officials "were concerned that the state's testing might discover problems that the Navy had not previously identified."[12]

The threat of enforcement action from the state appeared to serve as an incentive for a full-scale environmental investigation at Camp Lejeune. LANTDIV made the base a part of the Navy Assessment and Control of Installation Pollutants (NACIP) program that had been launched by Navy headquarters in 1982 in the wake of the national scandal over Love Canal, the toxic waste dump uncovered at Niagara Falls, New York, in 1978. The Pentagon thought it wise to check whether there were any ticking time bombs at its many installations around the country.

The NACIP process in the early 1980s required three steps: an initial assessment study, a confirmation study, and remedial measures. At Camp Lejeune, the Marine Corps hired Grainger Laboratories, a state-certified environmental lab based in Raleigh, North Carolina, to conduct a NACIP study in 1982.[13]

The effort was barely under way when Grainger engineer Mike Hargett called base chemist Elizabeth Betz on May 6, 1982, to report that in tests for THMs at both the Tarawa Terrace and Hadnot Point water systems, "peaks" of the cleaning solvents TCE and PCE had been found. It was essentially a repeat of the findings by the Army lab eighteen months earlier.[14]

Betz immediately notified her supervisor, Danny Sharpe, who sent the results "up the chain of command" to the base maintenance officer and the utilities director. About a week later, Betz was asked to brief Colonel Kenneth Millice and one of his assistants at base headquarters. But when she met with Millice and a lieutenant colonel on May 14, 1982, neither seemed to have been informed about the test results; Millice simply requested that Betz prepare a report for him to read later on the status of testing for THMs. "No mention was made of extra peaks [of the other contaminants, TCE and PCE] that Grainger found in the Tarawa Terrace and Hadnot Point systems samples," Betz wrote in a memo summarizing the meeting. Betz also noted that she didn't bring up the solvents issue because the meeting was focused on the contaminants that were being regulated.[15]

On August 10, 1982, Bruce A. Babson of Grainger wrote the base commander that his lab was continuing to have problems with the tests for THMs. "Interferences which were thought to be chlorinated hydrocarbons hindered the quantification of certain trihalomethanes," Babson said. "These appeared to be at high levels and hence more important from a health standpoint than the total trihalomethane content. For these reasons we called the situation to the attention of Camp Lejeune personnel."[16]

Babson later said he remembered the report because he had been congratulated by his managers for making such an important discovery for a new client. Grainger's contract with Camp Lejeune had been a "prize," and they wanted to be sure to obtain the most accurate results possible for the Marine Corps.[17]

Shortly after Babson sent his report to Camp Lejeune, his colleague Mike Hargett was asked by Betz to come to the base and explain the problem to top officers. Hargett readily agreed because he considered the presence of solvents in the base water to be a serious concern. Betz took Hargett in to meet with a lieutenant colonel whose name he could not later recall, but he did remember the brush-off he received. Betz introduced Hargett as an expert on water systems in North Carolina and state regulations under the Safe Drinking Water Act (which North Carolina began to implement in 1980); Betz said Hargett was there to discuss water-quality issues in residential areas of the base. "The lieutenant colonel responded that this was something he would have to look into and we were dismissed," Hargett testified years later to a congressional committee. "The total time in the Lt. Col.'s office chair was less than five minutes."[18]

At the time the solvents were discovered, the Environmental Protection Agency did not have regulations setting limits for TCE and PCE in drinking water, but the EPA had issued warnings about both chemicals in 1979 in the form of guidance known as a Suggested No Adverse Reaction Level. A SNARL was not an enforceable standard, but only a scientific guess of the amount of contaminant that could be unsafe for humans to consume.

For TCE, the SNARL was 2,000 parts per billion (ppb) if water containing that amount of the chemical was consumed for one day in normal amounts; it was 200 ppb if the water was consumed for ten days; and it was 75 ppb for long-term exposure to the water. For PCE, the SNARL was 2,300 ppb for one day of consumption, 175 ppb for ten days of use, and 20 ppb for long-term exposure.

By the end of the summer of 1982, the highest levels of solvents found in Camp Lejeune's water were 1,400 ppb of TCE in the Hadnot Point system and 104 ppb of PCE in the Tarawa Terrace system. But base chemist Betz said the average levels in eight different samples taken over the summer by Grainger Labs were 20 ppb of TCE at Hadnot Point, which was within all the SNARL limits for the chemical, and 90 ppb of PCE at Tarawa Terrace, which exceeded only the long-term SNARL.

Betz advised her bosses in an August 1982 memo that PCE, "in high doses, has been reported to produce liver and kidney damage and central nervous system disturbances in humans." Still, neither Betz nor any other official at Camp Lejeune recommended shutting down wells that showed measurable levels of contamination. Betz suggested instead that the problem might be in the pipes— that is, that PCE could be coming from coatings inside the pipelines serving Tarawa Terrace. She also believed that since the levels of contamination varied so greatly from month to month, there must have been flaws in the sampling methods. However, Betz later said she was unaware at the time that wells were being rotated in the base water systems—with some turned off for days at a time to spread the pumping around the aquifer. If she had known that the readings were high only when certain wells were being used, it would have been possible to pinpoint the sources of contamination, she said.[19]

For years after the water contamination was discovered, the Marine Corps insisted that there was no reason to shut down the water systems in 1981 or 1982 because none of them had violated drinking-water regulations then on the books. "At the time, no environmental standards or regulations in regard to the use and disposal of TCE or PCE were in place," Camp Lejeune's commander in 2007, Major General Robert Dickerson Jr., said at a congressional hearing. He noted that the first federal regulation for TCE went into effect in 1987, and the first limits on PCE took effect in 1991, both under the Safe Drinking Water Act.[20]

What Dickerson omitted from his testimony, though, was that the Navy had its own standards for drinking water that had been established in the early 1960s. These standards were largely ignored. Under rules written by the Navy's Bureau of Medicine and Surgery, known as BUMED, all installations were advised that "drinking water shall not contain impurities in concentrations which may be hazardous to the health of the consumers." More specifically, the regulations stated that "substances which may have deleterious physiological effect, or for which physiological effects are not known, shall not be introduced into the system in a manner which would permit them to reach the consumer."[21]

Navy regulations also required annual testing of water supplies using a method called Carbon Chloroform Extract (CCE), described in a Navy manual as a "technically practical procedure which will afford a large measure of protection against the presence of undetected toxic materials in finished drinking water." The Marine Corps was asked by the *Tampa Bay Times* in 2013 to provide evidence that CCE testing was conducted regularly at Camp Lejeune, and no records were found. "A cursory review of the more than 8,000 documents that have been produced did not yield any CCE analytical results," Marine Corps spokeswoman Captain Kendra Motz told the newspaper. "However, the absence of records fifty years later is not an indication that an action was or was not taken, only that no records are available."[22]

When NBC News asked Motz about past CCE testing in 2013,

she said the method would not have been effective in finding solvents such as TCE and PCE, because those chemicals would have evaporated before the test was completed. CCE testing was mainly good for detecting pesticides or other contaminants that were not as volatile, she said.[23]

While the leadership at Camp Lejeune continued to ignore the warnings about solvents in the water through the rest of 1982, base chemist Elizabeth Betz and the consultants from Grainger Laboratories continued to be concerned. Betz wrote a "memorandum for the record" on September 8, 1982, recounting the results of sampling at the Rifle Range the previous spring. A dozen different contaminants—none of which were regulated yet under the Safe Drinking Water Act—had been detected over a three-month period, she noted, including TCE, PCE, methylene chloride, toluene, and benzene; the highest reading was 182 parts per billion of 1,1-Dichloroethylene (1,1-DCE), a toxic compound that forms as TCE breaks down.[24]

In December 1982, Grainger's Bruce Babson reminded the base commander that the ongoing testing for THMs continued to be disrupted by the presence of solvents. Out of forty water samples tested at Camp Lejeune, five contained PCE and five others contained both PCE and TCE, Babson's memo said.[25]

If those warnings weren't enough, there were many other signs of environmental problems at Camp Lejeune that, had they been noticed, might have kept the base commanders up at night:

- In March 1977, SCS Engineers of Reston, Virginia, completed a study of oil pollution at the base that the Marine Corps had requested the year before. The survey found "problems associated with petroleum storage areas, maintenance facilities, grease racks, motor pool operations, parking lots, and other activities utilizing petroleum products," according to a brief description in a memo to base headquarters, but the Marine Corps has refused to release the full study.[26]

- On September 22, 1977, the Environmental Protection Agency cited Camp Lejeune as "a major polluter" for violating permit standards at its seven sewage treatment plants and for making illegal discharges to storm drains. The commander of LANTDIV responded to the EPA by ordering the commanding general at the base to take several hundred corrective actions, with a goal of getting into compliance by July 1, 1981.[27]

- A year later, in September 1978, the commander of LANTDIV sent a memo to Camp Lejeune's commanding general reminding him of the need to protect groundwater from contaminants that could leach from the installation's solid-waste and chemical landfills. "Thus, current land disposal facilities should be monitored to indicate, as early as possible, any movement of contaminants from either disposal facility into the groundwater," the memo said. "Monitoring is necessary to evaluate either the potential danger to or the impact on groundwater quality."[28]

- A leak of between 20,000 and 30,000 gallons of diesel fuel and gasoline was reported at Camp Lejeune in 1979, the first and largest of eight different fuel leaks that would be recorded at the base over the next decade.[29]

- In June 1980, in a report on Camp Lejeune's Hadnot Point fuel farm, Cal J. Ingram of LANTDIV told his bosses at the Naval Facilities Engineering Command that there were problems with the fuel depot. The depot was about thirty-five years old, he said, and many of the tanks and pipes exhibited general corrosion and deterioration. A number of leaks had been found.[30]

- In March 1982, chemist Wallace Eakes of the Naval Facilities Engineering Command wrote a "trip report" to his supervisors at LANTDIV describing a weeklong tour he had made of seventy different contaminated sites at Camp Lejeune. He had visited the sites with a team that was conducting an environmental study at the base. One of the sites, which he called "Bldg 712," had been the base's "Malaria Control Headquarters" in the 1950s and had later been used to store and mix pesticides such as DDT (dichloro-diphenyl-trichloro-ethane), which had been banned by the EPA in 1972. The building was now being used as a day-care center for babies and young children. "The findings concerning Bldg 712, the present day care center, was a shock to all concerned," Eakes wrote in his March 31, 1982, memo. "I recommend that, since this may pose a health threat to the children at the day care center, preventive medicine should be involved." It was agreed that the Navy medical officer, Norman Lachapelle, would take air and soil samples in the area "under the guise of a normal health survey" so that children and parents wouldn't be alarmed. The Navy's tests did not find pesticide residues inside the building, but in May 1982 tests by a private laboratory found that soils outside the center contained high levels not only of DDT but also of the pesticides DDE (dichloro-diphenyl-dichloro-ethylene), DDD (dichloro-diphenyl-dichloro-ethane), and chlordane. The day-care center was immediately shut down.[31]

- In June 1982, an "initial assessment study" conducted at Camp Lejeune under the Navy's environmental program, NACIP, found seventy-two sites on the base where "some form of waste disposal" had occurred. "Indiscriminate dumping in about every part of the installation" ranged from waste disposal in pits and landfills to the spreading of petroleum compounds on the roads for dust control, said the study by the Navy's contractor, Water and Air Research, Inc., of Gainesville, Florida. "Some 17 sites had potentially hazardous materials and reasonable potential for material migration, and thus warranted more analysis," the report said. Among their conclusions, the consultants included this one: "The water table aquifer is highly susceptible to contamination from hazardous waste disposal practices."[32]

- On October 5, 1982, a civilian equipment operator, Jerry "Ike" Rochelle, took Camp Lejeune officials to two areas on the base where he had buried at least fifty drums of mustard gas or nerve gas in 1953. He said that Marine Corps officials who hired him for the job told him to wear "extensive protective gear," including a gas mask.[33]

- On November 22, 1982, the new environmental manager at Camp Lejeune, Bob Alexander, received a telephone briefing from LANTDIV's J. G. Wallmeyer on information obtained from five people who were "knowledgeable of disposal" at the base. The interviewees reported two sites where drums of chemicals had been buried, two sites where pesticides had been dumped (including one that was now covered by a basketball court), and a hazardous-waste site in the Rifle Range area where a worker was so badly injured in an explosion and fire in 1970 that two years of medical treatment were required.[34]

All of this was occurring at Camp Lejeune during a time when water contaminated with TCE was turning up at military bases across the country. In at least a few of those cases, base officials took swift action. Wurtsmith Air Force Base in Michigan detected TCE in its water in October 1977 and within a month began closing wells. The Warminster Naval Air Development Center outside Philadelphia did the same thing in 1979. The Willow Grove Naval Air Station, also near Philadelphia, found both TCE and PCE in a well on the base in 1979. "After contamination was detected, this well was used mainly for fire protection, and not drinking water," according to a public health assessment done at the now-closed base in May 2002.[35]

Despite all of the alarms sounding on the base, Camp Lejeune officials decided in 1982 to reduce the testing for THMs from monthly to quarterly, because that was all that was required by state and federal regulations. And in 1983, the base asked the state for permission to reduce the testing to once a year in the Hadnot Point system because of the "low" contamination levels.[36]

One reason that commanders at Camp Lejeune were blithely trying to avoid the issue of well contamination was that they were already struggling to meet the demand for water. In March 1983, an operator of the base water plants wrote to the utilities director expressing concerns about high usage in two of the eight water systems. Based on flows from April to October 1982, wrote general foreman W. R. Price, "the water treatment plants at Tarawa Terrace and Camp Johnson could very well be unable to satisfy the demand during the summer of this year due to steady decrease in well yield." Because the aquifer was being drained more rapidly than it was being replenished, wells that had once yielded 350 gallons of water per minute were now producing only about 50 gallons per minute, Price said. "If they keep operating pumps at capacity there is a high risk of failure," he wrote.[37]

It was not until 1984 that any wells were first shut down on the base.

5

TROUBLE AT TARAWA TERRACE

I think we kind of caught it right at the beginning.
—CHUCK RUNDGREN, DIRECTOR,
NORTH CAROLINA DEPARTMENT OF HUMAN RESOURCES,
DIVISION OF HEALTH SERVICES, WATER SUPPLY BRANCH

Jeff Byron was on the threshold of his dreams when he moved to Camp Lejeune in early 1982. In the past year he had joined the Marines, survived boot camp, gotten married, and graduated from the Navy's air-traffic control school in Millington, Tennessee. Best of all, his wife, Mary, was pregnant with their first child.[1]

Byron loved the Marine Corps—two of his uncles were Marines during World War II, and a cousin fought in Vietnam— but he wasn't really thinking about joining when he graduated from Forest Park High School in Cincinnati in 1975. He went to Morehead State University in Kentucky, then left after a breakup with his girlfriend in his third year there. Back in Ohio, he made a living as a bartender (and met Mary when he was on the job in a bowling alley). Meanwhile, the state was going through economic doldrums, just like the rest of the country. "It was the second-largest recession since the Great Depression in 1981 and it was hard to find a job," he said. "I was overqualified for lower-paying jobs and under-qualified for higher-paying jobs." So the Marines became a good path toward a better career, and Byron signed up in June 1981. He and Mary were married in Hamilton, Ohio, after Jeff finished boot camp in South Carolina and before he started at the Naval Air Technical Training Center in Tennessee.

When Byron was assigned to Camp Lejeune in early 1982, no housing was available on the base, so he and his wife rented a place in Jacksonville while waiting for a vacancy. Andrea was born in June. She was two months old when the family moved into base housing at Midway Park, directly across from the main gate at Camp Lejeune.

Andrea seemed perfectly healthy before she lived on the base—her only visits to the doctor were for "well-baby" exams, Byron said. That quickly changed after the move into Midway Park, where the Byrons lived for a year. Things continued to go downhill when the family lived in quarters at 3114 Bougainville Drive in the Tarawa Terrace housing complex from August 1983 until June 1985. In that period of less than three years, Andrea was at the base hospital a total of fifty-seven times—an average of nearly twice a month—for treatment of a variety of ailments. There were rashes, ear infections, coughs, urinary tract infections, yeast infections, and unexplained fevers. "Most of the time the medical personnel on base did not have an explanation for her symptoms," Byron said. "We were told to give her tepid baths and children's Tylenol to reduce the fevers."

One of the worst episodes involved three visits to the emergency room on the weekend after Thanksgiving in 1983, when Andrea's fever soared as high as 105.8 degrees. Again, doctors had no idea what was causing the baby's temperature to rise so far above normal.

Around the same time, another family was struggling with the serious but unexplained illness of their own daughter. Janey Ensminger was the six-year-old child of Jerry and Etsuko Ensminger, a drill instructor and his Japanese wife who lived on and off of Camp Lejeune for eleven of the nearly twenty-five years that Jerry was in the Corps. He was a career Marine, having joined right out of high school in 1970 in hopes of avenging his older brother's severe wounding at the hands of the Vietcong.[2]

Born on the Fourth of July in Chambersburg, Pennsylvania, in 1952, Jerry Ensminger was the third of six children in a family that was anything but steeped in the military. His father was an orphan who became a pipefitter and part-time farmer in south central Pennsylvania; he had fought the Germans in Greenland during World War II. His brother Dave had signed up for service only because he wanted to get married and pursue a career as a veterinarian, but couldn't afford college. The Marine Corps offered to send him to officers' school after boot camp, but Dave wanted to do only a two-year stint to qualify for the GI Bill, so he was assigned to the infantry with orders for Vietnam.

There, in an orchard in the Mekong Delta, Sergeant Dave Ensminger was leading a team that was training Vietnamese fighters when he crouched down to look into some brush as his unit was putting down its gear nearby. An explosion ripped into his lower body. A Marine from New Jersey ran to help and was killed by a second powerful blast. Dave Ensminger survived, but he had shrapnel in his skull and was paralyzed on the right side of his body. He came home facing years of therapy to learn how to walk again; eventually he would be able to handle a job as a mechanic at a Navy shipyard. These events on the other side of the world changed the direction of Jerry Ensminger's life. Ensminger hadn't even waited for his high-school graduation ceremony to be over before he joined the Marines. Some of his classmates, caught up in the antiwar fury felt by many young Americans in the spring of 1970, derided his decision to sign up. One of them spit on Ensminger. "I knocked his ass out," Ensminger said.

"I wanted to go to Vietnam—it was a revenge motive," he said. "But in 1970 we were starting to pull out." Ensminger ended up as a mechanic assigned to Camp Johnson, one of the ancillary bases at Camp Lejeune, where he worked on equipment that was used in training Marines to drive military vehicles. Then he was sent to Okinawa, Japan, as part of the support teams for bombing runs to Vietnam and Cambodia. It was there that he met Etsuko Asako, who was working in the Navy mess hall, and the two dated for a year and a half while Ensminger was assigned to the base. After filing scores of documents required by both the Marine Corps and the Japanese government, including a translated transcript of Asako's family history, the couple was married and had a daughter in Okinawa.

When he got orders to return to Camp Lejeune in 1973, Ensminger was a sergeant in the 8th Engineer Battalion, "but even with a sergeant's pay it was shit housing," he said. His family initially rented a trailer on the base, but as soon as better quarters became available in Tarawa Terrace, Ensminger broke his lease and moved his wife and baby there. It was in Tarawa Terrace in 1975 that Etsuko became pregnant with the girl they would name Janey.

Jerry Ensminger volunteered for the drill field around that time and went to the boot camp at Parris Island, South Carolina, for training. Since he could end up anywhere after his graduation as a drill instructor, his wife would remain at Camp Lejeune until she found out where the family would move next. As it turned out, she was on the base for almost two months of Janey's first trimester of development.

On December 19, 1975, Ensminger graduated and was assigned to stay at Parris Island. He immediately headed north to Camp Lejeune to pick up his pregnant wife and daughter. When he arrived, Etsuko was working hard to clean out their quarters so it would pass the series of inspections the Marine Corps required before anyone could move out. But Jerry Ensminger was anxious to have his family back together again. "I said to hell with it and hired a company to clean it that guaranteed you'd pass inspection," he said. "There was a payoff of course; they operated with kickbacks. I just wanted to get out of there."

At Parris Island, twenty-three-year-old Master Sergeant Ensminger was in the best condition—both physically and mentally—of his life. "I had muscles in my shit," he laughed. And he knew how to work recruits, berating them during the rigorous drills with favorite phrases, such as "Did your mother have any children who lived?" and "You are a paraplegic piece of pig shit!"

Janey Ensminger was born on July 30, 1976, at the Buford Naval Hospital near Parris Island. The baby girl seemed perfectly normal, though she never crawled—she rolled, her father said. "She learned to get up on her knees and rolled to the left." By the time the family moved back to Camp Lejeune in 1982, she was a precocious, fun-loving, and very active child. The Ensmingers moved into a house off the base at the time, but Jerry and Etsuko frequently took Janey and her two sisters (another daughter, Veronica, had also been born at Parris Island) to use the swimming pools at Camp Lejeune.

The problems began in the late spring and early summer of 1983, around the same time the Ensmingers were planning a trip to Pennsylvania for the wedding of Jerry's sister. Janey, a few months shy of seven years old, came down with a case of strep throat that she couldn't seem to shake. "We were going to cancel the trip to Pennsylvania, and then she got better, so we went," Ensminger said. "But then in Carlyle I had to take her to the base hospital. She got worse."

The family returned to North Carolina and Janey was still not feeling well. "I stayed home with her when we got back," Ensminger said. "It was on a Sunday in July and she got really hot. I was putting cold compresses on her and when I took off her shirt I noticed little hickeys on her back." Ensminger didn't know what they were—he learned later they were petechiae caused by hemorrhaging beneath the skin—but he knew they were a bad sign, and he rushed Janey to the base hospital.

"It was crowded, on a Sunday, but luckily my battalion surgeon was on duty and he ordered blood work," Ensminger said. "I could tell something was wrong, the way they were looking at her."

After waiting for what seemed like an eternity, and with his patience wearing thin—"I was ready to leap over the desk to demand an explanation," he said—the doctor finally called Ensminger back behind the counter while Janey was brought back into the waiting room with a Navy corpsman. The doctor said he had been waiting for the head of pediatrics to come but felt he couldn't hold off any longer, Ensminger said. "Your daughter has leukemia," the doctor told him.

"I went to my knees right there on the tile floor and my forehead hit the tile," Ensminger said. "I started to sweat and shake. I was going into shock. The doctor got me up and I said, 'I've got to get hold of myself.' Janey was there with a female corpsman and I needed to go to her."

Janey's blood platelet count was very low. The hospital had to have a supply flown in so the girl could make it through the night. The next day, Jerry and his wife arranged to have their daughter transferred to the Naval Medical Center in Portsmouth, Virginia, one of the military's top medical facilities.

—ᴍ—

When the first state regulations for groundwater quality in North Carolina took effect in 1983, Rick Shiver of the state's Department of Environment and Natural Resources was charged with overseeing their implementation in Onslow County and other parts of the coastal region. Shiver had actually lived at Camp Lejeune as a boy from 1954 to 1963 while his father was stationed there, and he had made many visits back since joining the state agency in 1973, having been assigned to Onslow County in 1978. So he was well aware of the base's operations and the fact that for decades a variety of hazardous materials had been dumped at numerous locations around the 220-square-mile installation. Julian Wooten and Danny Sharpe, the two environmental supervisors on the base in the 1970s, had even taken Shiver on a tour of many of these disposal sites in the mid-1970s.

It wasn't until July 1984, though, that Camp Lejeune's recently hired environmental engineer, Bob Alexander, showed Shiver the results of the 1980 and 1981 tests for trihalomethanes that indicated the presence of solvents in samples from the Hadnot Point and Tarawa Terrace water systems. Shiver was surprised that base officials hadn't done anything since to try to pinpoint the source of the contaminants. The large water systems on the base were served by as many as thirty wells, and if a test for the entire system showed contamination, it was likely the amount was diluted by water from clean wells. "I would have tested the wells individually," Shiver said.[3]

Bert Mundt, a water plant operator at Camp Lejeune from 1973 to 2004, didn't find out about the tests until years later, but he was convinced that base officials knew some of the water contained potentially harmful levels of toxic chemicals in the early 1980s. "They were perfectly aware," Mundt said in an interview. "They were just hoping it was diluted enough that it wouldn't be a problem." Base commanders didn't want to know if individual wells were contaminated, Mundt said, as the general foreman, W. R. Price, had written in 1983 that any shutdowns would have made it very difficult to meet summer demands for water.

The top managers at Camp Lejeune also felt justified in not spending money to test each of the dozens of wells on the base because they believed that any problems would be found and addressed in the Navy's environmental assessment and cleanup program, NACIP. After the initial assessment study, completed in 1982, which had identified more than seventy dumping sites on the base and recommended further assessment, the second phase, a verification study, was started in May 1984 by another Florida consulting firm, Environmental Science and Engineering, Inc., "to determine existence and possible migration of specific chemicals" at twenty-two locations at Camp Lejeune. "The objective of the verification step is to determine whether specific toxic and hazardous materials identified in the Initial Assessment Study, and possibly other contaminants, are present in concentrations considered to be hazardous," according to the "work and safety plan" prepared for the consultants by LANTDIV, which was overseeing NACIP at Camp Lejeune.[4]

A notice about the study was placed in a base newspaper, *The Globe*, in June 1984 so that residents would be prepared for workers in spacesuits digging around various sites at Camp Lejeune. The crews would be wearing protective gear, but "we do not expect to expose anyone to any contaminants," advised Colonel M. G. Lilley, assistant chief of staff for facilities, in the article.[5]

In the meantime, Shiver of the state environmental department started snooping around on his own for possible sources of groundwater pollution. He noticed that within a short distance of one of the Tarawa Terrace wells that had tested positive for solvents, there were three cleaning establishments and a gas station that would have storage tanks for chemicals and fuel. It didn't take long to identify the worst operation of the bunch. ABC One-Hour Cleaners, a thirty-year-old dry-cleaning service at 2127 Lejeune Boulevard, was directly across the highway from Tarawa Terrace. Shiver went to the service and asked the workers to show him around. "I observed solvent leaking from a big tank or its piping system and draining across a cement floor to a sump," Shiver said in an interview with federal investigators in 2004. "The sump pumped the liquids to a septic field. I realized that ABC Cleaners was the probable source of contamination at Tarawa Terrace." His suspicions were confirmed after three test wells were drilled and sampling showed that a plume of solvents in the groundwater, including tetrachloroethylene (or perchloroethylene, PCE), was migrating directly toward the housing area on the other side of the highway.[6]

At this point, some in the Marine Corps leadership thought all the water problems at Camp Lejeune had suddenly been solved. A commercial polluter was responsible for contamination moving into the base wells and would be forced to clean up the mess at its own expense. It didn't take long for that bubble to burst.

On November 30, 1984, the environmental staff at Camp Lejeune received an urgent call from the Navy engineers at LANTDIV. A test on a drinking-water well very close to the Hadnot Point fuel farm showed the presence of benzene and several solvents. The levels found included 121 parts per billion for benzene, an astounding 1,600 ppb for trichloroethylene (TCE), 630 ppb for trans-1,2-dichloroethylene (or trans-1,2-DCE, a solvent contained in many products, including waxes and resins), and 24 ppb for 1,1,2,2-tetrachloroethane (1,1,2,2-TeCA, mostly found in oils and lubricants). The well was immediately shut down. But this time the problem could not be blamed on ABC Cleaners. Not only was the well far from the cleaning service, the benzene was a telltale sign of fuel in the water, not cleaning solvents.

Less than a week later, on December 6, 1984, LANTDIV provided test results on samples from seven other wells serving the Hadnot Point water system. One showed benzene at 720 ppb and both TCE and trans-1,2-DCE at levels above 300 ppb; another well had TCE at 230 ppb. Both of those wells were shut down. The other five wells had only small traces of solvents, including levels of methylene chloride, also known as dichloroethane (DCE), that were determined to be the result of laboratory contamination. But the findings at Hadnot Point were alarming enough for LANTDIV engineers and the base environmental staff to decide to have every water well at Camp Lejeune tested for volatile organic compounds, or VOCs, starting in January 1985.[7]

Those tests were barely under way one day in late January when the wife of Camp Lejeune's chief of staff smelled fuel in her water at the officers' housing on Paradise Point. The area was served by the Holcomb Boulevard water system, which also pumped water to housing areas at Berkeley Manor, Watkins Village, Hospital Point, Midway Park, and Stone Street. When maintenance workers checked the pumping station at Holcomb Boulevard, they discovered a fuel line leaking directly into a water tank, sending fuel throughout the system, including the tap water in the chief of staff's quarters. If that didn't get the attention of base commanders, nothing would.

Utility operators at the base, assuming that after LANTDIV's December 6 report all the contaminated wells in the Hadnot Point system had been discovered and removed from service, shut down the Holcomb Boulevard system and replaced it with water from Hadnot Point, using a tie-in line that connected the two systems.

The Hadnot Point water would be pumped into both systems for more than a week until the Holcomb Boulevard lines were flushed.

After several days of pumping from Hadnot Point, tests were conducted on water samples taken from taps throughout the Holcomb Boulevard system to make sure the fuel contamination was disappearing. What was found in samples pulled from drinking-water fountains at the Berkeley Manor Elementary School on January 31, 1985, was shocking: the solvent TCE was measured at more than 1,100 parts per billion.

The solvent had to be coming from the Hadnot Point system, and sure enough, another contaminated well was discovered there that had not been tested earlier. This one, located near an old dumpsite, would show levels of TCE at a whopping 18,900 parts per billion, DCE at more than 8,000 ppb, and PCE at around 400 ppb. Considering that three other contaminated wells were now shut down in Hadnot Point, and more than 1,000 ppb of TCE were still being found in a school's drinking water because of this one well, it can only be assumed that levels of TCE in the drinking water from the Hadnot Point system may have been even higher when all four contaminated wells were online.

By now, all the top officials at Camp Lejeune knew they had a very serious problem that required immediate action. The results of tests conducted on all wells at the base rolled in during February and March, and a dozen wells had to be removed from service owing to the presence of volatile organic compounds: one in the Rifle Range system; one in the New River system serving the air station; two at Tarawa Terrace primarily containing PCE, the solvent that had leaked from ABC Cleaners; and eight in the Hadnot Point system containing benzene, TCE, and other VOCs.[8]

As expected, the well closures posed a difficult supply problem for the base managers. The loss of two wells at Tarawa Terrace, which had about 6,000 residents at the time, meant they would be short about 300,000 gallons per day during the spring and summer months when water was in highest demand, according to a March 1, 1985, memo by the assistant chief of staff for facilities at Camp Lejeune, Colonel M. G. Lilley. Lilley outlined seven different options for replacing the water, including having it hauled in by tanker trucks at a cost of about $2,000 a day or building a new well at Tarawa Terrace for about $80,000. Lilley also noted that the two contaminated wells could be turned on when needed "to maintain adequate water levels" at no cost to the base, but he warned that "the potential health hazards must be weighed against the need and cost of providing water from other sources."[9]

It was ultimately decided that an auxiliary line would be built connecting the Holcomb Boulevard system to the Tarawa Terrace area. The line was to be completed by June 1985.

Meanwhile, Lilley began preparing a defense for not taking action years earlier when tests showed the presence of solvents in the water at Hadnot Point and Tarawa Terrace. Julian Wooten, the longtime environmental manager at Camp Lejeune who was demoted when engineer Bob Alexander arrived in the early 1980s, was assigned to write what was later described by critics of the base management as a "cover your ass" memo in March 1985. Wooten was told to contact Paul Hubbell, a top civilian official at Marine Corps headquarters, to gather information about standards existing in other places around the country for volatile organic chemicals in drinking water. "Mr. Hubbell expressed surprise at the lack of information," Wooten wrote in his March 11, 1985, memo. The intended implication was that Camp Lejeune did not appear to be violating any regulations even if it had measurable levels of VOCs in its drinking water.[10]

A more telling sign that the Marine Corps was worried about its culpability for allowing contaminated wells to be used for years is that test results from numerous updates to the NACIP confirmation study of 1984 have been kept under wraps for decades. That study, conducted by Environmental Science and Engineering, Inc., "to determine existence and possible migration of specific chemicals" at Camp Lejeune, was required to be updated on a monthly basis before the final report was issued in January 1985. *The Globe*, the newspaper on the base, had reported in June 1984 that as the report was being conducted that year, if any contaminants were discovered in the base water supply, "a review of alternatives will determine action necessary to meet health and environmental standards." Presumably, the contractor was sampling all the wells at Hadnot Point during this time and reporting the results to Lejeune officials. But when the progress reports for 1984 were requested years later under the Freedom of Information Act, the Marine Corps said they had been destroyed in a 1999 warehouse fire for which the cause was never determined. As a result, test results from wells conducted in August, September, October, and November of 1984—just months before eight wells in Hadnot Point were shut down—have never been made public.[11]

Residents at Camp Lejeune—or at Tarawa Terrace, to be precise—were finally told about the water contamination on April 30, 1985, in a "Notice to Residents of Tarawa Terrace" from the base commander, Major General L. H. Buehl. The notice was later described by veteran congressional investigator Dick Frandsen as "one of the most outrageous things" about the military's handling of the base's water problems. "Two of the wells that supply Tarawa Terrace have had to be taken off line because minute (trace) amounts of several organic chemicals have been detected in the water," the commanding general said in the signed notice. "There are no definitive State or Federal regulations regarding a safe level of these compounds, but as a precaution, I have ordered the closure of these wells for all but emergency situations when fire protection or domestic supply would be threatened." The notice went on to encourage Tarawa Terrace residents to do all they could to reduce water usage during the upcoming warm months, such as flushing the toilet "only for sanitation purposes" and taking shorter showers. Car-washing on the base was banned, and lawn-watering was limited to a few hours on weekday mornings.[12]

The general's notice was misleading and deceptive in several ways. The description of the contamination as "minute" and "trace" did not match the reality of PCE levels above 100 parts per billion found in the two Tarawa Terrace wells, not to mention the fact that levels of TCE above 1,000 ppb had been discovered in other base water systems that were undoubtedly used at times by residents of Tarawa Terrace. The omission of the word "volatile" with "organic chemicals" also made the pollutants seem less hazardous than they were; if they had been accurately defined as "volatile organic compounds," many more residents probably would have been concerned about what was in their water. And the statement that the wells would be closed "for all but emergency situations when fire protection or domestic supply would be threatened" left open the possibility that contaminated wells would be brought back online if water demands could not be met.

Ten days after the notice went out, the *Jacksonville Daily News* reported about the chemicals in the base wells. Gunnery Sergeant John Simmons of the public affairs department at Camp Lejeune was quoted as saying that "no state or federal regulations mandate an unacceptable level of these organic chemicals in drinking water."[13]

The following day, May 11, 1985, the *Wilmington (N.C.) Morning Star* also reported on the water problems at Camp Lejeune. The newspaper quoted Chuck Rundgren of the state's water supply branch as saying he did not think base residents needed to worry about bad water. "I think we kind of caught it right at the beginning," he said.[14]

—ɯ—

Just as Camp Lejeune was shutting down its poisonous wells, Jeff and Mary Byron—still living in Tarawa Terrace—had their second child. Rachel was born on April 27, 1985. Her newborn profile at Onslow Memorial Hospital in Jacksonville listed no abnormalities, but when the Byrons took her to the base hospital for her first checkup, there were numerous concerns.

The Navy physicians reported that Rachel Byron was slow to gain weight and had a heart murmur, a double ear infection, an umbilical hernia, brachial dimples, ears rotated toward the back of her head, a large hemangioma (raised birthmark) on her lower back, and an atrial septal defect in her heart, Jeff Byron recounted in testimony to a congressional committee in 2007. "She was labeled a 'failure to thrive' baby," Byron said.

But the worst was yet to come for the Byrons. Jeff's stint in the Marine Corps ended in June 1985, and the family returned to Ohio, where Jeff and Mary had grown up. Six months after they arrived back in the Cincinnati area, their oldest daughter, Andrea, who was three years old, was diagnosed with a rare bone marrow disease, aplastic anemia. Initially it was believed that she would require a marrow transplant, but fortunately the disease went into remission before that was required. However, Andrea spent the next nine years of her young life undergoing treatment at the Cincinnati Children's Hospital Medical Center, including painful bone marrow testing and regular blood and platelet transfusions.

Early in Andrea's treatment, the head of the hematology department at the Cincinnati hospital asked the Byrons if their daughter had been exposed to any toxic chemicals. "Our answer? None," Jeff Byron said. "They asked us for all of the names of cleaning and hygiene products that we were using. All of the products were ruled out." Byron had read the "Notice to Residents of Tarawa Terrace" that the commanding general had distributed in

April 1985, but at the time he never connected any illnesses in his family to the "trace amounts" of "organic chemicals" found in the base housing's drinking water. Looking back, Byron was more disturbed by something else in the general's notice: his advice that they store water in the refrigerator for drinking. "So they want me to store poisoned water for my children to drink," he told the congressional panel in 2007. "But they don't spell out that—No. 1, it says that these are—they found minute trace amounts of several organic chemicals. 1,580 parts per billion is not minute or trace."[15]

Jerry Ensminger's daughter Janey turned nine years old on July 30, 1985, exactly two months after Major General Buehl sent his notice about the wells being shut down. Janey's leukemia had gone into remission for more than a year after it was discovered in 1983, but her father received some crippling news when he asked the Marine Corps in 1985 for a transfer to a Reserve unit in Harrisburg, Pennsylvania, so that Janey could undergo treatment at the Penn State University Medical Center, closer to his family. One of the doctors who evaluated Ensminger's request wrote a letter saying that Janey's white blood count was over 150,000, "which put her in a high-risk category and limited the ability or the chances that she would have long-term survival," Ensminger said. "I lived that nightmare every day from the time I saw that letter. Every day that entered my mind."

Ensminger later transferred his daughter to the Duke Children's Hospital and Health Center in Durham, North Carolina, which specializes in pediatric cancer treatment. During a visit in September 1985, one of the doctors said that Janey had relapsed. "And that was the beginning of the end," Ensminger said.

"Janey was a lot like me," Ensminger told a writer for the *Daily Beast*, Lloyd Grove, for a story in 2011. "She's very forward. She asserts herself. Very alert, very aware of her surroundings. She wanted to know everything and she wanted her voice in everything."

The doctors suggested another round of chemotherapy for Janey, but they warned that it would be painful, with lots of sores and ulcers. "I said no, I don't want that," Ensminger told Grove. "Janey was laying over there in the bed, and she said, 'Hey, you're talking about me, and I want a say in this. If there's a chance I can live, I want to do it.' I told the doctors, 'You heard her.' They did it, and oh my God, I still have her purse and all the stuff she had in her room. She had little examining lights—these flashlights that doctors use—and a little compact in her purse with a mirror. And she was obsessed with these sores, and she would constantly shine that thing in her mouth."

Grove told Ensminger that he thought it was incredible that his daughter could face such a terrifying illness and the excruciating treatments with such courage and practicality. "With any kid that has cancer and who's been in treatment for a long time," Ensminger responded, "if you weren't sitting there looking at that child and knowing that they were a child, you would think you were talking to an adult. They're all that way."[16]

Janey's final days were horrific, Ensminger said in testimony before Congress in 2007. "Every time she got stuck with a needle, I was there holding her," he said. "She was screaming in my ear. Every time they stuck a needle through her bone in her hip to pull out bone marrow, I held her and she screamed in my ear, 'Daddy, Daddy, don't let them hurt me.' And the only thing that I could say to her was, 'Honey, the only reason they're hurting you is they're trying to help you.'"

In a later interview, Ensminger said he marveled at his daughter's strength in the face of death. "Janey told me she didn't want to die," he said. "She wanted to live so she could make a difference in this world." She even had a sense that her presence would be felt after she was gone. A few days before she died, Janey told her father, "Every time you see a rainbow, Daddy, it'll be me."

Janey died on September 24, 1985. "And then on the day of her death, I started crying," Ensminger told members of Congress. "I hadn't cried in front of Janey before that time because she was pulling her strength from me. And I had to be strong for her. If I had to cry, I went somewhere else. But that day I started crying, and she looked up at me, and she had pneumonia that bad she could hardly talk, but she said, 'Stop it.' And I said, 'Stop what?' She said, 'Stop crying, Daddy. I love you.' That was the last words my daughter said to me. She went into a coma. Thirty-five minutes later, she took her last breath."[17]

6

A PERILOUS MESS

You wouldn't want kids out there digging in the soil.
—WAYNE MATHIS, ENVIRONMENTAL ENGINEER,
U.S. ENVIRONMENTAL PROTECTION AGENCY

Toxic waste entered the American consciousness in a big way
in 1978. That's when news reports appeared saying that about
a hundred homes in Niagara Falls, New York, along with the
neighborhood school, were sitting on top of barrels and barrels of
poisons that had been buried in the early 1950s by the Hooker
Chemical Company. Love Canal and its leaky drums of industrial
waste became a symbol of the nation's worst environmental problems. A state study found five documented cases of physical and
mental deformities among children born there after 1958 and determined that one in five pregnancies at Love Canal had resulted
in miscarriages. More than three hundred homes were eventually
abandoned, and hundreds of millions of dollars were spent to clean
up and rebuild the neighborhood.[1]

Within two years of the disaster, a frightened Congress established a program for cleaning up dangerous waste sites around the country. Known as Superfund, the Comprehensive Environmental Response, Compensation and Liability Act (CERCLA) of 1980 for the first time required polluters to pay for removal of hazardous wastes, and if responsible parties could not be found, special taxes collected from oil and chemical companies would be used for cleanups. Over the next several decades, more than 1,600 toxic sites were placed on the national Superfund list, including 141 sites operated by the US Department of Defense.[2]

Public sensibilities about deadly chemicals were further heightened in 1983 when it was discovered that a contractor for the city of Times Beach, Missouri, had used liquids containing dioxin to oil roads in the early 1970s. The entire community had to be abandoned after the dioxin levels in the water and soils were found to be hundreds of times above the safe level set by the Environmental Protection Agency. Today, Times Beach is only a memory for the 1,240 people who once lived there. All the buildings—and the poisons—have been removed, and the land has been converted into a state park.[3]

So when word went out from Camp Lejeune in 1985 that drinking-water wells had to be shut down because of chemical contaminants, alarm bells went off at a number of government agencies. The city of Jacksonville adjacent to the base was especially concerned, because it and other communities in Onslow County were drawing water for more than 100,000 people from an aquifer just below the one used by the military. Colonel R. A. Tiebout, the facilities supervisor at the base, assured the city in a letter on June 5, 1985, that there was a natural barrier between the aquifer used by Camp Lejeune and the one used by the city. The Marines were tapping the aquifer at depths of between 200 and 250 feet, whereas the city's water was coming from around 500 feet below the surface, he explained. Tiebout said he had checked with environmental officials at both the base and the state water agency, and it was their opinion "that we are in no way affecting the aquifer that is presently used by the city of Jacksonville. As noted on the enclosure, there are several layers of clay which act as a membrane to prevent the groundwater from seeping into the middle sand aquifer."[4]

Despite the publicity surrounding Love Canal and Times Beach, however, Marine Corps officials were almost nonchalant about the fact that toxic contamination had forced the shutdowns of ten wells in two of the base drinking-water systems. It wasn't until June 21, 1985, that the results of tests for trihalomethanes, such as chloroform, a by-product of water treatment processes, were given to the Camp Lejeune utilities director, Gold Johnson, by Danny Sharpe of the environmental division. "Until this date, I was not informed that we had any problems with this," Johnson wrote in a memo that day—nearly five years after the first tests for the chemicals in the base water done by the Army lab. He noted that the data had not been submitted to the state either "and will probably result in a violation letter from the state."[5]

More appalling than the failure to communicate about the water problems was the fact that Camp Lejeune officials continued to allow the contaminated wells to be used after they were first turned off in early 1985. In late spring that year, base environmental engineer Bob Alexander reported to Marine Corps headquarters that all ten contaminated wells at Hadnot Point and Tarawa Terrace remained closed, though his report indicated that one of the tainted wells at Tarawa Terrace had been used three times in April to maintain the water supply to the nearly 6,000 residents of the housing complex.[6]

Federal health officials would report at a congressional hearing in 2007 that contaminated wells were used off and on for two years at Camp Lejeune after the presence of solvents was confirmed in 1985. Research by the Agency for Toxic Substances and Disease Registry (ATSDR), a part of the federal Centers for Disease Control (CDC) that was investigating whether people were affected by Camp Lejeune's pollution, showed "there may have been some much lower contamination in the finished water from 1985 through 1987," the agency's Tom Sinks said at the hearing. Asked if the levels of dry-cleaning solvents in the water at Tarawa Terrace after 1985 were above 5 parts per billion, which by that time had been set as a federal health standard for the solvents, Sinks said the levels were "probably between five and ten, but certainly nowhere approaching the levels of 180 which we saw prior to 1985."[7]

At least the Marine Corps was taking steps to solve the problem. An emergency water line to Tarawa Terrace from the Holcomb Boulevard system became active in June 1985. Soon after that, in early summer, the base asked the United States Geological Survey (USGS) for a study to help determine "groundwater use and management practices that will reduce the chances of further contamination and help assure that future water-supply needs are met." The USGS responded with a study proposal that showed the complexity of the task. Camp Lejeune has one of the largest groundwater withdrawals in North Carolina—8 million gallons per day to support a population of about 100,000, noted USGS hydrologist Orville B. Lloyd Jr. in the proposal. Lloyd added that there had been tremendous growth at the base over the years and a corresponding rise in the wastes generated: "As a result," he wrote, "significant amounts of several kinds of wastes containing hazardous and toxic organic compounds have been disposed of or spilled at numerous sites on the base." The sandy soils in the coastal area did little to prevent the wastes from moving into the groundwater. In order to fully understand the movement of contaminants and groundwater conditions below the base, the USGS would need to do a study in three phases over four years at a cost to the Marines of \$417,000, the hydrologist said.[8]

—⁂—

While the Marines were scrambling to maintain a clean water supply for Lejeune residents, the state of North Carolina was demanding immediate action on the contaminated groundwater. On May 15, 1985, the state's Department of Natural Resources and Community Development notified the base commanding general, Major General L. H. Buehl, that state standards had been violated in ten wells containing at least nine organic contaminants, including the degreaser trichloroethylene (TCE), the dry-cleaning solvent perchloroethylene (PCE, also called tetrachloroethylene), the TCE by-product vinyl chloride, and a carcinogen found in fuel, benzene. As a result of the violations, the Marine Corps had thirty days to provide the state with the base's plan of action for identifying the sources of the contamination, determining the extent of the contaminated plume, and completing remedial work.[9]

It took more than thirty days for the Marine Corps to respond. When Colonel Tiebout wrote to the state on July 19, 1985, he said the plan of action was simply to continue with the Navy Assessment and Control of Installation Pollutants program that had started in 1982 with an assessment of potentially contaminated sites at the base. The next steps planned in NACIP included retesting groundwater at twenty of the polluted sites, conducting new tests on samples from all water wells on the base, determining the size and movement of the contaminated plume, and developing plans to clean it up, according to an outline of the plan attached to Tiebout's letter to the state. The goal was to complete the NACIP process by the end of 1986, he said.[10]

The state's attention to Camp Lejeune's problems soon resulted in a public spotlight on the base contamination. The *Raleigh News*

& Observer published a lengthy report on September 15, 1985, headlined "Civilians, Military Investigating Waste Dumps at Camp Lejeune." The story began by describing the child-care center that had been housed in a former pesticide-storage building for nearly twenty years until it was shut down in 1982, when chemicals such as DDT and chlordane had been found in the soil outside. Wayne Mathis, an environmental engineer for the EPA, told the newspaper that he could not speculate about the risks to children who spent time at the site over the previous two decades, but he added, "You wouldn't want kids out there digging in the soil." In fact, there is little doubt that many children did just that, as there was a 6,300-square-foot playground outside the day-care center where the soils were found to be laced with pesticides.

The *News & Observer* went on to describe widespread dumping at the base, but noted that Camp Lejeune wasn't the nation's worst military site in that regard, or even the most polluted installation in the Southeast. EPA officials told the paper that bases in Tennessee, Alabama, and Georgia had sites that were even more polluted. They also made a point of saying that it appeared that no laws had been violated at the bases. "The military hasn't done anything that wasn't done in the private sector," said Arthur E. Linton, federal facilities coordinator for the EPA's southeast region in Atlanta. The Marines and state officials also downplayed the fact that at Camp Lejeune, ten wells serving two major drinking-water systems had to be closed because of the toxic pollution. Charles E. Rundgren, head of the state's water supply branch, was quoted in the story as saying that the base water would not cause someone to immediately become sick from drinking it, but he did warn that ill effects could result from long-term exposure.[11]

The story was an early signal that the Marine Corps was not going to be able to gloss over Camp Lejeune's environmental problems as some of its leaders hoped. "I anticipate considerable public attention to this problem and how we deal with it," a state environmental manager, Chuck Wakild, said in an October 1985 memo to Perry F. Nelson, chief of the groundwater section at the North Carolina Department of Natural Resources and Community Development. It also was becoming clear to state officials that the land and water, and possibly even the air, at the largest Marine base on the East Coast had become an utter, perilous mess.[12]

Rick Shiver, regional hydrogeologist in the state's Division of Environmental Management, prepared a detailed report for his bosses in October 1985 that said more than seventy sites with hazardous wastes had been identified at the base, and thirty-eight of them were potential sources of groundwater pollution. Already ten wells were permanently shut down, and the contamination posed a threat to at least eighteen others, he said.

Shiver's report was the main item of business at a November 1, 1985, meeting at Camp Lejeune between environmental managers from the base, the state, and the federal Environmental Protection Agency. The EPA had taken a lead role in the cleanup process because it was unclear whether the state had authority over pollution problems on federal land. At the meeting, the EPA's Wayne Mathis said that data from the contaminated wells in January 1985 showed health risks to people at the base, so Camp Lejeune should be eligible for placement on the National Priorities List for the Superfund program. The base environmental manager, Bob Alexander, pushed back, arguing that there may have been errors in the tests done on the water wells, and therefore a Superfund designation would be overkill. And so began a struggle that would continue for years over who would be in charge of the base cleanup, the EPA or the Navy.[13]

The military was determined to follow its own process, the Navy Assessment and Control of Installation Pollutants program known as NACIP, and tried to build a case for it by insisting that the water at the base was now clean and safe. The assistant chief of staff at Camp Lejeune, Colonel Tiebout, sent a memo to the commanding general on November 6, 1985, saying the contamination problem at Tarawa Terrace was under control. "We have not detected any organic compounds in the Tarawa Terrace finished water since we started taking weekly samples in July," Tiebout said, adding that the state was addressing the source of the housing area's pollution, ABC One-Hour Cleaners located off the base. Environmental manager Julian Wooten followed up in January 1986 with a report to the state saying that tests now showed "no immediate concern over the quality of water in the two systems at Tarawa Terrace and Hadnot Point."[14]

Navy headquarters tried to bolster its case for managing Camp Lejeune's cleanup by arguing that the NACIP process it would follow had the same requirements for public involvement as the Superfund program. The Navy's chief of information, Rear Admiral J. B. Finkelstein, issued a memorandum on July 1, 1986, stating that it was NACIP policy to keep all interested parties informed about every step of a cleanup project. "To assure the public that the Navy is not hiding information concerning former hazardous waste sites on Navy property, local and state officials, media and interested organizations should be fully apprised of NACIP activity at the commencement and conclusion of each phase of work," Finkelstein wrote.[15]

The EPA was not happy with the NACIP process, though. At a meeting on July 31, 1986, between sixteen officials from the base, the state, and the EPA, it was pointed out that NACIP was not nearly as demanding as the Superfund law known as CERCLA: the cleanup standards were lower, the deadlines for action were looser, and the requirements for studies were weaker. Under the Superfund program, each contaminated site would require a full "remedial investigation/feasibility study" (RI/FS) that would cost between $200,000 and $600,000, and Camp Lejeune was going to need at least twenty such projects. If the EPA had its way, it was going to cost the Navy a minimum of $4 million to do just the required studies at the base, and that was before any real cleanup work began.[16]

An overview of the base using environmental studies and reports produced in later years explains why the EPA in 1986 wanted to declare Camp Lejeune one of the worst toxic-waste dumps in America. As the state's Rick Shiver put it, "these were not the garden variety landfills." The contaminated sites included:

- The Hadnot Point fuel farm, which had been built in an industrial area near Ash Street that was only a short distance from a major housing complex. More than a dozen fuel tanks had been installed at this site when the base was built in 1941—a 600,000-gallon tank above ground and fourteen underground tanks, each one capable of holding 12,000 to 15,000 gallons of fuel. A break in one of the aging lines to the tanks in 1979 had caused at least 20,000 gallons of fuel to leak into the soils at the site, and a number of other leaks were documented in the 1980s, including two of more than 1,000 gallons each. The result was that large pools of diesel and gasoline, fifteen feet deep in some places, were floating on the top of the aquifer just below the surface. Groundwater in the area of the tank farm contained "extremely high levels of benzene."

- A site known as Lot 203, located near Holcomb Boulevard and Piney Green Road south of Wallace Creek, that was used for forty years to dispose of just about every type of hazardous waste imaginable. "There is everything from some aboveground storage tanks labeled 'diesel fuel' to minefield-clearing training kits to M-16 shells to . . . the DDT and PCB disposal area, and so on and so forth," environmental engineer Ray Wattras told a meeting of cleanup officials at Camp Lejeune in 1992.

- The Rifle Range Chemical Dump, on the south side of Camp Lejeune next to the New River, which was used from the early 1950s until 1976 to bury containers of pesticides such as DDT, wastes containing PCBs from transformers and other equipment, cleaning solvents such as TCE, chemical weapons, and gas cylinders. Investigators documented at least a dozen different "disposal events" at the dump. "Waste materials that were allegedly disposed of here include PCBs, pentachlorophenol, pesticides, gas possibly containing cyanide, chemical agent test kits, and fired and unfired cartridges," Wattras said at the 1992 meeting, continuing, without irony, "We believe that there is a high probability that chemical agents may be present."

- Two lots on Holcomb Boulevard between Wallace and Bear Head creeks—about midway between the Watkins Village and Hadnot Point residential areas—that were used to dump the now-banned pesticide DDT during the 1940s. Transformers containing cancer-causing PCBs were also stored at the same site.

- A pit off Center Road at the heart of the base that was used in the early 1950s to dump waste oil and liquids from transformers and other electrical equipment. From 1958 to 1977 the area was then used for mixing pesticides and cleaning pesticide equipment. Every week during those two decades, an estimated 350 gallons of pesticide-laced water from the cleaning operations flowed onto the ground.

- A burn dump for garbage, industrial waste, and construction debris at the center of Camp Lejeune, at Hadnot Point on the east bank of the New River. The twenty-three-acre site, in operation from 1946 to 1971, was graded and seeded with grass after it was closed and is now a recreational area with a fishing pond.

- A parcel of land adjacent to the New River, where about a gallon of mercury was poured on the ground each year between 1956 and 1966. The toxic metal that had been drained from radar units "was reportedly hand carried and dumped or buried in small quantities at random areas" around the four-acre site, according to one EPA report.

- A dump at Camp Geiger on the north end of the base that was used from 1946 to 1970 as both a landfill for hazardous wastes—including mortar shells and grenades—and as an open burn area for garbage, used oil, batteries, cleaning solvents, and ordnance. Tons of the insecticide Mirex, banned by the EPA in 1976, were buried at the site in 1964. It was also reported that two truckloads of drums containing pesticides, PCBs, solvents, and "chemical agent training kits" were unloaded at the site in the mid-1960s.

- The Mess Hall Grease Disposal Area, located in a wooded area east of Holcomb Boulevard in the northeastern quadrant of the base, which served as a dump for grease and food wastes from the mess hall in the 1950s. Dozens of drums were also found buried at the site, probably containing PCBs or pesticides.

• A disposal area at Courthouse Bay, a few miles inland from the ocean shore, where at least 400,000 gallons of waste oil and 20,000 gallons of battery acid were dumped.

• The French Creek Liquids Disposal Area on the southern end of the base, near a creek flowing into the New River, the dumping ground for as many as 20,000 gallons of waste fluids and oil from vehicle maintenance and up to 10,000 gallons of acid from used batteries.

• A point along a trail used for training exercises, near Sneads Ferry Road and Marines Road, where two 12,000-gallon tanks of sludge from fuel tanks were emptied on the ground while fuel-storage facilities on the base were being upgraded in 1970.[17]

Even with all that hazardous waste on the base, the worst contamination for residents of Tarawa Terrace was actually coming from off the base, from the dry-cleaning business at 2127 Lejeune Boulevard directly across the highway from the housing area. ABC One-Hour Cleaners had opened in the mid-1950s and did a booming business serving the base's active and mobile population. And while the owners, brothers Milton and Victor Melts, were cleaning uniforms and civilian clothes for Marines and their families, their business was dumping the highly toxic solvent PCE into the groundwater on an almost daily basis. The cleaning agent was stored in a leaky 250-gallon tank behind the business. A pipe to the tank also leaked regularly, and buckets of the used solvent were frequently dumped on the ground at the site, according to state and federal inspection reports. PCE-tainted sludge was even used to fill potholes in the establishment's parking lot. Chemicals that didn't seep through the soils directly into the shallow aquifer below ended up there anyway after they were washed into the business's septic tank, which was located 900 feet from one of the wells used for Tarawa Terrace drinking water.[18]

The EPA proposed ABC One-Hour Cleaners for the Superfund program in 1988 and formally added it to the list of the nation's worst hazardous-waste sites in 1989. The Marine Corps paid close attention to the proceedings because, as Colonel A. P. Tokarz of the Navy's Judge Advocate General's office told the North Carolina attorney general in early 1988, "the Department of Defense or the Federal Government may ultimately be required to seek contribution from ABC Cleaners for its on-Base clean-up costs." (That turned out to be wishful thinking: the business, which became only a drop-off location for dry cleaning in 2005, and was closed in 2011 after being damaged in Hurricane Irene, was unable to afford the extensive cleanup required. Taxpayers ultimately footed the $2.2 million bill through the Superfund program.)[19]

Camp Lejeune's command over its own environmental problems was in chaos, and its maintenance staff was overwhelmed in the late 1980s. The director of utilities, C. H. Baker, acknowledged as much in an "action brief" sent to base headquarters on March 15, 1988, that was tantamount to throwing up a white flag of surrender. Baker's plea for help said: "(1) Confusion exists regarding which organization or person is responsible for acting on environmental issues, implementing environmental policies and programs, and resolving environmental problems; (2) No single point of contact is available for consultation with State and Federal agencies; (3) Confusion exists among Base activities and State and Federal Agencies regarding who to talk to on various environmental concerns." There were also more than a dozen

"outstanding environmental concerns" that required action, Baker
said, including the need to address illegal discharges at four
sewage treatment plants and the need to notify people on the base
about "lead and other heavy metals in drinking water."[20]

It wasn't just the water that was causing environmental concerns at Camp Lejeune. Throughout the 1980s, workers in many
buildings complained about fuel odors and chemical smells inside
the workplace. Tests of indoor air were recommended by consultants at Environmental Science and Engineering in the summer of
1988 as part of a five-part plan "to deal with immediate health risk
in the Hadnot Point area of the base." The firm recommended
tests of air quality in areas "with the potential for high levels of
harmful volatile compounds," such as inside buildings near "hot
spots" of contaminated groundwater. Dangerous levels of benzene,
TCE, and other pollutants in the air could easily be detected using a
vapor analyzer or other equipment, the consultants said, adding
that if levels were above the limits considered acceptable to humans, "immediate measures, such as forced ventilation, should be
taken to reduce health risks until permanent remediation measures
can be taken."[21]

This was at a time when Camp Lejeune managers knew that
fuel was leaking from the tank farm at Hadnot Point at a rate of
1,500 gallons per month and that it was forming a pool of diesel
and gasoline, 15 feet deep in some places, just below the surface in
an area filled with offices and maintenance buildings. Base officials
were more concerned at the time with the cost of the wasted fuel
than with the health effects of the leaks. "The loss of 1,500 gallons
per month will be difficult for taxpayers to understand, and the extremely high costs of recovering that lost fuel exacerbate the problem," Colonel Tokarz wrote in a March 29, 1988, memo to the
base's assistant chief of staff.[22]

The head of the Naval Hospital at Camp Lejeune, H. P. Scott, told the base commander that summer that his staff would not be able to conduct indoor-air monitoring. It would take five people to do the job, or half the hospital's industrial hygiene staff, Scott complained, suggesting that the work be contracted out. Years later, when the Marine Corps was asked to produce results of the air tests, none could be found. A Marine spokesman, Major Nat Fahy, told the *St. Petersburg Times* in Florida in 2011 that an extensive search of records turned up empty. "The absence of records more than 20 years later does not necessarily mean action was not taken," Fahy told the newspaper. "We believe that any testing that may have been done was done in a timely manner."[23]

The paper found a woman who had worked as a computer specialist in a building that had to be evacuated several times in the 1980s because of fuel odors. The woman, Mildred Duncan, was furious that the base apparently never tested the air in her office. "This is a betrayal," said Duncan, now retired as a civilian employee for the Marine Corps. "It's like they lied to us. They kept us in those buildings, breathing all that. It's not right."[24]

On June 24, 1988, the EPA again proposed placing Camp Lejeune on the National Priorities List for the Superfund program, the first step toward a final designation and a full cleanup managed by the federal environmental agency. The extent of a "full cleanup" was a contentious point. Marine Corps engineers had suggested that it would take about five years to clean up the groundwater in the Hadnot Point industrial area, but EPA project managers commented that the Navy was being unrealistic—restoration work would take at least thirty years, they said.[25]

Nine months after the Superfund listing was proposed, another federal agency encouraged the EPA to move forward with a cleanup. The National Oceanic and Atmospheric Administration (NOAA), a branch of the US Commerce Department that serves as a trustee of the nation's natural resources, said it had determined

that Camp Lejeune represented "a potential threat to natural resources held in trust by federal agencies."[26]

As the official designation of Camp Lejeune as a Superfund site
came closer, Marine Corps commanders decided they should notify base residents before they were alarmed by a news announcement from the EPA. In September 1989, Corporal Dave Mundy
wrote a series of reassuring stories in the base newspaper, including one quoting chemist Elizabeth Betz saying the contamination
levels at Camp Lejeune were considered safe by the EPA and that
much of the pollution came from an off-base source, ABC One-
Hour Cleaners. A number of water wells were shut down, but
there was no effect on base operations, added B. W. Elston,
deputy assistant chief of staff for facilities at the base. "We closed
eight wells in the Hadnot Point Industrial Area and two in the
Tarawa Terrace area as a precautionary measure and still had an
adequate water supply," Elston said.

"We shut down some wells that were not near the EPA limit,"
Betz told the base newspaper. "Then we started looking at what
caused that contamination." The fact that one of the chemicals
found in the wells was the dry-cleaning solvent known as PCE
helped determine the source, she said. "We were puzzled when
that chemical showed up," Betz said. "At first we couldn't figure
out how it had gotten into the Tarawa Terrace system. Then we
looked across Highway 24. There was a dry-cleaning business
right across the road from the housing area."[27]

Elston was quoted again in a follow-up story by Mundy touting
the high standards at the Marine Corps base. "Very few munici-
palities, I'd say, are inspected as often or as thoroughly as our public works are," Elston said. "Violations are reported promptly and
corrected immediately. . . . We always take measures to go at least
a step beyond what is required by law and to ensure that we don't

provide water that is unsafe for those using it. The commanding general will not accept anything less."[28]

On October 4, 1989, a few weeks after the articles were published at Camp Lejeune, the EPA officially designated the base as a Superfund site. Among the reasons listed were fuel contamination and volatile organic compounds in the groundwater beneath the Hadnot Point Industrial Area, potential damage to wetlands from waste disposal areas on the base, and pesticide-contaminated soil outside a building once used as a child-care center.[29]

Rick Shiver, the environmental regulator representing North Carolina in negotiations on the cleanup, said that by this point the Marine Corps seemed resigned to the fact that it had a massive job ahead of it. The military lawyers and engineers worked closely with the state and the EPA to write a 172-page "federal facilities agreement" spelling out requirements for the cleanup and the responsibilities of all parties involved. "It was all very collaborative," Shiver said. "There was no animosity between the various groups."

7

THE STRUGGLE FOR DATA

You and I both know how this would "play in Peoria."
—KATHY SKIPPER, AGENCY FOR TOXIC SUBSTANCES
AND DISEASE REGISTRY, OFFICE OF POLICY AND EXTERNAL AFFAIRS

If the Marine Corps had been cooperative with regulators on cleanup plans at Camp Lejeune, the same could not be said for its efforts to find out who might have been harmed by the pollution.

Once the base was placed on the Superfund list, a required federal health study kicked in to determine if people had been exposed to unsafe levels of contamination. The task of conducting this Public Health Assessment fell to the Agency for Toxic Substances and Disease Registry, or ATSDR, created by Congress in the CERCLA law that established the Superfund program in 1980. Not intended as a regulatory agency, the ATSDR had a relatively small budget (less than $16 million for health assessments nationwide in 1990).[1] It had to rely largely on the polluters themselves for funding and data in order to study whether their pollution affected public health, hardly the ideal way to conduct scientific research. The science of defining chemical pathways, determining levels of human exposure, and taking into account other environmental influences is anything but exact, yet to have impact on policy it must stand up to rigorous standards and extensive peer review.

In the case of Camp Lejeune, there was an additional conflict. The ATSDR is assisted on many studies by a sister agency within the Department of Health and Human Services (HHS), the Public Health Service, which has its roots in the US Navy. Many in the so-called "commissioned corps" consider themselves part of the military, and even wear Navy uniforms and have similar ranks, operating under the command of the surgeon general of the United States. Thus, not only were the government scientists who were assigned to find out if the US Marine Corps had inadvertently poisoned people at one of its largest installations dependent on the military for the money and information needed to do the job, but they were at least loosely connected to the military themselves. It was kind of like the nerdy little brother being told to find out if the bullying star athlete in the family had been violating any of Mom and Dad's rules.

Though it was only twelve years old when it began studying Camp Lejeune's contamination issues in 1992, the ATSDR already had a questionable reputation. A joint study released by two environmental groups that year maintained that both the CDC and the ATSDR—two federal agencies most responsible for protecting Americans from harmful pollution—routinely produced health studies that were "inconclusive by design" because they used weak testing methods, inappropriate statistical analyses, biased contractors, and misguided assumptions about the kinds of health problems that might have occurred. The result was that very few of the ATSDR's assessments showed harmful exposures to toxic pollution.

ATSDR investigators also were known to avoid direct contact

with people in affected communities, the study found. "According to both local citizens and their physicians, ATSDR has lacked even the simple etiquette of returning their phone calls," the report said. "Agency officials have themselves acknowledged that 'Unless you are a senator or a senator's staff we won't respond.'" Environmentalists reached a damning conclusion about the CDC and the ATSDR. The Environmental Health Network and National Toxics Campaign Fund concluded: "They have become virtual propaganda tools of polluting industries—making public reassurance instead of public protection their foremost focus. One result has been an increase in public complacency and government inaction at many sites where further precautions to reduce toxic exposures are merited."[2]

To its credit, the ATSDR quickly determined there was reason to be concerned about people in Tarawa Terrace who had used water from wells contaminated with perchloroethylene, or PCE, that had been dumped by ABC One-Hour Cleaners across the highway from the base housing. A Public Health Assessment completed in 1990 on the dry-cleaners' pollution prompted the agency to start looking for health effects, especially on babies, in the Tarawa Terrace population. They began by compiling birth records from the base hospital going back more than twenty years.[3]

The ATSDR took much longer to zero in on potential exposures from the many sites on the base where land or groundwater was tainted by hazardous materials used in operations. A major reason for that delay was a lack of cooperation from the Marine Corps in providing information about base contamination. Nearly two years into the study, on February 23, 1993, the epidemiologist in charge of the Public Health Assessment at Camp Lejeune, Nancy Sonnenfeld, wrote the base's communications director, Neal Paul, saying she had received only one set of pre-1985 data on drinking water at the base. Even that data was flawed, showing some contaminants at levels so low it would not have been possible to detect them using available technology. Sonnenfeld tried to be reassuring about what the health agency might find if it had more information: "As the Navy has noted, the discovery of contamination in potable wells at these sites does not in itself imply that anyone actually drank or washed with contaminated water; the water was treated and diluted before distribution," she wrote. "Therefore, I would like to examine the data from samples of the tap water which was actually distributed to individual residences and housing areas on the base."

Sonnenfeld asked for information about Camp Lejeune's water treatment processes, about when tap water was analyzed, about the dates when contamination was first discovered in potable wells and in tap water, and about the frequency of sampling before and after the closures of contaminated wells. She added that she was also still in need of information about all the base housing areas, how many people lived in each, and which water systems they used. And she asked for rough estimates of the numbers of people who had been living at the base for longer than five years and those who had been there for more than ten years at the time the contamination was discovered.[4]

A couple of weeks later, on March 5, 1993, ATSDR environmental engineer Stephen Aoyama followed up with a letter to Paul asking for information about cleanup work that had been done so far at the base, along with documents from the Superfund program, such as site studies and work plans, and a full index of the administrative record for the cleanup effort. But the Marine Corps continued to stonewall for another year and a half, prompting the ATSDR's Carol Aloisio, in the office of the assistant administrator, to send a letter higher up in the Navy command. "As you are aware, we have had much difficulty getting the needed documents from MCB Camp Lejeune," Aloisio wrote on September 2, 1994, to Yvonne P. Walker at the Navy Environmental Health Center in Norfolk, Virginia. "We have sent MCB Camp Lejeune several requests for information and, in most cases, the responses were inadequate and no supporting documentation was forwarded. . . . For an ATSDR public health assessment to be useful, it is important that all pertinent information be provided for evaluation."[5]

The commanding officer of the Navy Environmental Health Center, W. P. Thomas, responded eleven days later by sending a letter to the commander of the Naval Facilities Engineering Command suggesting that Camp Lejeune's environmental managers cooperate with the ATSDR—but not ordering them to do so. "In general, we recommend that the Department of the Navy installations routinely provide ATSDR with documents distributed to the installation's Restoration Advisory Board," Thomas wrote. Base officials should keep the ATSDR updated with revisions to the administrative index for the Superfund cleanup and "should respond to requests for information promptly with appropriate supporting documents."[6]

Despite the limited cooperation, the ATSDR managed to complete a first draft of the Public Health Assessment for Camp Lejeune in September 1994. The authors of the assessment concluded that there were "probable health effects" from exposures to volatile organic compounds in the drinking water and recommended further study of babies born to women who drank the contaminated water during their pregnancies. "A study of birth outcomes, in particular of low birth-weight, pre-term births and fetal deaths, should further our understanding of the health effects of low-dose VOC exposure," the draft assessment said.

Navy officials threw a fit. Andrea Lunsford, head of the health risk assessment department at the Navy Environmental Health Center in Virginia, responded to the ATSDR's initial public health assessment with a "medical review" dated October 28, 1994.

Lunsford challenged the health agency's assumption that a study of birth outcomes would add to understanding about the effects of low-dose VOC exposure, saying it was difficult to determine "causal relationships" between specific contaminants and certain health effects, and even more difficult when the subjects of the proposed study were part of a "a transient, military population" exposed to many other harmful substances as well. Lunsford also said it was "somewhat misleading" to suggest that there were "probable health effects for VOC exposures" at the base, "since the risk estimates are based on personnel being exposed to these maximum detected values for a period of one year." In reality, people were exposed to varying levels of contamination throughout their time on the base, not always to the maximum levels, she said.[7]

There were other criticisms, including a complaint about the ATSDR saying that personnel involved in training exercises could be exposed to harmful contaminants without being specific about what areas of the base and what chemicals posed that threat. Of course, if the Marine Corps had provided full information about contaminated sites, the health agency could have given more precise assessments. ATSDR's scientists pressed on, and despite another delay when "the agency's entire file on Camp Lejeune was mistakenly thrown out—tossed in the trash—by a contractor," as a House investigation found in 2010, a final version of the Public Health Assessment was released to the public in August 1997.[8]

The report said there were ten sites out of ninety-four potential areas of contamination on the base that had potential for human exposure. And it found three past health hazards: volatile organic compounds in three drinking-water systems (Tarawa Terrace, Hadnot Point, and Holcomb Boulevard), lead in tap water in buildings with lead plumbing, and exposure to pesticides in soils at the former day-care center. On the drinking-water exposures, the agency said solvents including TCE and PCE "have been documented over a period of 34 months, but likely occurred for a longer period of time, perhaps as long as thirty years."

The biggest concern to the scientists was the fetal exposures. The agency said it had already begun investigating "pregnancy outcomes" at the base and had identified about 6,000 infants whose mothers lived in housing with contaminated water supplies. It had found a "statistically significant" decrease in birth weights for males in that group, particularly among babies born to mothers who lived in areas served by the Hadnot Point water system, but also among babies whose mothers lived at Tarawa Terrace. Low birth weights, generally below five and a half pounds, are warning signs of other potential health problems.[9]

Surprisingly, the ATSDR did not express concern about the poisoned aquifer at Camp Lejeune. "Groundwater contamination on base is considered no apparent public health hazard because several programs are in place to detect, monitor, and predict groundwater contamination flow before people could be exposed to any contaminated drinking water," the agency said. That finding seemed to conflict with a number of previous reports about the base aquifer, such as the 1988 confirmation study for the Navy by Environmental Science and Engineering, Inc., that described "extremely elevated" levels of benzene in water supply wells at Hadnot Point. And it seemed as if the agency was unaware of the large pools of fuel that that were floating on top of the shallow aquifer, fed by leaks from underground storage tanks and pipes at the rate of 1,500 gallons a month.

Nevertheless, the release of the report—with the startling news that federal health scientists had evidence that babies born at Camp Lejeune might have been harmed by contaminated drinking water—generated some newspaper stories and TV coverage in eastern North Carolina. On September 2, 1997, about a month after the report became public, the manager of the environmental restoration program at the base, Kelly Dreyer, distributed a memo saying that to date, "two individuals have contacted Camp Lejeune regarding abnormalities in their children." One was a woman who lived at the base in the early 1980s and had two children born with birth defects, Dreyer said. The other was Jerry Ensminger, whose daughter Janey had been conceived at Camp Lejeune in 1976 and died of leukemia in 1985.[10]

Ensminger, it turned out, had been sitting down to dinner in front of his TV one evening in August 1997 when he caught a report about the ATSDR study on a local North Carolina station. When he heard that children at Camp Lejeune had been exposed to cancer-causing chemicals in the water, Ensminger dropped his plate of spaghetti on the floor and stood in stunned silence. The former drill instructor, now retired from the Marine Corps after twenty-five years of service, had agonized for twelve years about his daughter's inexplicable death, and at last there was a possible explanation. "It was like God saying to me, here is a glimmer of hope that you will find your answer," Ensminger said.

Unknown to Ensminger at the time, the Defense Department was doing everything it could to avoid finding out how its pollution might have affected babies and children. It pushed hard against the ATSDR's proposal to study the health of infants born at Camp Lejeune, arguing that a lengthy and expensive investigation would still be inconclusive no matter what was found.

The director of federal programs for the ATSDR, Mark Bashor, tried to make a case for the study at the highest levels of the Pentagon. On July 16, 1997, he wrote to Elsie Munsell, deputy assistant secretary of the Navy for environment and safety, expressing concerns about the Defense Department's resistance to investigating possible childhood cancers linked to solvents in the water at Camp Lejeune. "It appears that some of this reluctance may be attributable to a lack of understanding regarding the need and requirement for the study," Bashor wrote.[11]

"ATSDR's investigation indicates that more than 6,000 children were probably exposed to TCE and PCE *in utero* between 1968 and 1985 in base housing at Camp Lejeune," Bashor explained. He went on:

> Based on an epidemiologic study recently completed by the Massachusetts Department of Public Health in the town of Woburn, Massachusetts, there is evidence indicating that these children exposed to TCE and PCE may be at increased risk of adverse health effects. The Woburn study observed an association between the mother's potential for exposure to TCE and PCE in drinking water and childhood leukemia, particularly when exposure occurred during pregnancy. To our knowledge, no other study has explicitly examined the potential association between the environmental contaminants and childhood leukemia. Although the solvent mixture was slightly different at Woburn than at Camp Lejeune, the levels of solvents found in the drinking water at Camp Lejeune were comparable to, or higher than, the solvents found in wells at Woburn.

Bashor acknowledged that no single study could prove a connection between maternal exposure to the solvents and diseases in the women's offspring, but because of the findings in Woburn, he wrote, "we feel that there is a substantial possibility that the children exposed to solvents *in utero* at Camp Lejeune are at increased risk of childhood cancer."

A full description of the study proposal attached to Bashor's letter described childhood leukemia as a disease in which white blood cells accumulate but fail to reach functional maturity, leaving the victim susceptible to infection, hemorrhage, and "inadequate cellular nutrition." At the time, the proposal said, there was an annual rate of 7.1 cases per 100,000 children under age four, and the disease was fatal within five years for about a third of the children diagnosed with leukemia before age ten and for half of all victims of the disease diagnosed after age ten.

There had been studies done up to that point linking leukemia to solvents, but most of those involved occupational exposures. Only three studies—all conducted at Woburn—focused on leukemia in children, and the last found "a very strong association" between TCE exposure in the womb and childhood leukemia. At Camp Lejeune, there were about 6,000 babies exposed to the solvent during gestation and about 6,000 others born to mothers who lived in areas not affected by the contamination. "This existing database presents a unique opportunity to examine this potential association in a cohort of moderate size where exposure is relatively well-defined," the study proposal stated.

The ATSDR's Jeanetta Churchill also sought support for the study from the White House through the Office of Management and Budget. Leukemia, her report said, was the most common cancer occurring in childhood and was of "tremendous public health concern." The studies in Woburn had shown an eightfold increase in risk among offspring of women exposed to TCE in water during pregnancy, it said.

"Epidemiology is not an exact science that easily lends itself to proving a definite cause-effect relationship between an exposure and outcome," Churchill's appeal to the OMB said. "Before the scientific community can accept the hypothesis that maternal exposure to VOCs causes childhood leukemia or birth defects, the cause-effect relationship must be seen consistently among studies. Therefore, this proposed project has the potential to greatly contribute to the body of scientific knowledge by possibly showing a consistent association between the exposure and outcome."[12]

The ATSDR's plan was to first locate as many of the children born to residents of the base between 1968 and 1985 as possible. The parents who were contacted would be asked in an interview about health problems to identify those children with cancer or birth defects. Any cases reported would then need to be verified through medical records. But the health agency faced a real challenge—the database of births at Camp Lejeune did not include Social Security numbers for either the children or their parents. So the ATSDR decided it would try to have the families come to them "by widely advertising our desire to locate individuals who were born, or whose children were born, at the USMC Camp Lejeune between 1968 and 1985 in publications targeting military personnel." If the agency did not hear from 80 percent of the 12,000 families with children born at the base hospital during those seventeen years, it would try to track enough others to reach that percentage of respondents, with help from the Navy and possibly credit-rating agencies like Equifax, the proposal said.[13]

The cost of the survey would be $1.6 million in fiscal year 1998 and another $190,000 in fiscal year 1999, for a total of $1.79 million, Bashor told Munsell in his letter. He argued that under the Superfund law, the Defense Department was responsible for covering those costs.

The Pentagon pushed back hard. Elsie Munsell sent back a terse rejection letter saying that "the volatile organic chemicals found in the water supply under investigation came from an off base source, ABC One Hour Cleaners. According to our investigation, this off site source of contamination is a National Priorities Listed Site under the jurisdiction of the EPA. Therefore, in accordance with CERCLA 107(a), it is more appropriate for you to seek funding for the study from the responsible party."[14]

In August 1997, Navy Environmental Health Center epidemiologist Jeffrey Hyman picked apart the ATSDR's study proposal in a ten-page review. Hyman started out by citing weaknesses in the Woburn studies—the sample sizes were too small, there were other contaminants in the water besides TCE, and there were other risk factors that were not evaluated, such as a father working in an industry with chemical exposures or a mother who used alcohol during pregnancy. "Unfortunately, every problem that existed in Woburn and limited the conclusions . . . exists in at least as severe of a form in the Camp Lejeune population," he said. Even if the ATSDR managed to contact 83 percent of the 12,000 families with children born at the base—"which seems virtually impossible," Hyman noted—"this study would have (at best) no more power than the Woburn studies," he wrote.[15]

The Navy's epidemiologist also argued that PCE, not TCE, was the major contaminant in the Tarawa Terrace water system, while the opposite was true at Woburn. Plus, Hyman said, there would be no way to determine through telephone interviews how much water people drank at Camp Lejeune; moreover, the rapid changes in the population at the base made the control group for the study suspect.

"In summary, it is very difficult to see how, even if successfully completed, this study could contribute anything to our understanding of the relationship between VOCs and childhood leukemia," Hyman wrote. The methodology, he said, was "extremely expensive, poorly thought out, has little chance of being successfully completed and providing useful information, and it lacks the detailed information that any competent funding agency would demand before considering it."

Hyman recommended small "pilot studies" to determine if there was a problem with childhood leukemia at Camp Lejeune. The names of children born at the base could be checked against cancer registries in states with high military populations, the records of military hospitals could be reviewed, and doctors who worked at Lejeune could be asked for their recollections about childhood cancer cases, he said. "These pilot studies would cost only a small fraction of the cost of the proposed ATSDR study," Hyman said. And if they showed an excess of leukemia cases among children born at the base, "the Armed Forces Epidemiology Board should be asked to offer their opinion on the feasibility of conducting a large study in this population, given the known problems," he said.

The Navy not only refused to provide money for ATSDR studies in 1998 and 1999, but it also refused to help locate residents of Camp Lejeune who gave birth at the base between 1968 and 1985. An official of the Defense Manpower Data Center, which keeps records on past and present military personnel, told the health agency that providing information from its database would violate the federal Privacy Act.[16]

Still, the ATSDR pressed forward, issuing a new report in August 1998 that verified its earlier statistics showing a significant association between exposure to contaminated water and adverse pregnancy outcomes, including low birth weights. The report said that birth certificates were studied for the children of 6,117 women who had drunk water tainted with PCE, for 31 women who had been exposed to TCE, and for 5,681 women who had been unexposed. Infants whose mothers had lived in housing with PCE in the water weighed an average of 24 grams (about 0.8 ounces) less at birth than those whose mothers had lived in unexposed housing, the report said. And for mothers over age thirty-five and mothers who had previously experienced fetal deaths, the babies weighed an average of 205 grams (7.2 ounces) less. "Because associations in these subgroups were not anticipated, these results should be considered exploratory," the ATSDR acknowledged. "They are, however, biologically plausible and deserving of followup."[17]

The agency made plans to begin the survey, using its own funds, at the beginning of 1999. But the launch was delayed, at least in part because of objections raised by the Marine Corps that it should not coincide with the December 1998 release of the movie *A Civil Action*, which was based on the childhood leukemia case in Woburn, Massachusetts. "Just a thought, with the movie coming out in Dec, can we delay the questionnaires until April/May time frame?" Camp Lejeune's information officer, Neal Paul, wrote in an e-mail to the Marine Corps public affairs manager in Washington, Kelly Dreyer, on October 23, 1998. The military got its way—the ATSDR survey wasn't mailed out until October 1999.[18]

Dreyer insisted in an e-mail to the ATSDR in April 1999 that the Marine Corps supported the study of childhood diseases at Camp Lejeune, but restrictions in the Privacy Act prevented the release of information. Kathy Skipper of the ATSDR Office of Policy and External Affairs responded to Dreyer with a warning that the agency had received permission from the White House Office of Management and Budget to move ahead with the study whether the Navy cooperated or not. "We very much need to work out a way that this can happen," Skipper told Dreyer. "With OMB approval a 'done deal,' this whole issue could prove very embarrassing and problematic for the Marine Corps if the public perception is that names aren't provided or needed information isn't being provided 'proactively.' As a former military [public affairs officer] and one married to a retired officer, I feel a strong allegiance to the military community and don't want this thing to go in this direction."

Skipper added, "However, you need to know that full-page ads for the *Federal* and *Navy Times*, and other publications are being discussed. I think you and I both know how this would 'play in Peoria' not to mention inside the beltway. What can I do to help prevent this scenario from developing?"[19]

Not much, apparently. It wasn't until the fall of 2000, when the ATSDR made plans for a "national media blitz" to try to locate more families who had babies at Camp Lejeune, that the Defense Department agreed to help. The agency had done pretty well on its own, tracking down more than 6,000 families, but it needed twice that many to make it a valid survey. It would not look good for the military to be absent when federal health scientists issued a mass appeal for help locating former Marines.

Finally, at a press conference on November 1, 2000, Colonel Michael Lehnert, head of the Marine Corps Facilities and Services Division, stood side by side with the ATSDR's chief of epidemiology and surveillance, Wendy Kaye, inside the Pentagon. Lehnert said he was there to ask the media for help in reaching some 10,000 former residents at Camp Lejeune. "The people we are trying to locate are the parents of children born or conceived while living in base family housing at Camp Lejeune from 1968 through 1985, who may have been exposed to contaminants in the water supply," he said, adding that the ATSDR was attempting to investigate "possible relationships" between exposure to contaminants and the health of the children.

"For your background, we began testing the water systems at Camp Lejeune in the early 1980s, in compliance with federal guidelines," Lehnert said. "The testing indicated we might have a quality concern with the water from both the Tarawa Terrace and the Hadnot Point water distribution systems. When we confirmed the contamination of the water, we took the necessary steps to close the wells and notified the appropriate authorities. News of the situation and what the Corps was doing to guarantee quality water for the residents was carried in the base paper and the local media."[20]

Lehnert added that some had questioned why the Marine Corps had waited until now—late 2000—to try to reach all the people who might have been exposed over the past several decades.

"That is a valid concern," he said. "It would be virtually impossible for me or anyone else to go back and analyze the many decisions that were made with regard to this situation since 1985. What I can tell you is that I truly believe that the decisions that were made were based upon the best information science could provide at the time."[21]

8

SLOW AWAKENING FOR THE VICTIMS

That's when I finally realized it wasn't me.
—LOUELLA HOLLIDAY,
MOTHER OF BABY BORN AT CAMP LEJEUNE IN 1973

The efforts of the Agency for Toxic Substances and Disease Registry to contact parents brought a grim awakening for some, and the hope of answers for many.

Mike Gros had joined the Navy for one reason—he needed help paying for medical school. Little did he know when he made the decision in the early 1970s that it would doom him to a lifetime of medical trauma.[1]

Growing up in San Antonio, Texas, in the 1950s and 1960s, Gros knew he wanted to become a doctor, possibly a psychiatrist, but he was good with his hands so he ultimately decided he should do something involving surgery. His family was not wealthy, so he worked his way through Trinity University in his hometown, living with his parents to save on room and board. He then signed up for a health professions scholarship in which the Navy would pay

113

for medical school on a one-for-one basis—for each year of school, the student would owe a year of active duty.

While earning his MD at Baylor College of Medicine in Houston, Gros met his future wife, Janie, then a part-time secretary in the psychiatry department at Methodist Hospital. They were married the week after he graduated from Baylor and spent their honeymoon driving through Virginia to the Naval Medical Center in Portsmouth, where he would do his internship and residency in the obstetrics and gynecology department.

When it came time to pick a duty station in 1980, Gros, who had a one-year-old son by that time, decided to ask for a family-friendly location on the mainland, thinking this preferable to one of the overseas bases, where security and safety issues always lurked in the background. He also knew some of the Ob/Gyn staff at the Camp Lejeune hospital from his time in Portsmouth, so he put the North Carolina base at the top of his Navy "dream sheet." His request was granted, and he and his wife and son, Andy, moved to the base in July 1980.

Life seemed good in the comfortable officers' quarters on Hospital Point, overlooking a marina in the New River. At no time, Gros said, did he or his wife suspect that anything was wrong with the water provided by the Hadnot Point treatment plant, even though tests conducted the year they arrived showed a heavy presence of solvents in wells serving that water system. "There were no taste or smell abnormalities," he said later. "That's the sinister side to this—a million people would never know they were drinking contaminated water." Gros had an especially high exposure level. As a hospital physician, he was scrubbing his hands in hot water from Hadnot Point many times each day. Studies show that solvents like TCE evaporate rapidly in hot water, and those who breathe the steam get a dose of chemicals five times more potent than if they drank it, Gros said.

In July 1983, after three years at Lejeune, the Gros family—now with two young boys—moved off the base to Chapel Hill, North Carolina, where Mike started a hospital fellowship at the invitation of a doctor there who had trained some of the residents at Camp Lejeune. But it wasn't long before he and Janie were headed back to Texas, where they always knew they would settle down. Mike set up his own Ob/Gyn practice in the Cy-Fair area of Houston, with Janie as his office manager, and eventually he joined with three other obstetricians in a partnership that lasted twenty years, he said. "It made life enjoyable not to be on call all the time," he said.

In 1997, Gros decided he was overdue for a checkup. "I felt fine but hadn't done one in a long time, so I went in for full blood work and a urine test." The results were startling. His white blood cell count showed a deficiency of the granular lymphocytes that gobble up bacteria and too many of the kind of lymphocytes that aren't needed as much. "I was flipped," Gros said. "I repeated the test in a month and found the same thing." Gros took his slides to a pathologist, who looked them over and immediately suggested a visit to an oncologist—it appeared to be a form of leukemia. A doctor at Baylor confirmed the worst: Gros most likely had B-cell chronic leukemia.

"He gave me all the stats, and said there was no chemotherapy for it," Gros said. "He basically gave me a fifteen-year life span. It was hard to digest. A transplant would have been an option, if we had a bone-marrow donor."

Devastated, Gros shared the diagnosis with his family, and none of them could believe what they were hearing. There was no history of cancer in their family, and Gros himself seemed as healthy as ever. About a week later, Gros sought some respite on the golf course. But during the round he got a call from the Baylor doctor, who apologized for a mistake in reading his slides. "It turned out it was not B-cell, it was T-cell, and it's worse," Gros said. "You die soon. It could be tomorrow."

Gros and his wife sought a consultation at the Mayo Clinic, where they met with an oncologist who confirmed the diagnosis of T-cell leukemia. The only possible treatment, the doctor said, would be a bone marrow transplant. Gros then decided that since he had one of the best cancer hospitals in the world in his own backyard—the MD Anderson Cancer Center at the University of Texas in Houston—he should go there. The head of the cancer center's Department of Stem Cell Transplantation and Cellular Biology, Dr. Richard Champlin, who had volunteered to assist victims of the Chernobyl nuclear disaster in Ukraine in 1986, was considered one of the best in his field.

Champlin and Dr. Michael Keating, a well-known specialist in leukemia, took on the case together. First they tried treating Gros with two types of drugs: interferon, which has side effects such as extreme drowsiness, and psoralen, which has a one-year regimen that involves the use of ultraviolet radiation. Neither of these drugs worked, however, and Gros was out of options. Champlin and Keating told Gros they needed to monitor his condition closely and would let him know when the time came for a bone marrow transplant.

Two years into the waiting period, in November 1999, Gros was working in his office when his secretary said someone from the CDC in Atlanta wanted to talk to him. Gros assumed he was being contacted about some emerging threat to public health. In a way, he was right, but it was a threat that had emerged years ago, when Gros was stationed at Camp Lejeune from 1980 to 1983.

The caller said the Agency for Toxic Substances and Disease Registry had recently discovered that some of the drinking water at the military base was poisoned during the time he was there. Gros said he knew immediately why he was ill. But rather than ask him about his health, the ATSDR representative started asking questions about his youngest son, Tom, who had been conceived and born at Camp Lejeune. Gros said that Tom was fine, thank you, "but let me tell you about me!" The response was that there was no indication that adults had been affected by the water contamination. "Are you serious?" Gros said he replied.

It didn't take long for Gros to confirm his suspicion that his leukemia was very likely caused by poisoned water at the Marine Corps base. The ATSDR's Public Health Assessment, published in .1997—the year Gros had been diagnosed—stated that people there were exposed to volatile organic compounds including TCE and PCE, possibly for as long as thirty years before the contaminated wells were shut down in 1985. Scores of studies available online linked both chemicals to cancer, including leukemia, with an incubation time of about ten years between exposure and effects. For Gros, it was twelve years. "It's well proven now," he said more than fifteen years after his diagnosis.

The doctor was grateful, at least, that neither of his boys or his wife appeared to have been harmed even though they had been exposed to the same pollution. "Each person has different genetic coding and some are affected, others not," Gros said. "Some are resistant, some not."

In the spring of 2002, Gros was advised that he needed to prepare for a bone marrow transplant. His son Tom turned out to be almost a perfect match, and he agreed to take a break from his studies at Texas A&M University to be his father's donor. The procedure, in which marrow from both of Tom's hip bones was transplanted into his father, was done in May 2002. Mike Gros was fifty years old and praying for a new lease on life.

—∞—

Around the same time that Gros was battling leukemia in Texas, three daughters of Joan and Eddie Lewis, who had lived at Camp Lejeune as babies or toddlers in the late 1960s, were having serious and unusual health problems, too. Now adults in North Carolina, the sisters had spent the years from 1966 to 1970 in three different homes in the Tarawa Terrace area while Eddie was doing two tours of duty in Vietnam. Those years were marked by frequent visits to the clinic for respiratory issues among the girls, but nothing as serious as what they would experience several decades later. One would have a baseball-sized uterine tumor discovered as she was delivering a baby girl; another underwent emergency surgery to remove more than a dozen noncancerous tumors from her uterus; and another would have half her lung removed because of a rare illness. And their younger brother, who had been born with two vertebrae fused together a year after his mother left Camp Lejeune, had been living for years with chronic back pain and headaches. In 2000—three years after the ATSDR report was completed—Joan Lewis read a newspaper article about the water contamination at Camp Lejeune extending over several decades, including the years her family lived there. She went online and requested information from the ATSDR, only to find when the packet arrived that every one of her children had experienced one or two of the symptoms listed as possible effects from the contaminants. Now convinced there was a connection between the water at Camp Lejeune and her family's array of health problems, Joan Lewis filed a claim for compensation with the Marine Corps in 2001. In 2013, she was still waiting for a response.[2]

The year 2000 brought similar revelations to others. Louella Holliday, whose baby conceived at Camp Lejeune died just hours after his birth in 1973, saw a news report about the base's water problems. "I was watching TV getting ready to go to work and heard about Camp Lejeune and contaminated water," Holliday said. "I didn't catch the whole report, so I went to work and looked it up on the Internet. All the sites directed me to ATSDR. I had no idea what that was. . . . A lot of information came in the mail. That's when I finally realized, it wasn't me." Not only did she and her husband lose a child after living at Camp Lejeune, but Louella lost the good health she had enjoyed as a girl and young woman. "I've been through a whole plethora of ailments," she said. "It's easier to say what I haven't had." The more she learned about the poisoned water—and the fact that the Marines had failed to inform her about it—the angrier Holliday became. "I could not imagine that Marine Corps officials had knowledge of this contamination for so many years without divulging it to the masses that had been adversely affected by it," she wrote on a website for victims of the base pollution.[3]

A report in 2000 on CNN about the contamination led Terry Dyer and her sister, Karen Strand, to ask for information from the ATSDR. They instantly saw a possible link with the sudden death of their father, John Fristoe, in 1973 at the age of forty-five, after he had worked for fifteen years as principal of an elementary school at Camp Lejeune. They also realized that their own spate of health issues, including bladder cancer, a miscarriage, hysterectomies, and cysts, and the severe mental and physical disabilities of their younger sister, Johnsie, might be linked to their childhoods at the base. "It all came together for me," Dyer told a reporter for *The Veteran* in 2004. "I was on the phone to ATSDR the very next day. That was when I understood that the Marine Corps had not been honest with us. And that we deserved answers."

Dyer and Strand concluded that the Marine Corps had robbed their father of his prime years. "He missed his children growing up," Dyer said to the reporter. "He missed our marriages; he missed his grandchildren. And I'm convinced the water deprived my [younger] sister of any kind of normal life. So what should we do? Nothing? Let it pass? What would you do if this was about you or your wife or sister or your children?"[4]

—␣␣—

Around the time that the Gros, Lewis, Holliday, and Dyer/Strand families were learning about the possible causes for their tragic illnesses, two hit movies appeared about heroes fighting corporate polluters, *A Civil Action* in 1998 and *Erin Brockovich* in 2000. Dyer contacted the model for the heroine of the latter movie, a California woman who teamed up with lawyer Edward Masry to win a $333 million settlement for victims of water poisoned by Pacific Gas & Electric. Masry's law firm wouldn't touch Dyer's case because it involved taking on the US military, Dyer said. She also called attorney Jan Schlictmann, the lawyer, played in the movie by John Travolta, who nearly went bankrupt suing W. R. Grace Corporation for contaminating the water in Woburn, Massachusetts, with trichloroethylene. Schlictmann didn't want to enter another lengthy legal battle over toxic pollution, but he offered some advice to Dyer over the phone: go to the media with your story, organize for political action, and start a website to spread the word. "He asked me if I was ready for a roller-coaster ride," Dyer said. "He said it's gonna tear your heart out; it will be very hard."

Inspired by the celebrated attorney's advice, the sisters went to work. Dyer set up meetings in Washington with members of Congress, including North Carolina's senators in the early 2000s—John Edwards, Jesse Helms, and Elizabeth Dole. The ultraconservative defense hawk Helms wouldn't meet with Dyer and her colleagues, but Dole, who succeeded Helms after his retirement, met with a group of Lejeune victims for more than an hour and at one point had tears in her eyes listening to their stories, Dyer said. Back home in Wilmington, North Carolina, Dyer and Strand organized a group they called The Stand, an acronym for Toxic Homefront Empowered Survivors Take All Necessary Defense. And in the fall of 2002, they set up a website named Watersurvivors.com to allow people who lived at Camp Lejeune to connect and share their stories. Dyer also had another goal in mind: "I started the website so I could help people get health care and compensation," she said.

Within a few months, more than 150 former base residents had landed on the site and posted tales of woe about problems that might have been caused by tainted water: cysts, tumors, ulcers, headaches, rashes, polyps, sore joints, birth defects, anemia, and diseases such as asthma, diabetes, and cancer. The numbers grew exponentially as word about Camp Lejeune's water spread through the media. Dyer and some of her newfound colleagues added documents about the environmental problems at the Marine Corps base to the website and posted forms that victims could use to file claims against the government.

Among the many victims who were drawn to the site after hearing about the ATSDR study was Sandra Carbone, who had lived at Camp Lejeune with her parents, four sisters, and brother from 1968 to 1971. The granddaughters of a Cherokee scout for the Army and the daughters of a Navy veteran, Carbone and a younger sister, Anita Roach, had both joined the Army to help pay for college. (Carbone said in an interview that she had passed the test for admission to the United States Naval Academy in 1974, the first year it was opened to women, but a sexist recruiter who didn't agree with the policy submitted her application late and she was disqualified.) Carbone served as a linguist with the Army Security Agency (ASA), as a clerk in the agency's communications division, and later as a specialist in electronics. Roach joined ROTC between her junior and senior years at Northwest Missouri State

University, but she suffered a severe spinal injury during officer training that required surgery. She had to drop out of college a semester before graduation.[5]

All that they gave for the military was nothing compared to what Carbone and Roach believe the Marine Corps took from them and other members of their family. Carbone summed it up in a posting on a website for Lejeune victims in which she listed a long series of serious health problems plaguing her, her mother, and her three sisters. In 2001, the ATSDR sent Carbone's mother a questionnaire asking about her health and that of her son, who had been born at Lejeune. When Carbone read the explanation for the survey, describing contaminated water at the base during the time her family lived there, "I just flipped," she said. "I think all of our health issues are related because we were all healthy before we moved to Camp Lejeune." Later studies by the ATSDR and other scientific agencies listed fifteen specific diseases that could be linked to the contaminants in Lejeune's drinking water. But given how frightening the initial information was about the contamination, there was a tendency for people to blame all kinds of health problems on their exposure.

"We've had crazy stuff in our family," Anita Roach said. "We never had any of these things in our family before we lived at Camp Lejeune. . . . My brother was born with lead poisoning. How else do you explain that? When we were growing up there it was instant milk, Tang and Kool-Aid, all with water right from the tap."

Carbone went online to search for information and came upon Watersurvivors.com, Dyer's website. She e-mailed Dyer to tell her about her family's health issues. "She replied that it was her, Terry Fristoe, which was her name in high school," Carbone said. "We had been best friends at Camp Lejeune." Reconnected, the two talked about their time at the base and all the problems they had while living there and in the years after they left. Dyer was angry about what had happened, but Carbone said she tried to turn something horrible into something positive. "Instead of getting super angry and mad, we can show the world what water contamination can do to you," she said.

Jeff Byron also linked up with Dyer and her group after he learned about the contamination in May 2000. Byron and his wife, Mary, had been preparing for a trip from Ohio to North Carolina to show his daughters, Andrea and Rachel, where they were born while he was stationed at Camp Lejeune. The Byrons had no idea what had caused their daughters' extensive health problems until they received a letter on May 27, 2000, from the National Opinion Research Center, on behalf of the US Department of Health and Human Services, asking them to participate in a health survey because they lived at Tarawa Terrace during a period when the water was contaminated. Once the Byrons got past the initial shock of learning the Marine Corps had apparently poisoned their two daughters, they had another major concern. The survey asked only for information about Rachel, who had been conceived and born while the family lived on the base; it did not ask about Andrea, who was born two months before they moved into base housing. Byron contacted the ATSDR to inform the agency that after moving into Tarawa Terrace, Andrea had two of the maladies listed as possibly being connected to the water contamination, cleft palate and spina bifida. He was later informed that at least one of those qualified as a birth defect of concern, so Andrea would be included in the survey as well. But what really gnawed at Byron was the fact that he was only hearing about the tainted water more than fifteen years after his family was exposed to it. "It was clear to me after reading the questions in the survey that the Marines had been aware of this situation for a long time," he said.[6]

Jeff Byron was angry, but not at the institution he loved, just its leaders. "I signed up to take a bullet for my country. My daughters didn't," he said. "I still love the Marine Corps. They did a lot of good things for me. We had good memories, and a lot of friendships." But now, Byron said, "I want them to be faithful to me." The Byrons filed damage claims against the Defense Department—$3.5 million for Andrea and $4 million for Rachel. "I don't care about the money," he said. "We want our children taken care of medically."

He also joined The Stand, volunteering to be on the group's board. "It's not just for the Byron family; it's for all these people," he said. "We want to make sure they get help."

—⚫—

Tom Townsend, now in Moscow, Idaho, learned about the water contamination from a veterans' newsletter, not a government health survey. Though he and his wife had lost their son, Christopher, less than four months after he was born at Camp Lejeune in 1967, the federal agency was studying health problems only among babies born at the base after 1968, when computer records became available. Townsend asked his wife, Anne, to contact the agency mentioned in the newsletter, the ATSDR, and soon afterward an official there told the retired Marine couple that their infant son would be included in the survey. "Some thirty-three years later we were learning that the death of our three-and-a-half-month-old son from a congenital heart defect was the result of in-vitro [sic] contamination from the drinking water at Camp Lejeune," Anne Townsend wrote shortly after discovering what had happened. "Now there is a certain sense of relief in knowing that the cause of the loss of our son was not our fault. We were just in the wrong place, at the wrong time—and drank the water."[7]

Tom Townsend did not take the news so well. "My wife spent 30 years wondering if she did something wrong," he told a newspaper reporter based in Montana. "I love the Marine Corps, but I'm suing them for big money. I'm talking Philip Morris dollars." Townsend proceeded to go after the Marine Corps with a vengeance, conducting a one-man investigation from his home in Idaho. He had been a logistics officer during his two decades as a Marine, so he knew something about how the military provided water on its installations. Townsend gathered enough information about mismanagement of the system at Camp Lejeune to put together a criminal complaint that he sent to the Department of Justice in Washington. Federal prosecutors told him they were actually looking into the case when along came September 11, 2001, and suddenly nearly all the department's resources were diverted to terrorism investigations. Townsend's complaint was handed off to the Environmental Protection Agency, and Justice Department attorneys transferred their files to EPA investigator Tyler Amon in North Carolina—with copies to Townsend. "All of a sudden out of the blue came a packet of information and I started piecing it together," Townsend said years later. "It was like a cathedral where the windows were blown in and I needed to put the pieces of glass back together." He learned how to use the federal Freedom of Information Act to request more documents and filed hundreds of requests—all handwritten on yellow legal pads— over the next few years.

Jerry Ensminger, now living not far from Lejeune in North Carolina, had also started digging for information about the contamination. His effort began as soon as he heard a TV report about the ATSDR study. The years since his daughter's death had been very difficult for Ensminger. He and his wife divorced, his small farm had put him deep in debt, and most of all, he was haunted by the mystery of his little girl being taken by a horrific disease. "When we did get divorced, right after Janey's death, I felt like I was going to come out of my skin," Ensminger told *Daily*

Beast reporter Lloyd Grove in 2011. "I started going to some of these grief groups. One time I told my story about Janey and about the divorce, that I felt my world was falling apart, I felt like a freak and that something was wrong with me, and when the thing was over with, as I was walking out, the moderator pulled me over to the side and said, 'Hey, Jerry, I want to show you something.' She pulled a book out. It was statistics of couples who lose a child through a long-term catastrophic illness, where you watch them go through the hell we watched Janey go through, watch them die a little bit at a time. And it was 87 percent of the couples ended up getting divorced. I said, 'Wow.'"[8]

When he found out about Lejeune's poisoned water, Ensminger never suspected anything sinister; he felt it had to be an innocent but awful mistake. "I wanted to believe the Marine Corps," he said. "I felt they'd step up to the plate and do the right thing. But the more documents we discovered, the reality came to me that they were covering their ass." Everyone in the Navy that Ensminger asked about the pollution downplayed its significance, he said. "They said the ATSDR was blowing it out of proportion, the chemicals were trace amounts—there's no way it could have caused my daughter's illness." The more denials he heard, the more motivated Ensminger became to seek the truth. His experience as a drill instructor equipped him perfectly for the job: he was relentless, determined, and very forceful. "They created me," Ensminger has said many times about the Marine Corps. "And now I've turned this weapon on them."

Ensminger expanded his arsenal in 2002 by connecting with Jeff Byron through the Watersurvivors.com website and by contacting Tom Townsend after reading his comment online about suing the Marine Corps "for big money." Townsend told Ensminger he had received a packet of documents from the government after filing a criminal complaint, so Ensminger headed to Idaho to meet with

Townsend. At his home in Moscow, Townsend pulled out a pile of Lejeune documents—and some disks that he hadn't even examined yet. When they popped the disks into Townsend's computer, Ensminger and Townsend realized they had struck gold. "This guy had sent Tom a master file of their document files," Ensminger said. "It hadn't been scrubbed." A full-bore investigation of the Marine Corps by a highly motivated group of former Marines was now under way.

—⁂—

The ATSDR survey that would be "virtually impossible" to complete, as Navy epidemiologist Jeffrey Hyman claimed in 1997, was in fact successfully completed in January 2002 after the agency and its contract employees had contacted the parents of 12,598 children who had been conceived or born at Camp Lejeune between 1968 and 1985. Of those who were reached, 10,040 agreed to participate—just under 80 percent of the total. The parents were all asked a number of questions about the health of their children, including whether they had birth defects or had developed childhood cancer. ATSDR investigators then set about trying to obtain medical records for those cases of serious illnesses identified by parents. By the summer of 2003, the survey findings were confirmed—and the results were stunning.

A total of 103 children with birth defects or childhood cancer were found among the 12,598 Lejeune babies surveyed, the ATSDR's chief of epidemiology, Wendy Kaye, announced on July 16, 2003. "These include anencephaly, spina bifida, cleft lip, cleft palate, childhood leukemia and childhood lymphoma," she said in a news release. In other words, out of 12,598 babies born at Camp Lejeune when drinking water on the base was known to be contaminated, one out of every 122 had either a serious birth defect or a deadly form of cancer. Jerry Ensminger did his own calculations using government statistics and found that for Lejeune babies, the rate of neural tube defects (spina bifida and anencephaly) was 265 times higher than the national average, and the childhood cancer rate was 15.7 times higher.[9]

Asked at a congressional hearing in 2007 how many of those children might still be alive, decades after their horrific starts in life, the ATSDR's Frank Bove said it was hard to say. "The neural tube defects, including in particular anencephaly, they die pretty much right after birth, so those would definitely be dead," he said. Bove's colleague at the ATSDR, Tom Sinks, focused on the bright side. "I was just going to add that most of the clefts—cleft palate, cleft lip—would not be fatal," Sinks said. "We've had a tremendous success in treating childhood cancers over the past fifteen to twenty years, so I would think that a significant number of the kids with leukemia would have survived."[10] Of course, that was no consolation to Jerry Ensminger, who was sitting just a few feet away when Sinks made his statement.

9

EPA vs. DOD

It is a World Trade Center in slow motion.
—DAVID OZONOFF, EPIDEMIOLOGIST, BOSTON UNIVERSITY

When the industrial cleaning solvent trichloroethylene was found in Camp Lejeune's water supply in 1980, toxicologists had a pretty good idea that TCE was a killer even if ingested at small doses. Government studies compiled that year in a handbook of toxic chemicals concluded that the widely used degreaser causes liver cancer, "attacks the heart, liver, kidneys, central nervous system and skin," and can be especially damaging to developing fetuses and young children. The effects of TCE on children were dramatically illustrated in 1981 when the Massachusetts Department of Public Health published a report saying that in the industrial city of Woburn, where drinking water was laced with TCE in the 1960s and 1970s, "the incidence of childhood leukemia was significantly elevated," with a dozen observed cases at that time in a community of only 35,000 people.[1]

A decade later, when the Agency for Toxic Substances and Disease Registry began investigating whether people had been harmed by chemicals in Camp Lejeune's water, even more was known about the dangers of TCE and its sister compound, the dry-cleaning solvent perchloroethylene, or PCE. Studies in New Jersey, where thousands were exposed to drinking water contaminated with the chemicals in the 1970s and 1980s, found "a statistically significant association between the concentrations of TCE and PCE and the overall leukemia rate among females from 1979 to 1984 in 27 towns," according to a report by the state Department of Public Health. And in Woburn, by 1986—the same year that W. R. Grace and Company reached an $8 million settlement with families whose children had died of leukemia or had experienced other serious illnesses linked to TCE-tainted water—twenty-one cases of childhood leukemia had been documented.[2]

With mounting evidence of TCE's toxicity, in 1989 the Environmental Protection Agency set a federal limit for the chemical in drinking water at 5 parts per billion—the equivalent of five teaspoons of the solvent in an Olympic-size swimming pool. Almost immediately, the EPA began pursuing further research to determine if the regulation needed to be even more stringent. It took more than a decade of studies and evaluation, but in 2001 the health scientists at the agency issued a new assessment saying that there was enough evidence linking TCE to a range of illnesses to indicate that the limit for public exposure should indeed be ratcheted down. "Under EPA's proposed (1996) cancer guidelines, TCE can be characterized as 'highly likely to produce cancer in humans,'" the report said. "TCE has the potential to induce neurotoxicity, immunotoxicity, developmental toxicity, liver toxicity, kidney toxicity, endocrine effects, and several forms of cancer."[3]

Bluntly translated, the assessment meant that thousands of cancer cases and birth defects could very likely be attributed to TCE exposure. "It is a World Trade Center in slow motion," said David Ozonoff, an epidemiologist at Boston University who had studied the chemical's effects extensively.[4]

The 2001 assessment, released in draft form to allow a period for public review and comment, did not suggest what the limit for drinking water should be—that would be a number for EPA scientists to determine later. But most informed observers of the process assumed the agency was headed toward a limit of just 1 part per billion for drinking water.

The authors of the report, led by V. James Cogliano, Cheryl Siegel Scott, and Jane C. Caldwell of the EPA's National Center for Environmental Assessment, knew the 153-page document would not be warmly received by the industrial and military sectors most responsible for TCE being the number one toxic pollutant in the United States. The Pentagon had more than 1,400 hazardous waste sites around the country, and most were contaminated with TCE. A fivefold increase in the safety standard for the chemical would significantly raise cleanup costs: the Air Force alone estimated that remediation expenses for its contaminated sites would go from $5 billion to at least $6.5 billion. Not surprisingly, an Air Force review of the EPA's risk assessment said the document "misrepresented" studies of TCE's effects and ignored the views of many scientists who did not believe the chemical was a serious threat to public health at the levels found in the environment.[5]

The timing of the EPA's report gave polluters good reason to believe that their concerns would be heard at the highest levels in Washington. Just six months before the assessment of TCE was released in August 2001, Republican George W. Bush had moved into the White House determined to rid the executive branch of what he and his aides considered anti-industry, antimilitary policies put in place during the prior administration of Democratic president Bill Clinton. Led by Vice President Dick Cheney, a former defense secretary with a background in oil and gas development, the Bush administration made the EPA one of its top reformation projects, installing political appointees at the agency who believed in less, not more, regulation. It also empowered other agencies, particularly the Department of Defense, to challenge the EPA's science.

"If you go down two or three levels in EPA, you have an awful lot of people that came onboard during the Clinton administration, to be perfectly blunt about it, and have a different approach than I do at Defense," a former Bush appointee at the Pentagon, Raymond F. DuBois, told the *Los Angeles Times* in 2006. "It doesn't mean I don't respect their opinions or judgments, but I have an obligation where our scientists question their scientists to bring it to the surface," said DuBois, who had been deputy undersecretary for installations and environment at the Defense Department.[6]

Knowing the TCE assessment would be fiercely attacked, the career staff at the EPA made sure it was sent to the agency's independent Science Advisory Board for a full review. The SAB issued its evaluation in December 2002 and extolled the TCE draft assessment as "groundbreaking" work by the EPA for a number of reasons. It was the first time an assessment of a chemical's toxicity focused attention on the risks to children, the board said, and it did so using "multiple kinds of evidence" and advanced research methods. "The Board advises the Agency to move ahead to revise and complete this important assessment," the SAB's cochairmen, public health scientists William Glaze and Henry Anderson, wrote in a cover letter to the EPA with the report. "We believe the draft assessment is a good starting point for completing the risk assessment of TCE."[7]

The SAB, acknowledging there was still "considerable uncertainty" about TCE's effects, also made some suggestions for further work by the EPA "to strengthen the rigor of the discussion" as it moved toward a final risk assessment. The Bush administration's new EPA research director, Paul Gilman, seized on the board's recommendations for revisions as a reason to put the TCE assessment on hold. Anderson, the SAB cochairman, who was also a doctor with the Wisconsin Division of Public Health, was surprised by the move. "I thought by and large we supported the EPA and that its risk assessment could be modified to move forward," Anderson said at the time.[8]

But Gilman interpreted the SAB's cautions as a "red flag" that "raised very troubling questions," and decided to have the TCE assessment evaluated by a higher authority—the National Research Council (NRC) at the National Academies of Sciences (NAS). Actually, it wasn't really Gilman's idea. The Defense Department, the Energy Department, and the National Aeronautics and Space Administration (NASA)—all faced with cleaning up TCE contamination at hundreds of sites—had offered to sponsor a study by the NRC, feeling confident that an independent panel of scientists would conclude that the EPA had gone overboard in assessing the chemical's threats to public health. The three federal agencies were backed by an industry group, the Halogenated Solvents Industry Alliance, made up of producers and users of TCE and other solvents in manufacturing. Paul Dugard, the group's director of scientific studies, had written a number of scathing critiques of the EPA draft, calling it "an example of extreme conservatism applied at every stage in the risk assessment that leads to an unbalanced outcome." Dugard had warned in public comments on the assessment that it would increase cleanup costs for the federal government and for many corporations by hundreds of billions of dollars.[9]

With equal confidence, one of the lead authors of the TCE assessment, V. James Cogliano, was sure the National Academies of Sciences, via the NRC, would put a significant stamp of approval on the EPA's work. "I expect them to like the draft assessment as much as the Science Advisory Board, whose favorable review triggered

DOD's 'appeal' to the NAS," Cogliano said in an e-mail to a reporter in 2005, not long after the NAS appointed a sixteen-member committee to evaluate the EPA assessment. The committee would be managed by the staff of the NRC and chaired by toxicologist Rogene Henderson of the University of New Mexico, with funding from the three federal agencies that proposed the study.[10]

The military and the industry made sure the committee was flooded with studies of TCE that reached different conclusions from the EPA. Paul Dugard of the solvents alliance sent the panel a memo in November 2005 describing "new information" showing that TCE could not be directly linked to kidney cancer. One was a study sponsored by the European Chlorinated Solvents Association, a sister organization of the US industry alliance, that concluded there was only a "weak association" between TCE exposure and kidney disease. That study and two others Dugard presented made the connection "an open question," he wrote.[11]

Research funded by the Department of Defense showed "no evidence" that TCE caused heart defects, dismissed any link between the chemical and non-Hodgkin's lymphoma, and raised doubts there was a connection to kidney cancer, the DOD's special assistant for emerging contaminants, Shannon Cunniff, told the committee in early 2006. Cunniff presented eight studies sponsored by the DOD, two collaborations funded by the Energy Department, and three NASA-funded studies—all casting doubts on TCE's toxicity.[12]

Jerry Ensminger, following all this debate, left no doubt about his opinion in an eloquent appearance at a public hearing held by a separate National Research Council panel that was reviewing the ATSDR's water-modeling studies for Camp Lejeune. "Here we have the EPA that was created by the government to protect our environment and our citizens from pollution being second-guessed by the world's largest polluter, the Department of Defense," he told the committee. "There is something fundamentally wrong with our system of government. I say this because here we have the DoD that was created to protect our country, its citizens and our way of life that is now attempting to manipulate legislation and/or regulations. If they are successful in their manipulation, it would allow them to do irreparable damage to the people and the land they were created to protect and not be held accountable for it."[13]

In the end, the industry/military push fell short—at least at the National Research Council. The NRC's committee issued a 379-page report in June 2006 that said not only that the EPA was correct in its assessment of TCE, but also that there was ample scientific research to show that the chemical was even more toxic than the EPA described in its draft report. "The committee found that the evidence on carcinogenic risk and other health hazards from exposure to trichloroethylene has strengthened since 2001," the panel said. The greatest risk posed by the chemical was kidney cancer, but a host of other diseases and deformities could also be linked to TCE exposure, the committee concluded.[14]

The path was now cleared for the EPA to issue a final risk assessment and presumably, based on its conclusions, stronger regulations limiting TCE levels in air and water. "We can't afford any more delays," Ensminger said after the NRC report was issued. Of course, when it comes to the military, where there's a will, there's a delay.[15]

10

THE PENTAGON TRIES FOR EXEMPTIONS

The Defense Department is supposed to defend
the nation, not to defile it.

—REPRESENTATIVE JOHN D. DINGELL (D-MI)

After the September 11, 2001, terrorist attacks, the Pentagon
reigned supreme in the administration of President George
W. Bush. Vice President Dick Cheney, who had been the secretary of defense under Bush's father from 1989 to 1993, focused
more on energy development in the early months of the younger
Bush's first term. But with the rise of al-Qaeda and escalating
threats from Iraq, Iran, and others in the Middle East, national security became the preeminent concern in Washington, as it was in
the nation at large. Anything that might detract from military
strength became a target.

Deputy Secretary of Defense Paul Wolfowitz wrote a memorandum on March 7, 2003, to the secretaries of the Army, Navy,
and Air Force suggesting the need to invoke the national security

exemptions allowed in many environmental laws. "While I believe we should be commended for our past restraint in this regard, I believe it is time for us to give greater consideration to requesting such exemptions in cases where environmental requirements threaten our continued ability to properly train and equip the men and women of the Armed Forces," Wolfowitz wrote.[1]

Wolfowitz cited sections of ten laws that allowed the president to exempt federal agencies from certain legal requirements for reasons of national security, including provisions of the Clean Water Act, the Safe Drinking Water Act, the Toxic Substances Control Act, the Endangered Species Act, and the Comprehensive Environmental Response, Compensation and Liability Act otherwise known as the Superfund law. He asked the civilian leaders of the military to develop procedures for seeking exemptions by identifying environmental regulations that threatened military readiness. Wolfowitz insisted his memo was "not intended to signal a diminished commitment to the environmental programs that ensure that the natural resources entrusted to our care will remain healthy and available for use by future generations." Exemptions would be "a high hurdle," he said. "However," he added,

> we cannot lose sight of the fact that these testing, training and other military areas and resources have been entrusted to our care—first and foremost—to provide for the realistic training and testing necessary to ensure that our Armed Forces are the best-trained and best-equipped in the world. In the vast majority of cases, we have demonstrated that we are able both to comply with environmental requirements and to conduct necessary military training and testing. In those exceptional cases where we cannot and the law permits us to do so, we owe it to our young men and women to request an appropriate exemption.[2]

The proposal was nothing new—after a series of lawsuits by environmental groups in the 1990s charging that military training exercises were harming endangered species or destroying valuable lands, the Pentagon had sought exemptions without success during the Clinton administration. But now, with the nation at war in both Afghanistan and Iraq—and with Republicans in control of both Congress and the White House—things were different. Wolfowitz gambled that the idea might gain traction in a political environment where national security trumped all else.

Instead, the idea of exempting military sites from environmental laws ended up calling greater attention to the toxic messes at many bases, including Camp Lejeune.

Senator James Jeffords of Vermont, a Navy veteran who left the Republican Party in 2001 to become an independent, said at a hearing of the Environment and Public Works Committee in April 2003 that the Defense Department had many bases sitting on aquifers tainted by fuel and chemicals from military operations. "There are numerous potential toxic effects that may result from the contamination that DOD is seeking to exempt from the hazardous waste laws," he said.[3]

A few months after the hearing, in July 2003, the Agency for Toxic Substances and Disease Registry released its study showing that children conceived or born at Camp Lejeune between 1968 and 1985 were three times more likely to have cancer or birth defects than were children in the general public. Jeffords called the results "chilling" and vowed to get a full assessment of the problems at the base. "At a time when the Department of Defense is seeking exemptions from the environmental laws that govern hazardous waste, we must also consider the health of the soldiers and families that serve our nation," he said.[4]

As alarming as the ATSDR report was, showing more than a

hundred babies born with birth defects or cancer after their mothers drank tainted water at Camp Lejeune, the problems were actually much worse. Because of incorrect data provided by the Marine Corps, the ATSDR study apparently missed hundreds, if not thousands, of other pregnant women who drank contaminated water at the base. The flawed data had been uncovered by Tom Townsend in 2000 as he dug into information about the water systems at Lejeune. Townsend found that the Marines had informed the ATSDR that housing areas at Holcomb Boulevard, Berkeley Manor, Paradise Point, and Midway Park had all been provided with water from a treatment plant for the Holcomb Boulevard system, where contaminated wells were never discovered. In fact, the Holcomb Boulevard plant did not go online until 1972, and before that all those housing areas were served by contaminated water from the Hadnot Point system. Townsend pointed out the mistake in letters to the Marine Corps after he discovered it in 2000, but it was never corrected. Kelly Dreyer at Marine Corps headquarters sent an e-mail in November 2000 to Camp Lejeune's environmental manager, Neal Paul, ordering him to provide the ATSDR with corrected information on the base water systems as soon as possible. But four months later, in March 2001, Dreyer had to write another e-mail to one of Paul's assistants making the same request. And more than a year later, when Jerry Ensminger mentioned Townsend's discovery of the flawed data to one of the ATSDR's lead investigators, Frank Bove, it was the first time Bove had heard about it.

It took another year for the ATSDR to figure out how to restore some integrity to its health studies at Camp Lejeune. Wendy Kaye, the agency's chief of epidemiology and surveillance, announced in 2003 that the agency would conduct a full-scale modeling study to determine exactly what housing areas received contaminated water, in what years, and at what levels. When the modeling was completed, scientists would have a much clearer picture of the base residents who had been exposed to tainted water. But the study would take several years, at least, since it involved developing a computer program that would re-create the flow of groundwater, the pumping of wells, and the delivery of water at the base over several decades. There was an added difficulty in that the base systems were unlike most municipal water supply operations, Kaye said. "If you lived in a town, you have a water meter attached to your house that shows how much water you use each month," she said at the time. "That's not true on base. There are no water meters, because residents don't have to pay for their water."[5]

The tag team of Townsend and Ensminger was just getting started. One day in 2003, Townsend was surfing through the Camp Lejeune website from his Idaho home when he came upon a treasure trove of documents that had been posted on one of the public web pages. There were nearly two dozen folders filled with reports, memos, e-mails, and other information, all focused on the water contamination issues. Townsend called Ensminger in North Carolina and told him to take a look. But when Ensminger tried to copy one of the folders using the slow dial-up connection he had at the time, it took hours just to download one set of documents. He called Townsend back and told him to tell his grandson to use his high-speed connection and put the data on disks as soon as possible. The boy did exactly that, and just in time. Within a few days the documents disappeared from the Marine Corps website. "I think the [National Science Foundation] or the EPA made them put these documents up so they could have access," Ensminger said. "And Tom got there at the right time."

Another big break for victims of the Lejeune pollution came in January 2004, when the *Washington Post* published a long story on page 3 under the headline, "Tainted Water in the Land of Semper

Fi; Marines Want to Know Why Base Did Not Close Wells When Toxins Were Found." After describing the tests done in 1980 and 1981 showing the presence of solvents in the base water supply, the story, by Manuel Roig-Franzia and Catharine Skipp, reported that it wasn't until 1985 that contaminated wells were shut down.

"The battle over the water contamination at Lejeune has strained age-old loyalties, matching Marine veterans against the power structure of an organization that prides itself in the motto *Semper Fidelis*, or 'always faithful.' The Marine Corps has not denied that contamination took place at Lejeune," the story said. It went on to describe the problem in more detail:

> In a written response to questions from the *Washington Post*, the Corps said the wells were not shut down for five years because there were no federal drinking-water regulations then for the chemicals found in Lejeune's water: trichloroethylene, or TCE, the metal degreaser that federal researchers say was kept in leaky underground storage tanks, and tetrachloroethylene, or PCE, which researchers believe leaked into the wells from a dry cleaner that still operates across the street from Lejeune's main gate. The Environmental Protection Agency had recommended levels—not enforceable standards—at the time, and the Corps said the average contamination readings for TCE were below those levels and that the PCE readings were "only slightly above" those levels.

The *Post* reported that criminal investigators at the Environmental Protection Agency were looking into what happened. Meanwhile, Senator Jeffords was calling for hearings. "I have very serious questions about why the Marine Corps, who knew the drinking-water wells were highly contaminated in 1980, didn't close them until 1985," Jeffords told the newspaper. "Sunshine is always the best disinfectant. . . . We have a strong obligation to provide all the information we already have to the Marines and their families."[6]

Jeffords kept the pressure on the Marine Corps and the federal health agency by demanding that everyone who lived in base housing at the time of the contamination be notified about it, and by requesting that the ATSDR's studies be expanded to include adults as well as children who may have been harmed. The Pentagon responded in February 2004 by saying it wanted to wait until the water-modeling studies (several years off) were completed so they could give people accurate information about their exposure. "Based on the ATSDR results, we will expeditiously consider the need for additional notification," the Marine Corps said in a statement. (At the same time, the Royal Netherlands Navy, which had an exchange program with Camp Lejeune to train members of its Marine corps, was trying to locate and notify any of its troops who had been at the base in North Carolina before 1985. "The least you can do is this: make up a list of people who had been there in those years and try to track them down," said Colonel Herman Dukers of the Dutch Marines.)[7]

The ATSDR insisted that there was a sound reason for its initial studies to look only at babies exposed to the contaminants in the womb. "They were the place where we were most likely to get results," said the agency's Scott Mull. "They are much more vulnerable than you or I as adults." If the studies clearly showed that the water could be linked to birth defects or cancer, they could be expanded, he said. "It was never meant that this would be the end of it. It is really just the first step in what could be [a larger study]," Mull said.[8]

Despite the ATSDR's insistence, the US Marine Corps, under pressure from Congress, federal agencies, and victims of the contamination, knew it had to do something to show it was being responsive. In February 2004, the commandant named a three-member panel to look into how the situation had been handled and report back to him. General Mike Hagee described the handpicked trio as an independent group of "private sector professionals" who would objectively consider all the evidence and assess what had occurred at the base.[9]

Almost immediately, there was an outcry that the blue-ribbon panel was anything but independent. The chairman of the panel was a former Republican congressman, Ron Packard of California, who had represented the district that included the largest Marine base in the West, Camp Pendleton, at the same time that Hagee was a general officer there. One of the members was former Navy administrator Robert B. Pirie Jr., who as assistant secretary for installations and environment in the Pentagon had denied that the Marines were responsible for the contamination at Camp Lejeune. The other was Richard Hearney, a retired four-star general who still served as a part-time consultant to the Marine Corps.

Jeffords was appalled by the lack of a water-quality specialist on the panel, and Republican senator Elizabeth Dole of North Carolina was angry about the members' close ties to the military. "The panel the Marines have chosen is outrageous," Dole said. She had written to the top brass at the Marine Corps before the panel was formed, insisting that it must be independent and impartial. "The Marines have failed on both accounts," she said.[10]

In response to the criticism, Hagee added two scientists to the panel, Robert Tardiff and William Glaze. Tardiff was president and CEO of the Sapphire Group, a consulting firm on pollution issues. "This company was nothing more than environmental hired guns," scoffed Jerry Ensminger. "They perform risk assessments on chemicals and products for the highest bidder." In contrast, Glaze, a researcher at the Oregon Health & Science University, was cochairman of the EPA's Science Advisory Board and had a sterling reputation in the research world. After just one meeting of the panel, however, Glaze quietly resigned without publicly stating his reasons. It was left to the panel chairman, Packard, to announce that Glaze had quit because he was concerned there could be a conflict of interest serving on both an EPA board and a Marine Corps panel. Ensminger, for one, wasn't buying it. "No, Dr. Glaze who cherished his position in the world of academia saw the handwriting on the wall after he attended the first meeting at Camp Lejeune," Ensminger told a congressional committee a few years later. "If he wanted to retain his high standing that he had attained in academia and the scientific community, he needed to distance himself from this fiasco."[11]

Ensminger was also skeptical about the limited assignment given to the Marine panel—to review only what happened from the time solvents were first discovered in the base drinking water in 1980 until the tainted wells were shut down in 1985. "I knew right then that this entire panel was nothing more than a farce," Ensminger said. "It was akin to placing a Band-aid over a sucking chest wound: too little, too late."[12]

The Marines were put further on the defensive in early 2004, when aides to Congressman John Dingell of Michigan spotted the *Washington Post*'s coverage of Jerry Ensminger and Camp Lejeune just as Dingell, the ranking Democrat on the House Energy and Commerce Committee, was preparing for a hearing on the military's requests for exemptions from environmental laws. "I saw the *Post* article and tracked Jerry down and took him in to see Mr. Dingell," said attorney Richard Frandsen, an investigator on Dingell's staff for more than thirty years. "He turned to me and said, 'Help 'em.'" Ensminger recalled that Dingell had started the meeting in his office by saying, "This is why we're here," and explaining the military's exemption requests. Ensminger said he reached into his pocket and pulled out photos of his daughter Janey and her gravesite, and said, "This is why I'm here." A few days later, Ensminger got a call from Dingell's office asking if he would appear as a witness at an upcoming congressional hearing. "It turned out the meeting was a job interview," Ensminger later said.[13]

The hearing, held on April 21, 2004, had been called by Energy and Commerce Committee Chairman Joe Barton (R-TX) to consider the requests from the military for exemptions from environmental laws. Unless Barton's committee approved the requests, the House Armed Services Committee would not be able to include language in legislation to authorize the exemptions. But with Republicans in control of both panels, it seemed almost a sure bet that the Defense Department would get what it wanted.

Dingell was determined to block the deal. "This is clearly not in the public interest," he said in his opening statement at the hearing. "The administration's proposal to exempt the Defense Department from important environmental laws will imperil drinking water supplies and eliminate vital state and federal authorities necessary to protect the public health and the environment. Nowhere has a single set of legislative proposals had so much audacity and so little merit. I would note that the Defense Department is supposed to defend the Nation, not to defile it."[14]

Dingell, an Army veteran of World War II with a strong environmental voting record, said regulations on pollution had never affected military readiness, "but the Defense Department like an old maid rushes around looking under the bed to find about what they may complain or what might threaten them. I could understand this from somebody else but I expect our Defense Department to be made of sterner stuff." He noted that the Marine Corps had argued that virtually all of Camp Lejeune was an "operational range" that needed to be exempt from hazardous-waste laws, even though the base was filled with housing areas, recreation sites, and other areas that needed to be protected from toxic contamination. Not to mention the fact that Camp Lejeune was already on the federal Superfund list requiring extensive and costly remediation.

Later in the hearing, Dingell introduced his ace in the hole, Jerry Ensminger. "From my own past experiences it makes me shudder to think that the military would be granted immunities from any environmental regulations or the oversight by the federal and state agencies that were created for these purposes," Ensminger said after describing Lejeune's history of pollution problems and the Navy's reluctance to address them. "To grant immunities we would be affording the Department of Defense a license to kill their own personnel and their families in a far more terrible way than any foreign enemy could ever kill them with bombs or bullets."

Ensminger pointed out that 141 military installations around the country were on the Superfund list. "This alone should be testimony enough for the disregard that the Department of Defense has for the environment and the welfare of their own people," he said. "However, if this fact is not enough of a deterrent, perhaps this next fact will convince you. My daughter, Jane, fought a courageous battle against her malignancy for nearly two and a half years. She literally went through hell and all of us that loved her went through hell with her. The leukemia eventually won that war. On 24 September 1985, Jane succumbed to her disease. She was only nine years old."

One member of the committee who was deeply moved by Ensminger's testimony was Republican Richard Burr, soon to be elected as a senator from North Carolina. "I am curious if there is anybody in the audience from DOD or from the Corps who was assigned to come here and listen to Mr. Ensminger's testimony as it relates to what I think is a tragedy at Camp Lejeune?" Burr asked the packed crowd at the hearing. No one responded, and the congressman said he was disgusted that military leaders responsible for the problems at Lejeune would not send a representative "to listen to the testimony from somebody who is willing to take their time, and probably pay their way, to come and sit through a very lengthy hearing and to wait to make one very, very important statement. Not just for you and not just for your daughter," Burr told Ensminger, "but potentially for every man and woman who serves and every family who could potentially live on a base that is faced with this type of problem."

After the hearing, most members of the committee came down to the witness table to shake Ensminger's hand, he recalled. Dingell's aide, Dick Frandsen, stood off to the side watching and waiting, "and when they were all done he came over and hugged me and said, 'You knocked it out of the park.'" The story of his daughter's death had a huge impact. Frandsen later told Ensminger that his testimony caused fourteen Republicans to change their minds and oppose the military exemptions. Two weeks after the hearing, Barton's spokesman said his committee would reserve the right to object if the exemptions were added to any bill authorizing programs for the Department of Defense.

—∞—

Camp Lejeune was still a mess. More than twenty sewage spills occurred at the base between 1997 and 2004; two occurred within two days in May 2004, including one that sent 47,500 gallons of raw sewage into a creek feeding into the New River. Cleanup crews specializing in treating and removing toxic wastes were also at work around the installation performing studies, installing monitoring equipment, and beginning remediation on dozens of contaminated sites. Most of the projects were expected to take years to complete.[15]

Into this environment waded the special panel appointed by the Marine Corps commandant to find out how the water contamination problems had been handled in the early 1980s. The committee called a public hearing for June 24, 2004, at the base USO center to allow interested parties to provide information. About fifty former residents of Lejeune showed up to testify, mostly in an angry, emotional manner.

"In the private sector this would be a felony . . . leaving people injured, sick and dying," said Ellen Harris, who returned to the base where she had lived for five years from her current home in Fort Plain, Georgia. "We all looked like we had the mange."[16]

The chairman of the panel, Ron Packard, urged calm and order, saying each person who wanted to speak would have five minutes to do so. "We think that it would be inappropriate to play to the media," he told the audience. "We have to carefully evaluate the Marine Corps' concerns and the concerns of the families."

"As a victim who has suffered the ill effects of this contamination for over 30 years, I resent and am appalled at being allotted all of five minutes to provide you with my questions and concerns," responded Paula Orellana of Chambersburg, Pennsylvania, who was born at Camp Lejeune and had lived there as a child in the 1970s. "This leads one to wonder: how many facts do you really want to find?"

Ensminger used his time to tell the four panel members that the group before them was just "a fraction of those affected by this travesty and tragedy." He began telling his version of how the Marine Corps failed to protect the base water supply by placing supply wells dangerously close to heavily contaminated waste sites. Packard allowed Ensminger to continue for ten minutes and then tried to cut him off. The audience hollered for Ensminger to continue, so Packard relented. By the end of the hearing, the panel was asking Ensminger for information. "I would ask you to screen your database and provide the names of all those we can interview," said Richard Hearney, a retired Marine general.

Packard, the Marine Corps panel chairman, met later with a reporter for a Vietnam Veterans of America publication, Richard Currey, and tried to explain that the panel's assignment did not include examining health problems among former Lejeune residents. "We're listening very carefully to the concerns of the people who feel they or their families suffered as a result of the solvents in the water," Packard said. "But it is not, however, the mandate of this panel to address those issues specifically or offer any form of redress. We're strictly a fact-finding group."[17]

Currey pointed out that "the inescapable heart of the matter" was the Marine Corps' failure to act for five years after learning that solvents were present in the base water supply. "The commandant has asked us to look very hard at that period of time, and determine if appropriate decisions were made in the context of the early 1980s," Packard replied. "There wasn't as much known about toxins or their effects back then. This panel has to make a decision about how it looked to the Camp Lejeune leadership at that time." It was not an easy task to piece together records of decisions made two decades earlier. "And in many cases we're dealing with people's memories," Packard said. "That can get pretty hazy. We've had people who said they were not involved, but then we produced documents confirming they were. At which point they say they just don't recall the details."

Packard insisted that his panel was operating under no constraints except for its specific mandate. "The commandant has not limited our range in terms of what we can look at or who we can talk to or consult with," he said. "In fact, after we got under way, the Marine Corps has left us alone to do our work. But definitive

Jerry Ensminger testified numerous times before congressional committees about the contamination at Camp Lejeune.

Courtesy of Jerry Ensminger.

Nine-year-old Janey Ensminger (in wheelchair) and her cousin Matt Ensminger, not long before Janey's death from leukemia in 1985.

Courtesy of Eileen Ensminger.

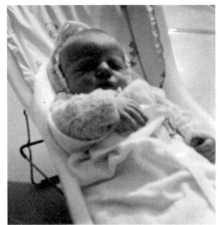

Christopher Townsend was born at Camp Lejeune on March 16, 1967, and died less than four months later of multiple health problems.

Courtesy of Tom Townsend.

Breast cancer victim Peter Devereaux at his home in North Andover, MA.

Courtesy of North Andover Citizen/David Sokol.

Poster for *Semper Fi,* a documentary on Camp Lejeune's water
contamination by Rachel Libert and Tony Hardmon.
Courtesy of Tied to the Tracks Films, 2011.

Breast cancer victims from Camp Lejeune posed for a calendar in 2011. Front row (L to R): Kris Thomas, Chet Sisky, Joe Moser, Ed Hughes, and Mike Muller. Back row (L to R): Jim Fontella, Jesus Carlos Marroquin, George Holmes, Peter Devereaux, Teddy Richardson, Mike Partain, Doug Palmer, and Ralph Burkeen.

Courtesy of David Fox for ArtBECAUSE Breast Cancer Foundation.

Mike Partain was born at Camp Lejeune in 1968 and diagnosed with breast cancer in 2007.

Courtesy of David Fox for ArtBECAUSE Breast Cancer Foundation.

Tom Townsend, whose son died a few months after being born at Camp Lejeune in 1967, pores over documents at his home in Moscow, ID.

Courtesy of Tom Townsend.

David Ozonoff, a professor of environmental health at Boston University, was part of an expert panel advising federal health investigators on Camp Lejeune.

Courtesy of Boston University.

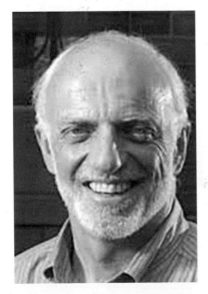

Richard Clapp, an epidemiologist and professor of environmental health at Boston University, volunteered his time to assist victims with health problems from Camp Lejeune's water.

Courtesy of BU School of Public Health.

Former Senator Elizabeth Dole, R-NC, sponsored legislation to assist victims of Camp Lejeune's contamination.

Courtesy of Richard A. Bloom.

Representative John Dingell, D-MI, demanded that the military be held accountable for contamination at its bases.

Courtesy of Richard A. Bloom.

Jerry Ensminger, Erin Brockovich, and Mike Partain pushed for passage of a bill to provide health care for Camp Lejeune victims in 2012.

Courtesy of Jerry Ensminger.

President Barack Obama signed the Janey Ensminger Act
Tony Hardmon and Rachel Libert, producers of the *Semper Fi*
documentary; Representative Jeff Miller, R-FL; Jerry Ensminger;
Representative Brad Miller, D-NC; and Mike Partain.

Courtesy of Jerry Ensminger.

conclusions about water contamination and human illness are simply not within this panel's purview."

And so it was that the commandant's panel issued a report and recommendations in October 2004 that carefully avoided making any judgment about whether Lejeune's pollution could be linked to health problems. The main conclusion was that the Marine Corps had "acted responsibly" in its management of the base water supplies but could have done more to provide information about the contamination to base residents. Base officials also should have assessed the potential health risks of the water pollution after it was discovered, the panel said, though there were understandable reasons why the military did not recognize there was a serious problem, including a lack of regulatory standards, inadequate testing methods, and an absence of complaints from residents about the quality of their water.[18]

"Camp Lejeune made every effort to comply with existing water quality regulations and related schedules but did not anticipate or independently evaluate health risks associated with chemicals that might be subject to future regulation," the Marine Corps panel said. Among the reasons that nothing was done about the volatile organic compounds in the water, according to the panel, were the following: the Naval Facilities Engineering Command Atlantic Division, or LANTDIV, apparently did not alert base officials to the significance of the problem; the environmental staff at Lejeune was not adequately informed about the chemicals; and there was poor communication between water system operators at the base and the environmental and health managers who knew about the presence of solvents.

"In the early 1980s, evidence continued to accumulate within the scientific community that synthetic chemicals, such as VOCs, created significant health risks as a result of long-term exposure," but there was no indication the Marine Corps was aware of the evolving science, the panel concluded. "Given that more than two decades have passed since the initial indications of VOC contamination, a lack of complete information on related decisions was expected. The scope of the Panel's interviews and research makes it unlikely that new information coming to light would indicate a cover-up."

The *Washington Post* tried to reach the Marine Corps commandant, General Hagee, for a comment on the panel's report, but none was forthcoming. "Hagee declined repeated requests for interviews and would not respond to written questions," the *Post* reported. Jerry Ensminger was not surprised. "We gave the Marine Corps a chance to police themselves," he told the *Post*. "It's obvious that they do not want to and they are not going to unless they are forced."[19]

The federal health agency studying the effects of the contamination, the ATSDR, was a long way from finishing its work, though. At the end of September 2004, agency director Henry Falk notified Richard Frandsen of Congressman John Dingell's staff about a four-part plan for expanding study efforts at Lejeune. "In response to questions and concerns raised by you and others, ATSDR has been exploring a variety of options for enhancing our understanding of health effects associated with exposure to contaminated drinking water at Camp Lejeune, and for more effectively communicating related information to the public," Falk wrote to Frandsen.

The plan included convening an expert panel "to explore the feasibility of additional epidemiological research" on the tainted water; increased research on the effects of the two most prevalent contaminants at Lejeune, TCE and PCE; "enhancing communications to the affected community" by adding materials to the ATSDR website; and clarifying the 1997 Public Health Assessment for Camp Lejuene about the risks of health effects from the base's water. The most promising news for victims was the formation of an expert panel, independent of the ATSDR, to evaluate the government's research and perhaps give it a much-needed kick in the pants.[20]

As it turned out, the public meeting before the seven scientists who were selected for the expert panel, held in Atlanta in February 2005, became something of a two-day catharsis for dozens of former Marines and their families who believed their lives had been irrevocably damaged by the poisoned water at Camp Lejeune.[21]

"My name is Hilda Rose," said the first witness:

> I'm a parent. We arrived at Camp Lejeune, North Carolina, in January of 1984. We could not get into base housing at Tarawa Terrace until a few months later. My son Daniel was born on December 8, 1984. . . . Daniel was born with a heart valve defect. . . . In March of 1985, I became pregnant again. . . . Nathan was born two weeks premature. He had so many problems. . . . He was admitted to the hospital for a high fever and ear infection. That's when they discovered that Nathan had two holes in his kidneys that caused urine to build up and cause an infection. . . . Now Nathan is nineteen years old. I just took him to a urologist and he told me Nathan needs a kidney transplant.

Lita Hyland, a native of Peru, described an array of health problems. "I have a letter from the hospital and I am going to read it," she said. "I am sorry about my bad English, but I'm very nervous, too. This is a big thing for my family and I want to be my best— okay." From the letter, she read, "Ms. Hyland has had multiple medical therapies . . . including chronic abdominal pain, chronic diarrhea, oral ulcerations, multifocal joint pain, fatigue and depression. She continues to require close follow-up. An attempt to determine her exact diagnosis presents a unique learning opportunity for the military physicians and might help in the treatment of similar patients in the future."

Statements by Jeff Byron and Mike Gros were read by Jerry Ensminger, the first describing the years of serious medical problems for his two young girls, the second outlining a life that turned into a battle with incurable leukemia and a host of related health issues. Then came Denita McCall, a Mexican American from Colorado who joined the Marines immediately after high school to follow in the footsteps of her father. "I'll begin by telling you that right out of boot camp for the Marine Corps, I was stationed at Camp Lejeune," she said. "I was eighteen years old." The year was 1982. "Seventeen years later I was diagnosed with parathyroid cancer. This is my radiation mask. . . . Before I came here I didn't think that anybody would listen, just because of the direction ATSDR has taken with this whole situation. So, I don't even know why I say this." Nevertheless, she continued:

> It's a horrible thing to have your head strapped down to a table and receive radiation, but I [also] had a radical neck dissection and part of my esophagus removed. . . . I've had several surgeries to restore my voice. . . . Needless to say, it's been a very hard six years, because this just happened to me six years ago. Aside from the cancer, I have a lot of other health problems, but I'm more focused on the one that's potentially going to kill me. . . . My oldest son who's twenty, he's also a Marine. He's been diagnosed for the past seven years with some kind of liver disorder—they're not sure what it is. . . .
>
> I really think it's important that somehow, someway, we contact most everybody that lived on that base. We were very young. We were eighteen years old, to me that qualifies as a child. I was—I was right out of high school. I don't know. Some of the

data from ATSDR that I've read states that the latency period for cancer would be ten to twenty years, and I got mine about seventeen years later. So, maybe they're getting sick right now and they don't know what's happened to them.

Just from the websites that I've visited, from some of the people here who started them, there are a lot of people who have cancer. But I need—I would like you guys to really get that information, so that we can prove to the Marine Corps. At this point I don't—I'm not eligible for any life insurance or health insurance. I'm not eligible for any service-related disability through the VA. So basically you know I'm at the mercy of public aid and the VA to help me out. It's just—It's been a struggle. Sorry, I'm so upset, crying. I just didn't think anybody cared. Thank you very much.

One by one the speakers presented a direct challenge to the Marine Corps and the Pentagon. The scientists listened with concern and expressed their sympathy for the victims. "I think I probably speak for everybody telling you how moved I am by your stories, you survivors," said Richard Maas, an environmental science professor at the University of North Carolina in Asheville. "How absolutely admiring and respectful I am of your persistence, your creativity and your hard work to do something about this. Your patience and letting your good sides flow." Maas also offered a bit of advice: "You have to be nice to your friends and tough on your enemies. One of the hardest wisdoms is to know, to recognize the difference, and know that enemies can become friends."

The experts also made clear that it was time for the ATSDR to move past the investigation stage and start drawing some conclusions. After all, it had been fourteen years since the agency began looking into potential health problems at Camp Lejeune, and all it had to show for it was a Public Health Assessment and a report on pregnancy outcomes that were both badly flawed.

"Where we stand right now is that you know that this Health Assessment is incorrect in some major ways," said Maas. "I think what we're all concerned about and trying to get at here—is [whether] there [is] some way to not sit around for a long time until this new hydraulic modeling and the exposure assessment is finished? To acknowledge that there are some problems here that we already know are problems, in terms of areas of the base that were served by contaminated water." Speaking to the ATSDR scientists at the hearing, Maas said, "Probably now in 2005, you might take another look at the kind of out-of-hand dismissal of adult cancers. So there might be some reason to, at least in the interim, put some kind of addendum or something that acknowledges that there's new evidence that's come out here and there are some problems."

"Let's face it," said David Ozonoff, a physician who had been chairman of Boston University's Department of Environmental Health for more than twenty-five years and had worked on scores of epidemiology studies for areas contaminated with TCE and PCE, including the community in Woburn, Massachusetts, that was made famous by the book *A Civil Action*. "Underlying this is sort of an issue of trust." Directing his comments to the federal health agency scientists, Ozonoff said:

> Although ATSDR has a long record of saying great things about how they're working for their community, there's been a very rocky history here—goes back years and years. It's often not at the level of headquarters. It's what goes on in the field often. Part of that is because people out in the field are asked to do almost impossible jobs. You've got a couple of people who maybe just got a degree in earth science somewhere, and now they're asked to do epidemiology and toxicology and so on, on all these sites. It really is impossible. Whatever the objectives here might be . . . you're also going to have to try to figure out what to do about the trust issue.

Ozonoff suggested that perhaps the ATSDR needed to get away from doing a "strictly scientific study" and "open up the process more and allow some participation by people at Lejeune in some meaningful way." If the agency had done that earlier, it probably wouldn't have been so dismissive of adult cancers in its earlier studies, he said. "To say that you don't expect them was just, in my view, was not a good way to generate trust, certainly didn't generate my trust," he said.

"I understand that this is going to be a difficult thing to study," Ozonoff said, adding:

I don't think anybody expects you to do anything but the best that you can do. So, nobody's expecting you to do the impossible, but by having a sort of a real partnership with the affected folks you can get two things. You can get, on the one hand, buy-in and understanding of all the difficulties involved, which I think will help the trust issue a lot. At the same time you can get the benefit of the tremendous amount of raw brain power that there is out there in the community. We know from our study that . . . I didn't mention this when I introduced myself, but I was a plaintiff witness in the Woburn case. I'm sorry to say that some of the stories I've heard this morning, the testimony I've heard this morning[,] was very reminiscent of stories that we heard in talking to the Woburn families, which was absolutely just heart-wrenching. You never get used to hearing it. When we worked with them, they had some really good ideas that we hadn't thought of because they know their community and they know their lives. You can take advantage of that. It can make the study better. Maybe you can do some things that you thought you couldn't do.

Later in the meeting, Ozonoff had a final message about the agency's tentativeness in accepting the risks of exposure to TCE and

PCE. "I don't know what it takes to convince ATSDR about the science of some of these things," he said. "You have to have a nuclear device set off underneath you in order for you to say, 'Oh gee, I guess maybe those things are bad.' It's a problem. I can't believe that people are arguing about TCE. I really can't believe it. I know they are because I run across those people all the time. But, give me a break. And I left out a word before break."

Four months later, the scientific advisory panel issued its report with one very strong recommendation: first and foremost, everyone who lived at the base in the two decades before 1985 should have their health evaluated at government expense. The experts also suggested that future studies of the base contamination should be done "in full partnership with the exposed community." New studies should begin without waiting for ongoing studies to be completed, and there should be immediate recognition that the water contamination could cause health problems for adults as well as for children. "All persons potentially affected by exposure to VOC in the drinking water at Camp Lejeune should be notified," the scientists said. And there was one final recommendation for public officials in Washington: "Future funding for Camp Lejeune health studies should come through direct congressional action, not DOD, to avoid even the appearance of a conflict of interest."[22]

Panel member Richard Maas summed up his concerns in an interview with the Associated Press after the report was released. "Camp Lejeune presents a groundwater contamination site of unusually high level of concern," he said in the July 1, 2005, story. "It became clear to me from my work on the panel that our country had treated these people unfairly. There should immediately be legislation passed that offers health care compensation to the thousands of people who were exposed to this contaminated drinking water and are now experiencing severe health effects." (Maas died in December 2005 after a short illness at age fifty-four.)[23]

In response to the panel's recommendations, the ATSDR formed a Community Assistance Panel (CAP) made up of victims of the contamination to provide input for federal health studies. They included Jerry Ensminger, Terry Dyer, Tom Townsend, Jeff Byron, Denita McCall, Dave Martin, and Sandra Bridges. The panel held its first meeting on February 1, 2006, at ATSDR headquarters in Atlanta. (Townsend participated by phone from his home in Idaho, as his wife of fifty-one years was in hospice care after being diagnosed with terminal liver degeneration. Anne Townsend was seventy-three when she died on February 22, 2006, and her husband was convinced that exposure to toxic chemicals at Camp Lejeune had everything to do with the rare disease that took her life.)

The CAP members made their purpose clear to ATSDR officials at their opening session. "None of us are scientists," said McCall, who had delivered an emotional statement about her cancer treatment at the expert panel hearing a year earlier. "We don't care about science, we want services." Byron said, "If the DOD poisoned my daughter, I want health care for my daughter. That's what we're leading up to. We are here because we want answers and we want this kind of stuff to stop." Ensminger was angry that the Marine Corps didn't send a representative to the first meeting. "They need to be up here and they need to have input," he said. "We're beating around the bush and chasing our tail because we're depending on them for information."[24]

The CAP would also become a source of frustration for some members. Terry Dyer said she quit the panel in 2007 "because we weren't getting anywhere. We were talking about the same exact things every time." David Martin, a North Carolina man who was a member of Dyer's Water Survivors group, left the CAP at the same time as Dyer.

There was a development in 2006, though, that gave Dyer hope. The Senate approved legislation that eventually made its way through the House as well, ordering the National Academy of Sciences to do a study of possible links between the water contamination at Camp Lejeune and health problems in base residents. "I think I literally screamed," Dyer said at the time. "It's like something good has finally started coming out of this thing."[25]

The legislation was proposed by Senator Elizabeth Dole, with backing from Senator James Jeffords. Dyer described the meeting that she and other victims of the contamination had had with Dole. "She wanted to hear and listen to each one of our stories," Dyer said. "She was shaking her head in disbelief. She couldn't believe what she was hearing. She looked at us and said, 'What can I do? What do you need?'"[26]

"I have heard from constituents and other Marine families whose children have suffered birth defects and even fatal illnesses, and these families believe that their tragedies were caused by water contamination at Camp Lejeune," Dole said in a news release. "We must uncover and evaluate the facts about this incident—and I am hopeful that this provision will help those families who are seeking answers." In his own release, Jeffords described the legislation as "the minimum that our government should be doing to address the grievous failure on the part of the Marine Corps to adequately protect its service members and their families."[27]

Jeff Byron, who also was gratified by the planned study, said simply, "I am very pleased, and I think the creator has smiled upon us."[28]

11

OBSTRUCTED JUSTICE?

I personally would have been using different water.
—THOMAS SINKS, DEPUTY DIRECTOR,
AGENCY FOR TOXIC SUBSTANCES AND DISEASE REGISTRY

In 2006, twelve years after the "Republican revolution" under Newt Gingrich had given the GOP a majority in Congress, Democrats regained control of both the House and the Senate. Democrat John Dingell of Michigan resumed chairmanship of the House Energy and Commerce Committee, a position he had held from 1981 to 1994. One of Dingell's first priorities was to hold the military accountable for its environmental problems, and Camp Lejeune's escalating health crisis topped the list. Another Michigan Democrat, Congressman Bart Stupak, took over the panel's Oversight and Investigations Subcommittee. Stupak scheduled a hearing for June 12, 2007, entitled "Poisoned Patriots: Contaminated Drinking Water at Camp Lejeune." It would mark the first time since the contaminated water issues had surfaced more than two decades earlier that all the major players in the unfolding drama were together on the same stage.[1]

Stupak opened the hearing by noting that one of the principal pollutants at Lejeune, TCE, was the same volatile organic compound that had poisoned people in Woburn, Massachusetts, in a case made famous by the book and movie *A Civil Action*. "As bad as the contamination was at Woburn, the concentrations of TCE at Camp Lejeune were as much as ten to fifteen times higher," he said. "We have a chart. . . . There is a current standard, five parts per billion; Woburn is 267; Hadnot, which is one of the wells [at Lejeune], was 3,400. In Hadnot on February 7, 1985, over 18,000 parts per billion [were found] in the water."

The lead witnesses at the hearing were Jeff Byron, Mike Gros, and Jerry Ensminger, who by this time had assembled their own website—"The Few, the Proud, the Forgotten"—which was filled with stories and documents related to Lejeune's water. Testimony by these three relentless advocates for victims of the contamination was a fitting start for an event intended to expose to the public— and more importantly to members of Congress—what was probably the biggest water-contamination case in history, both in terms of the levels of pollution and the number of people exposed to it. Their heartrending personal stories captured the wide range of health problems apparently linked to the tainted water. Driven by anger and grief, Byron, Gros, and Ensminger—along with Tom Townsend in Idaho and others who believed they had been harmed by the pollution—had managed to uncover more information about Lejeune's water issues than two federal agencies and the Navy itself had compiled during twenty-two years of investigation.

"From documents that we obtained through Freedom of Information Act requests," Byron testified, "we were able to determine that the Marine Corps/DOD environmental personnel on base were well aware of the VOC contamination before our family moved into base housing, and therefore could have intervened and prevented the adverse health effects suffered by my family as well as other families, whose medical history is very similar to my own."

After providing more background information, he said, "I was raised to believe that to get something done you had to do it yourself. That is what I and others are doing."

Gros described how the group of former Marines had found the lab reports that first indicated the presence of solvents in Lejeune's water in 1980, along with other test results given to the base's water system managers in the years that followed. "In spite of multiple handwritten warning notes on repeated test reports over several years' period of time, the advice of the base's outside water consultants to further identify and quantitate the poisoning chemicals was repeatedly ignored," he said. "Amazingly, no tests were ever done in follow-up to identify the nature of these compounds or their sources. Even more incredible was the Marine Corps' attempt to later justify this gross neglect with the tack that no law existed requiring them to exercise the normal good judgment and caring that any other contemporary water supplier would have had for its customers."

Ensminger told the subcommittee members how he had had to notify the health agency conducting studies at Lejeune, the ATSDR, that the Marine Corps had provided the agency with incorrect information about the base water systems, a mistake that had caused the ATSDR to overlook thousands of people who had been exposed to the contamination. "The credit for the discovery of the incorrect water system data belongs to Major Tom Townsend, United States Marine Corps, retired," Ensminger said. "It was through Major Townsend's diligent and aggressive letter-writing and Freedom of Information Act request campaign that much of the factual information about Camp Lejeune was uncovered. Major Townsend lost an infant son and, more recently, his wife of more than 50 years to this contamination."

Their testimony, rich in details about the military's attempts to downplay its pollution problems, was in sharp contrast to that of Major General Robert Dickerson Jr., the commander at Camp Lejeune in 2007. "This unfortunate situation happened over 20 years ago," Dickerson said. "And while there are still large gaps of knowledge on potential health implications due to exposure to TCE or PCE today, these gaps were even greater back in the 1980s." Dickerson said that two federal investigations, and one by an independent panel appointed by the Marine Corps commandant, had all exonerated Lejeune officials of any wrongdoing. "Ultimately, everyone is here today for the same reason, to determine whether or not our Marines and their families were harmed in any way by contaminated water," he said. "We fully complied with environmental laws and regulations, and we remain committed to working with ATSDR and other Federal agencies involved with the study."

Using information discovered by Ensminger, Stupak pointed out that the Navy had issued its own regulations for drinking water in 1972, and that compliance with these regulations had required regular testing. The regulations had specifically set a limit of 3 parts per billion for chlorinated hydrocarbons such as TCE. "Is it a violation of your military code if you ignore the regulations?" he asked Dickerson.

"No, sir. We do not ignore any regulations," the general responded. "We hold ourselves to the highest standard."

Sitting beside Dickerson, the environmental restoration manager at Marine Corps headquarters, Kelly Dreyer, interjected that wells were shut down at Camp Lejeune as soon as they were found to be a source of contaminants, but it took some time to track down which wells were tainted.

"Are you telling me the military's response is—even though we know we are extremely higher than 3 parts per billion, way over our Navy regulations, we would continue to expose people because we can't find the source?" Stupak said. "That's ludicrous. If you are concerned about the health and safety of the people you are dealing with, if they're being exposed to it, you would bring in potable water, you would take other action. . . . Your people were exposed to it, and you didn't do anything."

"I wouldn't say that the Marine Corps, that Camp Lejeune didn't do anything at that time," Dickerson said. "I will say that they did work closely with the state of North Carolina environmental [regulators] to detect and find out what was contaminating the water, see what the level of contaminants were and what the impact was. They didn't know. There were no standards for these contaminants at that point in time."

Asked about the levels of contamination in the drinking water, Dreyer said the results varied. "That was part of the problem," she said. "In many instances they would have non-detect [of any measurable levels of contaminants]. We have seen as high as 1,400 in tap water. I will point out that 18,000 figure is from a well sample. And that well would not have been provided directly to anybody to drink. It would have been transported to the water treatment plant and mixed with other wells that were pumping at that time."

"Everybody did the best with the information they had at the time," Dickerson insisted. "Unfortunately, some of the levels on a day-to-day basis were above the acceptable levels for drinking water."

Stupak and other members of the subcommittee also were flabbergasted that the Marine Corps had not made aggressive efforts to contact everyone who had lived on the base when the water was contaminated to inform them that they had been exposed to toxic chemicals. Dickerson said there had been outreach through the media, and that information had been provided on the Camp Lejeune website. "Not the media," Stupak said. "I'm talking about notice to those individuals who lived there. Why not contact them?"

Dickerson: "Some people, we haven't got an address to get to. Some of the records are not complete on everybody that was stationed there."

Stupak: "Have you made an effort?"

Dickerson: "We have made every effort to get the word out. That is why the website was set up."

Stupak: "No, no, not the word out. Notice directly these people."

Dickerson: "We have a media campaign to go out, based on the study."

Stupak grew increasingly frustrated. "My chief of staff here sits here and says, 'Man, I moved three times in the last few years, but still I get a recall notice on a car that I owned three moves ago.' And if a private company can still notify you about your clunker, which is probably already no longer on the road, but can give you recall notices, I would think the military could contact people who were exposed. And I would go from 1957 until 1987, that 30-year period. I just can't believe you can't do that. That's inconceivable to me."

Next, it was the ATSDR's turn to report on its studies. Thomas Sinks, the agency's deputy director, said that in the modeling that had been done on the Tarawa Terrace system, which mostly had been contaminated with the dry-cleaning solvent perchloroethylene from a nearby business, the highest PCE reading had been 180 parts per billion—thirty-six times the maximum exposure level set by the Environmental Protection Agency in 1992. "There were approximately 83,000 people exposed to this water from 1958 through 1985," Sinks said. Modeling had not been completed on the Hadnot Point system, but one sample of tap water there had 1,400 parts per billion of TCE, hundreds of times higher than the safety level, he said. Sinks also said the ATSDR had begun a modeling study for the Holcomb Boulevard system, which the agency only recently discovered had been served by the Hadnot Point treatment plant for years before its own plant was built in 1972. Sinks estimated that at least 10,000 people living in the Holcomb Boulevard area from 1968 through 1985 had been exposed to contaminated water from the Hadnot Point system.

Congressman Greg Walden, a Republican from Oregon, asked Sinks whether, if he had been living at Camp Lejeune during the time of the contamination, he would have felt comfortable drinking the water.

"Well, I think that I personally would have been using different water and I think that I would have been recommending that an alternative water source was used at that time," Sinks responded.

"I don't know anybody that would say the opposite of that," Walden said.

Ensminger and his crew had uncovered another ominous part of the story before the hearing: the Environmental Protection Agency's enforcement division had spent a considerable amount of time looking into whether Marine Corps officials had obstructed government investigations of Camp Lejeune pollution, but the Justice Department had determined that there was not a strong enough case to bring criminal charges.

EPA investigator Tyler Amon appeared before the subcommittee with the agency's top enforcement officer and verified that he had found some evidence of obstruction, mainly in the way Navy engineers appeared to have been coached in how to answer questions about the contamination. "So criminal charges were considered on obstructing justice?" Stupak asked Amon.

"That is correct, sir," the EPA investigator replied.

"Okay. And then who determined not to bring forth the charges?" Stupak asked.

"The Department of Justice ultimately makes decisions on what is charged," Amon said.

Peter Murtha, director of the EPA's Office of Criminal Enforcement, said the agency's investigation had spanned eighteen months and had included twenty-six interviews with personnel from Camp Lejeune and the Navy Facilities Engineering Command, Atlantic Division, or LANTDIV. In addition, thousands of documents had been reviewed, and investigators had consulted "extensively" with an expert in drinking-water regulations. "I think one also has to bear in mind, although clearly there is some derogatory information in the investigation that we put together, that it is really a higher bar to bring criminal charges," Murtha said.

"Under the principles of federal prosecution, the Department of Justice prosecutors need to make sure that they have a reasonable probability of succeeding on the charges that they bring," Murtha told the subcommittee. "And I think the feeling must have been here that, even though there was evidence of not being forthcoming, that that evidence didn't quite reach the level where there could be a reasonable probability that convictions would be obtained."

Congressman Ed Whitfield, a Republican from Kentucky, was troubled by the fact that the Navy's environmental engineers had been coached by their superiors on how to handle investigators' questions. "There may not have been any criminal charges, but I think it is a sad day that the investigation shows quite clearly that people were not forthcoming," Whitfield said. "And like I said, we are very proud of our military, but I think, in this incident, the military leadership failed the men and women who serve this country and their families."

Another EPA official, Franklin Hill of the Superfund office in Atlanta, provided an update on the source of all the problems at Lejeune. "During the eighteen years that EPA has been involved in cleanup at Camp Lejeune, we have made significant progress in cleaning up contaminated soil and groundwater," Hill reported. "To date, we have selected remedies at thirty sites within Camp Lejeune and anticipate selection of the last remedy in the year of 2011." Sixteen other contaminated sites were still under investigation at the base, he said, and all "remedies" were expected to be in place by 2014.

Stupak was not impressed. "Camp Lejeune was listed [as a Superfund site] in 1989," he told Hill. "That was when it was final, you said. Here we are eighteen years later, and nothing has been cleaned up, has it?"

Hill responded: "Well, we have a couple of sites that we have removed, or we have decided that they have reached their remedial goals. We have had some soil . . . "

Stupak interrupted: "You are close?"

Hill: "We have had a number of cleanups on the site. So the answer to your question, sir, is yes, there have been some cleanups."

Stupak: "Of the 46 sites, how many have been cleaned up?"

Hill: "That is a good question. I don't want to guess at that, but I know that there are several removals that have been completed."

Cleanup was also continuing at the property owned by ABC One-Hour Cleaners, which had dumped dry-cleaning solvents over a period of several decades, contaminating the water at Tarawa Terrace, Hill said. "It will go on until we achieve the remedial goals for that site," he said. "And right now, we are looking at North Carolina standards, which is about 2.8 parts per billion for TCE. So that is quite a conservative number. And it will take us some time to achieve that."

Finally, a representative of the Navy's Office of the Judge Advocate General (JAG) gave a status report on claims that had been filed to that point seeking damages from the military for health problems—and in some cases, deaths—that were believed to have been caused by the Lejeune pollution. "As of this date, we have received a total of 853 claims that allege either personal injury or death as a result of exposure to contaminated drinking water while living or working on board Marine Corps Base Camp Lejeune," said Pat Leonard, director of the claims, investigations, and tort litigation division at the Navy JAG office. "The majority of the claims are from family members of former service members stationed at Camp Lejeune. Included in that total number are 115 claims from civilian employees who worked on board the base."

Leonard said none of the claims had been addressed because of the "very complex scientific and medical issues" involved. "It is the Navy's intention to wait for the ATSDR study to be completed in order to insure that we have the best scientific research available so we may thoroughly evaluate each and every claim on its own merits," she said. "We truly believe this approach is in the best interests of both the claimants and the Department of the Navy."

Dingell, chairman of the full Energy and Commerce Committee, sat in for part of the subcommittee hearing and summed up the proceedings with a single statement. "I find myself somewhat troubled that the military—and I was an infantry man in World War II—doesn't adhere to the maxim that the Marine Corps has, and that is that the Marines take care of their own," he said.

12

"FLORIDA MAN HAS BREAST CANCER"

They brought me a pink smock with flowers on it.
—MIKE PARTAIN, SON OF US MARINE
STATIONED AT CAMP LEJEUNE

Born in 1968 to a Marine who was headed into the teeth of the Tet Offensive in Vietnam, Mike Partain aspired to a military career like his father and his grandfather. But in a perverse twist, it might well have been the very fact that he was born at Marine Corps Base Camp Lejeune that would block Partain from following that path.[1]

Partain's grandfather, Warren Partain Sr., had been a Marine in both World War II and Korea. He had enlisted in the Marines in 1939, largely to escape the hardscrabble life of farming and ranching in his hometown of Olney, Texas. He ended up on radio duty in Iceland when the war started, and then he was reassigned to the states as a communications officer. His son, Warren Jr., was born in 1943 on Parris Island, the Marine training base in South

Carolina. At age seventeen Warren Jr. received an appointment to the United States Naval Academy, signed by President John F. Kennedy and Texas Governor John Connally. There was an eerie connection there. When Kennedy was assassinated in Dallas in 1963, Connally was seated directly in front of the president in the limousine, and Warren Partain Jr. would be part of the Naval Academy contingent that marched in his funeral procession in Washington. Following graduation from the academy in 1966, Partain went all over the world as a Marine officer. "His roots were in the Marine Corps; the Marine Corps is family to him," Mike Partain later said of his father.

Mike Partain's mother was a French Canadian, Lisette Pampalon, whom his father had met while on a training cruise aboard the aircraft carrier USS *Shangri-La*, which made a stop in Quebec City in the summer of 1964. Warren and Lisette were married in June 1966, right after Warren's graduation, and a year later the couple moved to Camp Lejeune, where Warren was assigned as a communications instructor. It was there they conceived their first child while living in the housing at Tarawa Terrace. Mike Partain was born on January 30, 1968, a seemingly healthy baby except for one inexplicable detail: he had a red skin rash all over his body.

Partain's mother hated Camp Lejeune. It was too far removed from the forested vistas of Canada, her son said. "Lejeune is a swamp," he said. "The butt-crack of the South." His mother didn't like the taste or smell of the water there, either, "but my Dad said, 'Just boil it,'" Partain recalled.

When it came time for her husband to ship off for Vietnam in the spring of 1968, Lisette told Warren that if he left her at Lejeune, she and the baby wouldn't be there when he returned. So before he went to war in May, Warren Partain moved his family to California, where his parents had a home near Camp Pendleton, the headquarters of the 1st Marine Division.

Warren returned unscathed from Vietnam in July 1969 after serving in a relay battalion for division communications between Da Nang and Okinawa, Japan, the island launching pad for US troops and aircraft during the war. He took an assignment at the Pentagon, and in 1970 he and his wife had their second child, a daughter who was born at Bethesda Naval Hospital outside Washington, DC. Warren Partain retired from the Corps that year, landed a job with Johnson & Johnson in Michigan, and then moved in 1972 to Florida, where he settled with his family in nearby Winter Haven when Mike Partain was four years old.

Besides the strange skin rash at birth, Mike Partain had a number of other health issues growing up. Some seemed routine, such as frequent infections of the nose, ears, and throat, but others were highly unusual. "My toenails were described as rotten," Partain said. At age thirteen—and four more times over the next five years—he experienced painful swellings in the testicles, a problem most often experienced by sexually active older men. "The doctor asked if I had sex and I asked him what that was," Partain recalled. There were other problems, usually ones that were never understood by his doctors, throughout his teens and twenties. "I just remember being sick all the time," he said.

Partain followed a path not atypical for young men in Florida in the 1980s—he worked at Disney World, went to Florida State University and dated a girl there, then, when she broke up with him, let his grade point average slip to 1.9. His father told him he was on his own, so Partain joined the Navy in January 1988. He was assigned to the nuclear program and was sent to the Naval Training Center in Orlando.

Not long after he arrived, the rash Partain was told he had as a baby returned with a vengeance. "It exploded all over my body," he said. "The only way I could get [the itching] to stop was to jump in the shower and stand in scalding hot water. The Navy sent me to

the hospital and accused me of drinking. But it wouldn't go away."
Partain was diagnosed with atopic dermatitis, which disqualified
him from being in the nuclear program. "They discharged me as
an erroneous enlistment because I had the rash when I was born,"
he said.

Partain recalled that the rash had turned up only periodically in
his younger years, and he realized it often recurred whenever he
wore suits that had been dry-cleaned. He also discovered years
later that there was a plume of groundwater at the Orlando training base contaminated by the dry-cleaning solvent perchloroethylene, with PCE concentrations as high as 28,000 parts per billion. "I
think that's why it came back," he said of the skin rash that cost
him a Navy career.

He came back home in March 1998 and went to work again at
Disney World, and married a young woman from Indiana named
Margaret in the spring of 1989. They had their first child later that
year, and Partain returned to Florida State to earn a history degree
in 1992. The couple had a second child, and Partain worked for
about five years in sales and as a store manager, then, in 1997, he
started teaching high-school history. Kids three and four arrived
during his tenure as a teacher, before Partain started a full-time career as an insurance adjuster in 2001. He was promoted to State
Farm's office in Tallahassee in 2007.

It was there that Partain's life took an unwelcome turn. "I
started feeling tired more than usual," he said. "I felt drained a lot.
Then I went turkey hunting one day, and that night Margaret and
I hugged, and her hand hit a bump on my chest. I'm a hairy guy
and it felt like a cyst you get with an ingrown hair, but she didn't
like it. It was at 2 o'clock above the nipple."

When the bump didn't go away after two weeks, Partain's wife
insisted he have it checked out. The doctor who examined Partain,

he said, "gave me that look that said, 'I don't really like this,' and asked me to get a mammogram."

Partain is a tall and burly man who wears a dark goatee—not the kind of patient one would expect to see visiting a treatment center for breast cancer. "You feel stupid, a guy going for a mammogram," he said. "They thought I was waiting for my wife. When I went in they brought me a pink smock with flowers on it. It took a long time after they did it for them to call me. Then the nurse came in and had that look on her face. Something was really wrong. She said they needed more pictures, a sonogram. You couldn't sledge-hammer a pin up my ass. There was a big white mass, with dots all over it—calcification, a calling card of cancer."

A biopsy was ordered and Partain went home to await the results, feeling "like death warmed over," he said. The diagnosis of breast cancer came on the date of his eighteenth wedding anniversary, April 25, 2007. Partain was thirty-nine years old. For some reason it occurred to him that he had just gotten a new ringtone for his cell phone that suddenly seemed prophetic. It was a song by REM entitled "It's the End of the World as We Know It (And I Feel Fine)."

The mastectomy was done on May 4, 2007; the surgeon removed a 2.5-centimeter tumor and a big chunk of tissue from the left side of Partain's chest. As he lay in the recovery room—and for weeks afterward—Partain could not come to grips with what had happened to him. Statistics he found online showed that men accounted for just one out of a hundred diagnosed cases of breast cancer, and there was no history of the disease in his family, even among the women. He even had himself tested later for a genetic mutation that is found in most of the men who do get breast cancer, and the results came back negative.

Less than two months after the surgery, the most plausible explanation for Partain's rare diagnosis was revealed to him, thanks to the House Energy and Commerce Committee's Subcommittee on Oversight and Investigations hearing held in Washington on Camp Lejeune's water contamination. Partain was walking back to his car after a follow-up visit with his doctor in mid-June when he got a call from his father. "I was not used to hearing emotion in his voice, him being a former Marine officer and all that, but when he called he asked me where I was," Partain said. "I immediately thought something was wrong with Mom. He said you need to get your ass home and turn on your TV—that was more like him—and when I got home about twenty minutes later I turned on CNN and there was the lead-in to Jerry Ensminger testifying at Congressman Stupak's hearing."

One statement in the CNN report struck Partain like a thunderbolt—that federal investigators were looking for health problems in babies born at Camp Lejeune between January 1968 and December 1985. "January 1968—that was the month I was born," Partain said. "I knew immediately what had happened." He dug out photos of his mother holding him in her room just after he was born at the Camp Lejeune hospital; on the bedside table was a glass of water sitting next to a baby bottle.

Sifting through information about the base contamination, Partain realized that he and his mother had been hit with a double dose of toxic chemicals on an almost daily basis. His family had lived at Tarawa Terrace, where the water was tainted by the dry-cleaning solvent PCE, and his mother—who didn't drive—spent much of her time on the base in areas served by the highly contaminated Hadnot Point system: the hospital, the Officers' Club, the PX. "Everything my mother needed was on the base, so she never left it," he said.

Partain contacted Ensminger through Stupak's office, and the two talked on the morning Partain was scheduled to begin chemotherapy. It was one of the scariest days of his life. "I never drank, except in college, never smoked pot or used drugs. I never put anything in my body that could be harmful," Partain said, "and here I had to have these injections of drugs." But Ensminger gave him something positive to think about before he was put down for the chemo. "He was shocked and said he didn't know what to say," Partain said, "but that I needed to worry about getting better and then we'd talk more. And he told me about the website"—"The Few, the Proud, the Forgotten."

For the next six months Partain and Ensminger burned through thousands of minutes on their cell phones, going over every detail that had been uncovered so far about the Lejeune contamination and the Navy's handling of it. Partain also contacted a reporter at the *Lakeland Ledger* in Florida, which ran a story about him in September 2007 under the headline, "Florida Man Has Breast Cancer." The article ran online, and a few days later Partain got a call from a man in Birmingham, Alabama, Kris Thomas, who said he had lived in Tarawa Terrace as a boy at the same time as Partain, in 1968, and had been diagnosed with breast cancer in 2005. "This was incredible," Partain said. "The whole fact that I had male breast cancer and how rare it is—especially since we had no history of it in our family, people said it had to be a fluke—but this helped confirm for me that it had to be connected to Camp Lejeune."

Partain finished chemotherapy in November 2007 and was declared cancer-free, but it was a victory that took a heavy physical toll on him. Ensminger had asked him to join the Community Assistance Panel that was providing input on the federal health studies of Lejeune being conducted by the Agency for Toxic Substances and Disease Registry, and Partain agreed to go to the next CAP meeting in Atlanta on December 6, 2007. "I had just finished chemo, my hair was gone, and I looked terrible," Partain said. He arrived at the meeting late, and though the two had not yet met in person, Ensminger knew it was Partain as soon as he walked into the room. "Jerry didn't say it but his face said, 'You look like hell.' . . . And he told me later that the Marine Corps people looked like they'd seen a ghost."

From that point on, Partain became fully immersed in the saga of the tainted water at Camp Lejeune. Borrowing from his years as a history teacher, when he would write a couple of dozen facts on the chalkboard and have his students use them to put together a broad narrative, Partain gave himself the same kind of assignment to tell the full story of the base contamination. It would be a task that would consume virtually all of his free time for the next seven months. "I laughed because it was like the kids getting their revenge," he said.

Ensminger, he said, had an "encyclopedic knowledge of Camp Lejeune," which actually gave him an advantage over the Marine Corps, because every time someone left a key post involving the Lejeune contamination, a new person would have to come in and learn everything from scratch. "But in order to be effective I realized that you have to communicate that knowledge to people, like members of Congress," Partain said. He asked Ensminger if the victims of the pollution had a timeline of events that had occurred, similar to the highly selective list that had been put together by the Marine Corps. "He said, 'No we don't and you need to write it,'" Partain said.

"So I spent from December 2007 to July 2008 working on it all the time," he said. "I still had to work every day and had to do all the stuff I usually did for the kids, then I worked on it in the evenings." All the effort paid off with a detailed chronology documenting the pollution problems and actions by the Marines, federal and state regulators, and others involved with the waste problems from the time Camp Lejeune opened in 1941 to the day it was declared a Superfund site in 1989. The timeline was posted on "The Few, the Proud, the Forgotten" website in time for the CAP meeting in July 2008. "And we got immediate validation it was effective," Partain said.

During the meeting, a Defense Department lawyer, Lieutenant Colonel Michael Tencate, made a statement that the Marines had notified people immediately in 1985 when the water contamination was discovered. Partain raised his hand and said, "Wait a minute, this article published in the base newspaper in 1985 says that 'people were not directly exposed.'" During the next break in the meeting, Tencate and a Marine Corps spokesman, Scott Williams, approached Partain and asked him where he got the information. "I told the colonel it was on our website and, unlike yours, it's all annotated," Partain said. "He went away in a huff and Williams said, 'You won't find any smoking guns.' These two clowns doing that made me realize it really bothered them. The timeline really pulled together Jerry's knowledge and all the documents. I felt like, how could they dismiss us now?"

Some of the Marine Corps officials had actually publicly ridiculed Ensminger and his colleagues, knowing there were fewer than a hundred members of their loose-knit organization, "The Few, the Proud, the Forgotten," Partain said. "The Marines were making fun of us, telling us we should notify all our members," he said. But after the timeline went up and word spread about it, membership soared to more than 5,000. "The website became the rallying point," Partain said. "And that was how we started finding the men with breast cancer."

Among the men who contacted Partain to say he wasn't the only man from Lejeune with a type of cancer that overwhelmingly affects women was Peter Devereaux. A former Marine who was stationed at the base from December 1980 to April 1982, serving in the 8th Communications Battalion, Devereaux lived in the French Creek area of the base, which got its water from the contaminated Hadnot Point system.

Devereaux said in an interview that as a young Marine, he never suspected there were any problems with the water at the base. "You were nineteen or twenty years old and that was the last thing on your mind," he said. Working and training in the North Carolina heat and humidity, though, he and the other young Marines "would drink a quart at a time," he said.

One of the main reasons Devereaux joined the Marines was that he hoped it might serve as a path to his real dream: becoming a boxer on the US Olympic team. He was a self-described "psychotic" about physical fitness—running marathons, boxing regularly, constantly working out—and he absolutely loved it. "The Marines were right up my alley," he said. "So much teamwork; I loved serving my country. Even through all this stuff it was my best job."

After Devereaux left the Marines he returned to his home outside of Boston and started work as a machinist, earning extra money on weekends by doing landscaping and taking on small construction projects. Life was beautiful for more than twenty-five years, with a happy marriage and the birth of a healthy daughter, until the morning of January 11, 2008. "I got up early for my ten-year-old child," he said. "I was forty-five then. I felt like I was getting a little fat, and I came across this lump on my breast and thought it was just fatty tissue. My wife and I talked and we scheduled an appointment—we took immediate action, which is not common for a man. Within a week the doctor called and said I had breast cancer. I couldn't believe it. I'm a guy. I was like invincible. I was training for a marathon. To have any kind of cancer, that's tough, but for a guy to have a woman's cancer, my wife and I were reeling. We had no idea how it happened."

Devereaux underwent a mastectomy on his left breast and had twenty-two lymph nodes removed. All were cancerous. In the months to follow he endured twenty-nine rounds of chemotherapy and thirty radiation treatments. "Then in August 2008 I got a letter from the Marines about the contaminated water," he said. "A light went off. It was like one and one is two. It was clear." His wife, Fiona, went online and found more information about the Lejeune problems, including the website run by Terry Dyer's group, Water Survivors. She posted a message on the site about her husband's breast cancer, and within minutes there was a reply from Mike Partain. "You need to call me immediately," Partain wrote, and provided his phone number. "I think I was number seven," Devereaux said.

Partain recommended that Devereaux apply for benefits from the Veterans Affairs Department to pay for treatment of his illness, if only to start a paper trail that he might need to fight for health coverage down the road. Devereaux applied in November 2008 and was denied in April 2009—just as the second stage of his disaster struck. "On April 9, 2009, I was supposed to finish my last treatment, but I could feel in my back and neck a pain that was like a pinched nerve," Devereaux said. "The doctor said we'll do a scan, and when he got the results he said the cancer had spread to my bones." Now Devereaux had metastatic breast cancer, for which there is no cure; the doctors told him the average life expectancy was two to three years.

Mike Partain was deeply affected by Devereaux's story, not only because it hit extremely close to home, but also for the support it gave as he built a case that Camp Lejeune had caused a cluster of male breast cancer victims unprecedented in the annals of medicine. Since the publication of the *Lakeland Ledger* story, he had found eight other cases in addition to his own. "That was still a lot for male breast cancer," he said, "but after seeing how the *Lakeland* story got nine, I realized a national story would do more." After a Community Assistance Panel meeting in April 2009 in Atlanta, Partain headed to the nearby headquarters of cable news giant CNN and asked to talk to a reporter. As he described his rare disease and said it was probably connected to drinking poisoned water at Camp Lejeune, Partain said, he could tell the reaction was as if he had said an alien spaceship had landed in Georgia. "They blew me off," he said.

"Then in May 2009 we had a big break," Partain said. He got a call from Bill Levesque, a reporter at the *St. Petersburg Times* in Florida, who had heard about Partain's quest to find cases of male breast cancer linked to Camp Lejeune. "I talked to him for about two hours and he was really interested in my story," Partain said. When it was published in the big regional newspaper and went online, suddenly the number of breast cancer cases jumped from nine to twenty men who had spent time at the North Carolina base—many of them now retired in Florida. Levesque followed up with a report about that, too, and within days CNN was calling Partain. "With 20 men they were very interested now," he said.[2]

13

A STONE WALL CRUMBLES

Sir, there are a number of actions that I would have changed.
—MAJOR GENERAL EUGENE G. PAYNE JR.,
ASSISTANT DEPUTY COMMANDANT, MARINE CORPS HEADQUARTERS

More than twenty years after the contaminated wells were shut down at Camp Lejeune—twenty-seven since solvents were first discovered in the water—victims of the toxic chemicals had nothing but frustration and anger and grief. By 2007, pain and anguish were deeply embedded in those most affected by the pollution, the Terry Dyers and Jerry Ensmingers who were now going into their second decade of demanding that the military and the government acknowledge the harm done to their families and to potentially thousands of others who had been exposed to the tainted water at the base. And some key people in Washington were beginning to share their concerns.

Democratic senator John Kerry of Massachusetts had been hearing regularly from Sally and Tom McLaughlin, a couple from the western part of his state whose infant son had been born with part of his brain missing in 1966, two years after the end of Tom's eighteen-month tour at Camp Lejeune, where they had lived in housing at Tarawa Terrace. The McLaughlins convinced Kerry that the baby's fatal birth defect was the result of Sally drinking contaminated water from August 1962 to February 1964, when Tom was stationed at Lejeune. And Senator Hillary Clinton, the former first lady who had moved from the White House to the Senate at the beginning of 2001, had become concerned about TCE contamination in the water supplies of several upstate New York communities, where high-tech companies used the powerful solvent to clean computer chips. Kerry and Clinton teamed up in July 2007 to introduce legislation that would give the Environmental Protection Agency a year to draft new health standards for TCE in drinking water. The National Academies of Sciences had given the agency a ringing endorsement for its 2001 assessment showing that regulations for TCE should be strengthened to protect public health, but it still had not acted on the matter. "The EPA has dropped the ball in giving this issue immediate attention," said Kerry. "In light of the tragedy at Camp Lejeune, where the TCE levels in drinking water caused sickness, birth defects and death, it is urgent that we update the standard today."[1]

Around the same time, Republican senator Elizabeth Dole of North Carolina pushed an amendment to a Defense Department bill to require the Marine Corps to contact everyone who had lived or worked at Camp Lejeune over several decades before the mid-1980s and inform them about the water contamination. "We cannot correct a past mistake by pretending that this contamination did not take place," Dole said in a statement on the Senate floor. "We cannot hope to protect the sterling reputation of the Corps by avoiding the hard and unpleasant facts associated with this tragic situation." Dole said she understood it would be an enormous task to identify and directly notify each Marine, family member, and civilian employee who had lived or worked on the base since the mid-1950s. But not reaching out to them would be "a profound disservice," she said. "We count on them to protect us. They count on us to do the right thing. Every member of this body has many, many constituents who served at Camp Lejeune."[2]

The frustration among victims of the contamination was turning to outright anger. At an August 2007 meeting of the Community Assistance Panel set up by the federal Agency for Toxic Substances and Disease Registry to provide input on its Lejeune studies, scientists from the agency reported that it would be months before they could complete a study of how many people had been exposed to contaminants at the base and at what levels. The ATSDR was now into its fourth year of designing computer models to re-create the flow of contaminants in the base's water systems over a period of thirty years, with no clear end in sight. "These studies have not been easy," said the agency's senior scientist, Frank Bove. "And the future studies will take time, too."[3]

Members of the CAP who had traveled long distances to attend the meeting in Atlanta did not hold back their rage. "Nothing is happening here," said Terry Dyer, who had been actively following the studies by the ATSDR for nearly a decade, after discovering that her father, a school principal on the base for fifteen years, might have been killed by the tainted water, and that the water could have also accounted for the severe health problems suffered by her and her two sisters. "I'm tired of coming here. I'm tired of time away from my family. I'm tired of not knowing from day to day whether I'm going to die. I don't want to waste this time here because I want to be with my family."[4]

Jeff Byron also let loose on officials from the ATSDR and the Marine Corps. "When are you going to divulge what you know? Why are you still holding back on Freedom of Information documents that we are requesting, instead of citing national security?" Byron asked. "I'm sick of wasting my time with people who won't give us the truth."[5]

The fury increased in the fall of 2007 when the National Research Council—a part of the National Academies of Sciences that was tasked by Congress to study whether illnesses could be linked to Lejeune's contamination—dispatched a committee of researchers to the North Carolina base to begin an investigation. Members of the panel arrived on Wednesday, November 14, for a tour of the sprawling installation, followed by a reception and dinner at the Officers' Club. Jerry Ensminger heard that the committee was being "wined and dined" by the Marine Corps as it launched its study of the effects of the base contamination and immediately suspected the results would be as tainted as Camp Lejeune's water had been in the 1970s. "I fully intend to write an official letter of protest to what we, the victims of this tragedy, view as a direct violation of the ethical standards which should guide the activities of the National Academy's work," he wrote to one of the administrators of the study in Washington.[6]

The day after their inaugural meeting in the most comfortable accommodations the Marine Corps could provide, the scientists were confronted with the cold, harsh realities of the issues they were assigned to study. At a meeting with victims of the contamination, Mary Freshwater of Greenville, North Carolina, stood before the panel holding a cardboard box carrying a stained piece of clothing and a bottle that had been used by her infant son, who had been born with an open spine at Camp Lejeune in 1977. Fighting back tears, Freshwater said the tiny outfit was all she had to remember her baby boy, who had died on New Year's Eve only a month after his birth. The doctors had said it was a fluke, she said, and encouraged her to get pregnant again. That she did, and another son was born—this time without a cranium. "I'd appreciate it if you take into account that we are not just numbers in a study," she told the scientists. "We are people that have had great tragedies, and the pain is no less."[7]

But even if the problems at Lejeune were viewed only through statistics, it seemed no less a tragedy. This is what was so infuriating to Freshwater and others who were certain they had suffered horribly from drinking poisoned water at the base. The ATSDR survey completed in 2003 found that of some 12,000 babies conceived or born at Lejeune between 1968 and 1985, more than 100 had suffered from birth defects or childhood cancer. About half of those cases had been confirmed by medical records. This was an unusually high rate, meaning that 1 in every 240 children who had been exposed to the contamination had experienced a devastating health problem. Furthermore, separate studies in communities where drinking water was contaminated by the toxic solvents TCE and PCE, in both New Jersey and Massachusetts, also showed increased rates of childhood leukemia, birth defects, and other serious illnesses. And evidence was growing that adults were affected, too: a study released in January 2008 by researchers at the University of Kentucky pointed to "a clear-cut link" between TCE exposure and development of Parkinson's disease.[8] Yet in its studies at Lejeune, the ATSDR was still studying only the chemical's effects on children, insisting that there was insufficient evidence to show that adults also could have been harmed.

It shouldn't have been surprising that the effects of Camp Lejeune's water contamination were being downplayed by the administration of President George W. Bush. Questions involving the effects of toxic chemicals were no longer the sole responsibility of experts at the Environmental Protection Agency and the Department of Health and Human Services, the ATSDR's parent agency. The producers and users of hazardous substances—industries and the military—had a greater role in assessing the risks from their own pollution than ever before.

The EPA had established a program in 1985 to evaluate the safety of new substances introduced into the marketplace that ultimately ended up in the environment. Assessments of more than five hundred chemicals had been completed in the first fifteen years of this program, called the Integrated Risk Information System, or IRIS, but the numbers dropped below an average of five per year between 2000 and 2007, according to a March 2008 report by the investigative arm of Congress, the Government Accountability Office. "GAO concluded that the IRIS database was at serious risk of becoming obsolete because EPA had not been able to complete timely, credible assessments or decrease its backlog of seventy ongoing assessments—a total of four were completed in fiscal years 2006 and 2007," said one of the authors of the report, John B. Stephenson, in testimony to a House committee. A major reason for the slowdown in completing chemical-safety studies, according to the GAO, was that the Bush administration had imposed new requirements: the EPA now had to submit every risk assessment to the White House Office of Management and Budget for review before it could be added to the IRIS database. Many assessments that went to OMB were held there indefinitely, often to give industries an opportunity to comment on the EPA's conclusions about harmful levels of exposure. Some assessments never again saw the light of day.[9]

The delays in assessing chemical threats can have disastrous effects on public health, said Lynn Goldman, who had been head of the EPA Office of Prevention, Pesticides and Toxic Substances under President Bill Clinton, speaking to a Senate committee investigating the IRIS system in April 2008. Take the example of formaldehyde, a long-used wood preservative, Goldman said. In 2006, an international research agency had recommended that it be classified as a known cancer-causing agent rather than just a probable carcinogen. "As evidence has accumulated, many countries and the state of California have proposed strict enforceable standards for formaldehyde in buildings," she said. Goldman, who later became dean of George Washington University's School of Public Health and Health Services, and at the time of the hearing was professor of environmental health sciences at Johns Hopkins University's Bloomberg School of Public Health, noted that:

> for years, the scientists at the EPA have been trying to update the agency's assessment of formaldehyde on IRIS. In 2004, this was nearly complete, but the process was postponed. The formaldehyde industry persuaded members of Congress and the EPA's political leadership that "new" scientific findings would soon be forthcoming, justifying a delay. At the same time, the CIIT (Chemical Industry Institute of Toxicology) published its own formaldehyde cancer assessment. In an unprecedented action, in 2004 EPA incorporated the CIIT assessment into its fiberboard hazardous air pollution rule, without the concurrence either of EPA's scientists or the EPA's independent Science Advisory Board.[10]

While stricter limits on formaldehyde were being held back, Goldman said, the 2005 hurricanes Katrina and Rita struck the Gulf Coast, leaving thousands homeless. The Federal Emergency Management Agency (FEMA) stepped in to provide 120,000 travel trailers for temporary housing, without realizing the trailers had been built with materials soaked in formaldehyde. "You know about the rest of the tragedy, and the slow response to the problem by the federal government," Goldman told the Senate committee. Thousands of hurricane victims now had a new disaster—health problems from breathing the toxic fumes of formaldehyde—and multimillion-dollar lawsuits were soon in the works. (The trailer manufacturers and contractors ultimately settled a class action suit for $42.6 million, but cases seeking damages from the government were still in the appeals process in 2013.)[11]

"Like formaldehyde, several other major chemicals under assessment by the EPA, like the dry cleaning solvent perchlorethylene, also have been held hostage," Goldman said at the 2008 hearing. "Withholding information about chemical hazards does cause harm to the public."[12]

A couple of months later, a House committee looking into the same issues at EPA invited Jerry Ensminger to testify about the military's role in assessing the risks from chemicals such as TCE that had been found in the water at Camp Lejeune. "It is a known fact that the United States Department of Defense is our nation's largest polluter," Ensminger told the committee. "It is beyond my comprehension why an entity with that type of reputation and who has a vested interest in seeing little to no environmental oversight would be included in the scientific process. Not only are they obstructing science, they are also jeopardizing the public health for millions of people all around the world . . . and yet this administration and past Congresses have allowed DOD's tentacles to infiltrate the realm of science."[13]

Political pressures were also taking a toll on the federal scientists most responsible for protecting the public against health threats of all kinds, including those in the environment. At the Centers for Disease Control and Prevention and its Superfund branch, the ATSDR, more than a dozen top managers and researchers had left between 2004 and 2006, and morale among the remaining staff was in the tank, according to a lengthy story published by the *Atlanta Journal-Constitution* on September 10, 2006. "You're seeing a gradual erosion of the scientific base, and that's very worrisome," a former CDC director, David Sencer, told the newspaper. Sencer and four other past directors wrote a joint letter to the director at that time, Julie Gerberding, saying they were alarmed by the depth of problems at the CDC, which had long been considered one of the premier public health agencies in the world. The paper had obtained a copy of the letter and included quotations from it in the story. "We are concerned that so many of the staff have come to us to express their concerns about the low morale in the agency," the five former directors had written to Gerberding. "We are concerned about the inability of many of the partners to understand the direction in which CDC is headed." CDC employees told the newspaper in interviews that one of the reasons for the low morale was "a general lack of confidence that CDC's leadership will 'do the right thing' when faced with political pressure from Washington."[14]

If there was a sense that Washington was calling the shots at the CDC, it was most certainly felt among staff members at the health agency's stepchild, the ATSDR, which also was headquartered in Atlanta. Nearly all the tiny agency's studies dealt with the effects of pollution that had been caused by two of the most powerful forces in the nation's capital, the US military and corporate America. Researchers working on studies at the ATSDR had to know there would be hell to pay if they pressed too hard to link illnesses or deaths to contamination at a Superfund site where the Pentagon or Big Business had liabilities.

In the case of Camp Lejeune, the ATSDR was continually being bullied by the Navy. At one point in 2007, the Pentagon simply stopped providing funds for the computer modeling being done by the ATSDR to replicate the flow of contaminants at the base over several decades in order to better understand how many people had been exposed and at what levels. In May 2008, the ATSDR's deputy director, Thomas Sinks, was forced to remind Navy headquarters that it had not made its promised payments for the agency's studies at Lejeune in eight months. "You are requested to provide full funding of $1,570,409 to ATSDR by June 1, 2008, and not hold these funds contingent upon final resolution of our project and budget tracking differences," Sinks said in a letter to the Navy. After the Associated Press obtained Sinks's letter and reported that the military was stonewalling the ATSDR's studies at Lejeune, the Navy paid up, and officials dismissed the AP story as exaggerating a routine budgeting delay. Jerry Ensminger knew better. "In a nutshell, the DOD, DON, and the USMC do not want to see the water model for the Hadnot Point and the Holcomb Blvd. water distribution systems at Camp Lejeune to ever be completed," he said in an e-mail to the ATSDR and others on May 29, 2008.[15]

Yet in the midst of all this pressure, there was one senior scientist at the agency who was determined to see the Lejeune studies through to completion. Frank Bove had worked earlier in his career as an epidemiologist at the New Jersey Department of Health, spending years investigating the effects of industrial pollution on people in dozens of communities. He had earned a master's degree in environmental health science in 1984 and a doctorate in occupational health science and epidemiology in 1987, both at the Harvard University School of Public Health. But more important to his later career, Bove had majored in both political science and philosophy at the University of Pennsylvania and went on to study philosophy in graduate school at Boston University in the late 1970s. During that time, Bove had been an organizer in the Boston area on issues involving the environment, public health, housing, and welfare rights. With that background of social consciousness, he was not just a representative for the ATSDR sitting in dispassionately on more than two dozen meetings of the Community Assistance Panel set up in 2006 to give victims of Camp Lejeune's contamination input into the agency's studies. The hundreds of stories about children with cancer, babies born without parts of their brains, former Marines dying of rare diseases, and cases of men with breast cancer had to have an impact on Bove, even with all his training as a scientist to develop strong evidence before drawing firm conclusions.

On June 23, 2008, Bove and a colleague at the ATSDR, Perri Zeitz Ruckart, issued a document that would give new hope to the victims of Camp Lejeune's poisoned water. It was a forty-page paper, with almost as many pages of attachments, entitled "An Assessment of the Feasibility of Conducting Future Epidemiological Studies at USMC Base Camp Lejeune." Partly in response to the recommendations of an independent panel of scientists in 2005, and partly as a result of pressure from Lejeune victims through the Community Assistance Panel, the paper urged the ATSDR to expand its studies of Lejeune's contamination to include adults who had been exposed to the tainted water. So far, the agency had focused its research solely on the children who had been exposed to the contamination in their early years of development and on babies who had been exposed in utero.[16]

Bove recommended both a mortality study and a cancer incidence study of Marines, Navy personnel, and civilian employees who had been stationed on Camp Lejeune between June 1975 and December 1985. The mortality study would assess "all causes of death" among those who had lived at the base during that ten-year period, while the cancer study would evaluate all confirmed cases of cancer in the study group, using state and federal cancer registries and the results of a separate health survey of former personnel at the base to be conducted under a congressional mandate. And in order to improve the credibility of the studies, the ATSDR would conduct the same surveys on Marines and civilian employees who had been stationed at Camp Pendleton in California from 1975 to 1985. This group would have the same type of population of former military personnel as the Camp Lejeune group, with one key difference—the Camp Pendleton group had not been exposed to volatile organic compounds in its drinking water.[17]

It would take some time for Bove's recommendations to be digested by leaders of the ATSDR and its parent agencies—the CDC and the Department of Health and Human Services—as well as by top brass in the Navy, who would have to find the money to pay for the new studies. In the meantime, while the study proposals slowly worked their way through the pipeline to Washington, a Democratic senator from Illinois, Barack Obama, was ascending to the White House as the nation's first black president. The stunning results of the 2008 election would bring sweeping changes to Washington, including a transformation in how the civilian leadership viewed the military and national security. The Obama administration would begin to wind down wars in Iraq and Afghanistan, put pressure on the Pentagon to cut its bloated budget, and make a concerted effort to focus more on scientific integrity, rather than economic consequences, in addressing environmental problems, including those at military installations.

Howard Frumkin, who had been appointed director of the ATSDR in the first year of President Bush's second term in 2005, could see that change was coming to his agency. Frumkin, already the subject of scathing criticism for his agency's failure to respond to the concerns of hurricane victims living in formaldehyde-tainted trailers, made what appeared to be a desperate effort to save his job just a few months after Obama took office. He launched what he said would be an eighteen-month "national conversation" to address public concerns about exposure to toxic chemicals and the way his agency had addressed those concerns. "He committed to a voluntary, participatory, inclusive, and transparent process, aligned with President Obama's commitment to open government," said an ATSDR description of Frumkin's plan. Jerry Ensminger wondered why, if the conversation was to be

"participatory" and "inclusive," Frumkin had never contacted anyone from the Camp Lejeune Community Assistance Panel, which
had been set up by his own agency just six months after he had
taken office, to ask for their input. "I can answer my own question," Ensminger said in an e-mail to the ATSDR. "Dr. Frumkin
does not want anyone who has a dissenting view in attendance at
his meetings."[18]

Frumkin's plan for a public dialogue might have been a publicity stunt, but in May 2009, there was a surprising development at
the ATSDR that showed he was listening to some of the concerned
scientists within his agency as well as some of the critics outside it.
Twelve years after it had issued the Public Health Assessment
(PHA) for Camp Lejeune, a document that greatly downplayed the
health threats from the base water contamination, the ATSDR
posted a statement on its website saying that the 1997 document
had been taken down. The notice said that "additional information has emerged related to exposures to volatile organic compounds (VOCs) in drinking water at Camp Lejeune." Specifically,
the agency had learned through its modeling and through other
sources that contaminated wells had been used to supply water to
the Holcomb Boulevard area of the base for a period longer than
acknowledged in the 1997 assessment. This was a reference to the
fact that the Marine Corps had failed to tell the agency that the
Holcomb Boulevard area had been serviced by contaminated water
from the Hadnot Point system before a new treatment plant was
built in 1972. As a result of the incomplete data, the ATSDR had
missed thousands of exposures to contaminated water in assessing
the risks in its 1997 report.[19]

More significantly, the ATSDR said it had learned since 1997
that at least one well in the Hadnot Point system had been contaminated with benzene, a known carcinogen found in gasoline
and diesel fuel. "The PHA should have stated there were not

enough data to rule out earlier exposures to benzene," the agency admitted in its May 7, 2009, statement.[20]

Even though it removed the 1997 PHA from its website, the ATSDR wouldn't dismiss it entirely as a flawed document. "The PHA spurred beneficial public health research, including the ongoing water modeling, exposure reconstruction, and epidemiological studies," the statement said. "Although the drinking water section needs to be updated, the PHA contains valuable and accurate historical information about nine other exposure pathways"— that is, nine of the ten contaminated wells that were shut down in 1984 and 1985. "Much of what we now know about the potential for adverse health effects related to exposures at Camp Lejeune is owed to this 1997 document. Once we have completed the water modeling and exposure reconstruction studies, ATSDR will re-analyze the drinking water pathway for the Camp Lejeune site, communicate findings to the public, and update the public health assessment. Exposures to VOCs in the drinking water occurred at Camp Lejeune. ATSDR declared those past exposures a public health hazard and we maintain that position today."[21]

The fact that benzene contamination had been overlooked in the 1997 PHA infuriated the two senators from North Carolina, Republican Richard Burr and Democrat Kay Hagan. Burr and Hagan wrote to the acting secretary of the Navy at the time, B. J. Penn, demanding to know what had happened. "Nothing is more important than protecting the health and quality of life of our military personnel and families," the senators told Penn in a May 13, 2009, letter. "Victims and their families have been patiently waiting for closure on this issue for over two decades. There have been persistent delays in ATSDR's epidemiological studies and water modeling. The inability to provide key documentation delays the completion and accuracy of these studies."

Documents uncovered later by Jerry Ensminger and Mike Partain made clear that the Defense Department had had ample opportunity to provide information about the benzene contamination but had failed to do so. It also appeared that officials at the ATSDR had bent over backward in 1997 to make sure the Marine Corps was happy with the results of the Public Health Assessment.

Two months before the PHA had been publicly released in August 1997, a draft copy of the report had been sent to Rick Raines at Camp Lejeune under a cover letter on ATSDR stationery. (The signature on the June 6, 1997, letter was redacted in the copy obtained by Ensminger. However, a response from the Navy a few weeks later, also obtained by Ensminger, indicated the letter had been written by the ATSDR's Carole Hossum, an environmental health scientist at the agency.) The June letter had asked for Navy officials to informally review the draft PHA, practically begging for any revisions the Navy's environmental officials felt were necessary. "Although such a review at this phase of our public health assessment process is not agency policy, I felt that too much time had past [*sic*] since the last release and additional information added to the document," the letter to Raines said. It continued:

> Therefore, I expect this to be an informal review. If you prefer a different approach, I ask that you give me your "informal" comments so that I can go ahead and address them in the document, then if you choose to send formal signed comments for the record, the time delay will not affect the release date. I need to receive your "informal" comments by June 23, 1997, preferably by phone. If I haven't heard from you by then, I'll call you Tuesday, June 24. Ideally, I'd like to discuss your comments over the phone so that I can make the changes to the document at that time to quicken the process.[22]

The request for a review ended up with Katherine Landman at the Naval Facilities Engineering Command, Atlantic Division (LANTDIV), who sent a July 21, 1997, memo to David Mc-Conaughy at the Navy Environmental Health Center, forwarding a copy of the ATSDR's draft PHA along with eight pages of "informal" comments that Landman had already sent to the health agency. The draft PHA, Landman said in the memo, had been provided by Carole Hossum of the ATSDR "for an 'informal' review prior to formal issuance of the report." Landman added, "I have discussed these comments with Ms. Hossum on the phone, and she has indicated to me that substantial changes will be made to the document regarding most issues that I mentioned in my comments. . . . Because Ms. Hossum requested only an informal review from a limited list of people, please provide any comments or concerns you may have about this document to me (informally), and I will forward to ATSDR with additional specific comments of my own that I am still generating."[23]

In her eight pages of comments on the ATSDR's draft report, Landman provided a list of documents from Camp Lejeune's Superfund cleanup files. This was in response to the health agency's request for "updated records for particular sites" on the base. None of the listed documents dealt with the benzene contamination in the Hadnot Point water system. Most of the remaining comments focused on all the efforts Camp Lejeune was making to ensure that contamination never got into the base drinking water again.[24]

On the day the PHA was released, August 4, 1997, the director of the ATSDR's Division of Health Assessment and Consultation, Robert C. Williams, sent a letter to the commanding general and the brigadier general at Camp Lejeune to notify them about the report. "The data and information in the U.S. Marine Corps Camp Lejeune Military Reservation Public Health Assessment have been evaluated, and ATSDR has placed the U.S. Marine Corps

Camp Lejeune Military Reservation in the category of no apparent public health hazard."[25]

Christopher Portier, who took over as director of the ATSDR in August 2010 and left in May 2013, admitted in an interview after his departure that agency researchers could have been more aggressive about tracking down all the contaminants, including benzene, when they started investigating Lejeune's water problems in the early 1990s. He also admitted the Marine Corps wasn't exactly screaming that health officials had overlooked significant fuel leaks from underground storage tanks and pipelines in the Hadnot Point area.[26]

"My sense of it was that in 1991 we were called in to investigate the 'Perc' [perchloroethylene] contamination coming onto the base from ABC Cleaners, and did a fairly good job of that," Portier said. "But ATSDR did not recognize the magnitude of the contamination that was coming from a different direction, that's from the underground storage tanks, until later on. It is unfortunate that the team that was looking at it early on dismissed the benzene readings that were right in front of their eyes and did not further investigate it because that might have cut the amount of time spent on this particular issue." But, Portier added, "there were difficulties getting some of the records over the years that made it hard for us to do our work."[27]

The ATSDR's acknowledgment that its 1997 report on Camp Lejeune was badly flawed was met with a mixture of relief and concern from both Jerry Ensminger and Mike Partain. Ensminger ridiculed the ATSDR's statement that it was still trying to determine whether benzene had made it from a contaminated well into the base drinking water. "We have analytical results from samples taken on 6 July 1984 which show high contamination levels of benzene in well HP-602," Ensminger said in an e-mail to the ATSDR's deputy director, Thomas Sinks. "By the DON/USMC's own admission, this well wasn't removed from service until 30 November 1984. We do know there was benzene contamination in that well when it was still active, [so] why is ATSDR 'muddying' the facts here?" Partain noted in an e-mail to Sinks that a test done in December 1985 on finished water from the Hadnot Point water treatment plant showed benzene present in the drinking water at 38 parts per billion.[28]

Still, Partain applauded the agency in his note to Sinks for taking a major step toward acknowledgment of the damage done by Lejeune's contamination. "Withdrawing the PHA as a viable document from your agency's database demonstrates a sincere effort to involve the community and not just accept the statements and assertions of the polluters as fact," Partain said. Ensminger, as usual, was more emphatic than his partner in describing his reaction to the ATSDR's removal of the 1997 report from its website. "We are in Day 99 of change, and by God we're starting to see it," Ensminger told the Associated Press for a story about the agency's action, roughly a hundred days after Obama had promised a greater emphasis on scientific integrity in his administration.[29]

—m—

The new optimism that Partain and Ensminger shared was quickly shattered by the June 13, 2009, announcement from the National Academies of Sciences that a lengthy study by a committee of the National Research Council had found no conclusive evidence that illnesses could be directly connected to contaminated drinking water at Camp Lejeune.[30]

"It cannot be determined reliably whether diseases and disorders experienced by former residents and workers at Camp Lejeune are associated with their exposure to contaminants in the water supply because of data shortcomings and methodological limitations, and these limitations cannot be overcome with additional study," reported the NRC committee, which had been funded by the Navy under a mandate from Congress. "Thus, the committee concludes that there is no scientific justification for the Navy and Marine Corps to wait for the results of additional health studies before making decisions about how to follow up on the evident solvent exposures on the base and their possible health consequences. The services should undertake the assessments they deem appropriate to determine how to respond in light of available information."

The committee's 317-page report reviewed epidemiologic studies of solvents and their effects, studies of other communities that had had contaminated water supplies, laboratory research on TCE and PCE, and the studies that had been done so far on the population at Camp Lejeune. In each category, the committee had concluded that there was "inadequate/insufficient evidence to determine whether an association exists" between exposure to the chemicals and adverse health effects.

The committee had also evaluated whether further health studies of former Camp Lejeune residents, as recommended in June 2008 by ATSDR epidemiologist Frank Bove, would be useful in determining the effects of the water contamination at the base. "After reviewing the study plans and feasibility assessments, the committee concluded that most questions about whether exposures at Camp Lejeune resulted in adverse health effects cannot be answered definitively with further scientific study," the panel reported.

> There are two main reasons for this. First, it is not possible to reliably estimate the historical exposures experienced by people at the base. Second, it will be difficult to detect any increases in the rate of diseases or disorders in the study population. Most of the health effects of concern are relatively rare, which means that very

large numbers of people are needed to detect increased cases. Although the total number of people who have lived at Camp Lejeune while the Tarawa Terrace and Hadnot Point water supplies
were contaminated is sizeable, the population is still unlikely to be
large enough to detect effects, other than common diseases or disorders, of concern.

The committee also had a message for some of those who had
spoken at the three public hearings on Camp Lejeune's contamination. "Many of the people who addressed the committee have
suffered from serious diseases or have family members or friends
who have suffered," the panel's report said. It went on:

> The committee was moved by the testimonies it heard and under-
> stands that some may have been looking for the committee to
> make a judgment on their particular case. However, science does
> not allow the committee to determine the cause of a specific case
> of disease. This may be hard to understand. Why would scientific
> experts not be able to determine whether a child's birth defect or a
> parent's cancer diagnosis was due to a chemical exposure? Unfor-
> tunately, for diseases that have multiple causes and that develop
> over a long period of time, it is generally impossible to establish
> definitively the cause in individual cases.

To sum it all up, the committee's chairman, David Savitz of the
Mount Sinai School of Medicine, issued a statement in a press release sent out by the National Research Council when its report
was released. "Even with scientific advances, the complex nature of
the Camp Lejeune contamination and the limited data on the concentrations in water supplies allow for only crude estimates of exposure," Savitz said. "Therefore, the committee could not determine
reliably whether diseases and disorders experienced by former resi-

dents and workers at Camp Lejeune are associated with their exposure to the contaminated water supply."[31]

Almost immediately after the report came out, a political and scientific firestorm erupted.

"The NAS study released Saturday is simply a review of previous scientific literature on hydrocarbon solvents, reports on Camp Lejeune water contamination, and published epidemiologic and toxicological studies," said Democratic senator Kay Hagan of North Carolina. Hagan condemned the study on several grounds:

> It failed to take into account the conclusions of previous epidemiological studies that found an association between volatile organic compounds (VOCs) exposures and childhood leukemia, and presents some direct contradictions to the EPA's maximum containment levels of VOCs in drinking water. Moreover, the NAS study barely mentioned benzene and vinyl chloride and severely downplays the established links between adverse health effects and exposure to VOCs that were present in the water at Camp Lejeune. For these reasons, I cannot stand behind the validity of the NAS study.[32]

"It's clear that the water at Camp Lejeune was contaminated by a number of hazardous chemicals at unsafe levels," said her colleague in the Senate from North Carolina, Republican Richard Burr. "I am deeply concerned about the conclusions in the report from the National Academy of Sciences. This latest report still raises more questions than it answers."[33]

"We are disappointed and dismayed at the report," said five scientists who had worked closely with victims of the contamination: Ann Aschengrau, Richard Clapp, and David Ozonoff of the Boston University School of Public Health; Daniel Wartenberg of the Robert Wood Johnson Medical School; and Sandra Steingraber of

Ithaca College. In a June 17, 2009, statement released to the media, the scientists said the report "reached puzzling and in some cases erroneous conclusions. . . . The NRC doubts that 'definitive' answers can come from any study, but this sets the bar too high—no one study can provide definitive answers, and all studies must be considered in the light of other scientific evidence. From our experience in other settings, we believe that useful studies of the Camp Lejeune population are possible and furthermore that the Marines and their families deserve our government's best efforts to carry them out."[34]

The victims of the contamination were dumbfounded by the report. "We couldn't figure out why the NRC was so in bed with the Navy," said Partain. A little digging shed some light on the possible reasons for the committee's blanket exoneration of the Marine Corps for causing health problems at Camp Lejeune.

Ensminger discovered, in talking with Clapp, a highly regarded epidemiologist who had been asked to review the NRC report before it was released, that Clapp's dissenting comments had been left out of the document. He also learned that as the NAS report was being prepared for publication, the scientific panel had assigned a scientist at the Honeywell Corporation—a company second only to the US military in the number of Superfund sites for which it is a responsible party—to manage peer-review comments by independent scientists. The potential conflict raised concerns that any conclusions saying that health problems could not be linked to contaminants would benefit Honeywell's defense in Superfund cases. Not only was there no mention of Clapp's disagreement with the committee's conclusions in the report, but the National Academies told Ensminger that the peer-review comments would never be released to the public.

Ensminger and Partain uncovered an even more damning document as well, one implying that the National Research Council report had been soft on the Marine Corps for a reason. In May

2009—a month before the report was released—the National Academies of Sciences had signed a $600,000 contract with the Navy agreeing to serve as consultants in helping the military to explain the effects of the water contamination, or lack of them, on people who had lived at Lejeune. Bill Levesque, the reporter who had written about Mike Partain at the *St. Petersburg Times,* obtained a copy of the contract and wrote a story about it in November 2009, five months after the release of the report. "Federal scientists and critics of the Marine Corps say the contract . . . is a blatant conflict of interest, and some critics say it calls into question the accuracy of an NRC report that already has been criticized by some scientists," Levesque wrote. "They've beaten us to death with the NRC report and pulled the wool over everybody's eyes," Partain was quoted as saying in the story. "The NRC report smelled rotten," he said, "and now we have a deal that smells even worse."[35]

The article quoted the response of a spokesman for the Marines, Captain Brian Block, who said the contract was part of its continuing relationship with the NRC and would aid the Corps' efforts to better understand the potential health effects of polluted water. "The Marine Corps initially declined to confirm the existence of the contract when the *Times* asked about it earlier in the week," wrote Levesque. "Block, the Corps spokesman, said in an e-mail, 'We will not discuss future contracts until they are finalized.' In fact, the contract was finalized on May 1. The Marine Corps also provided, at the *Times* request, a financial breakdown of the $14 million the Corps has publicly maintained it spent on Camp Lejeune research. The list did not contain the $600,000 NRC contract. When asked about it, the Corps did not respond."[36]

Officials at the ATSDR, whose plans for further studies of health problems at Lejeune had been discouraged by the National Research Council committee, were furious about the consulting contract between the NRC and the Navy. "The direct funding of peer review by the agency responsible for contaminating the Camp Lejeune drinking water creates a perceived conflict of interest unacceptable to the community of veterans and their families exposed," wrote Thomas Sinks, deputy director at the health agency, in a letter to the Marine Corps and Navy.[37]

Regardless of the seemingly tainted process for evaluating the effects of Camp Lejeune's water pollution, the committee's report was a severe setback to the slow but steady progress that the ATSDR had been making in its studies. It also dampened the ability of the affected victims to get their story out. "When the NRC report came out it sucked the air out of the Camp Lejeune story," Partain said. CNN canceled its plans for a story about the male breast cancer victims. "It was probably the darkest time I remember because we were pretty much on the brink of being wiped out," Partain added.

But Levesque wasn't giving up. On July 3, 2009, another story on the male breast cancer cases was published under his byline in the *St. Petersburg Times*. Six more cases had been found in just the past week in Florida, all with time spent at Camp Lejeune, Levesque reported. "Male breast cancer is exceedingly rare," his story said. "Just 1,900 men are expected to be diagnosed with breast cancer this year compared with nearly 200,000 women, the American Cancer Society says. A man has a 1-in-1,000 lifetime chance of getting the disease. Men who get it are often over 70, though it is rare even in older males."[38]

Boston University scientist Richard Clapp told Levesque that he was very concerned. "My gut tells me this is unusual and needs to be looked into," he said. "I'm sure there are still more out there in other states."[39]

CNN came back again, and this time the national cable network did the story in a big way—in two segments that ran on September 24 and 25, 2010. The stories featured Partain and other men who had spent time at Lejeune and now had breast cancer, now numbering more than twenty. "Jerry [Ensminger] called me and was blown away," Partain said. "He told me it was the anniversary of Janey's death."

ATSDR epidemiologist Frank Bove told CNN that the level of contamination in one sample taken at Camp Lejeune was "the highest I've ever seen in a public water system in this country." But he was cautious: "Whether exposures were long enough and high enough at Camp Lejeune to cause disease—that's the question." Clapp also appeared in the CNN stories and was more emphatic. "I think if cancer of the breast in men or other kinds of cancer have been linked to this exposure, that we ought to know about that," he said. "The families deserve that. The veterans themselves should know about that, and they should be compensated if the link can be made."[40]

Soon after the stories ran, the number of male breast cancer cases tracked down by Partain rose to fifty. "The media was fascinated by the story," he said. "It was such an irony that the roughest, toughest men in the world were being affected by a women's disease."

The tide was starting to turn against the Marines and in favor of the victims. The ATSDR, facing increasing criticism in Congress for declaring in 2007 that trailers containing high levels of formaldehyde posed no threats to the health of hurricane victims who were using them for temporary housing, was like a battleship slowly changing direction. The agency was forced to back off its position on the trailers and admit that the chemical fumes were making people sick. The health agency was also backing away from another report, which had been issued in the spring of 2009. In that document, the ATSDR had said that heavy metals and the remains of explosives at the Navy's Vieques Island base in Puerto Rico could not have been a health hazard for the residents there.

The ATSDR reversed course in November 2009, however, saying that it had found gaps in its original environmental data from Vieques. Key members of Congress stepped up the pressure. "It seems to have gotten into their culture to do quick and dirty studies and to be willing to say there are no public health consequences," said Congressman Brad Miller, a North Carolina Democrat who chaired a House subcommittee investigating federal health research and reports. "People should be able to count on the government to tell them the truth."[41]

Miller and the two senators from North Carolina, Republican Richard Burr and Democrat Kay Hagan, were already pushing legislation to require the Department of Veterans Affairs to provide health coverage for enlisted personnel, veterans, and family members who had been harmed by Camp Lejeune's pollution. "We owe those who are sick the benefit of the doubt and the health care they need," Burr said. But when their bill was considered by the Senate Veterans Affairs Committee in January 2010, VA Secretary Eric Shinseki warned that coverage might be needed for as many as 500,000 people at a cost of more than $4 billion over ten years. Democrats on the committee, including then-chairman Daniel Akaka of Hawaii, argued that the Defense Department, which was responsible for the contamination, should be footing the bill for the health problems it caused. Burr and Hagan argued that the Pentagon could no longer be trusted to care for its own. "I can't in good conscience agree to give these brave men and women a false hope that they'll get health care," Burr said. "Do you really believe the Department of Defense will accept responsibility for this health care when it still doesn't accept responsibility for the contamination?" He vowed to block every nominee for a Navy appointment who came before the Senate until the impasse on health coverage for Lejeune victims was broken.[42]

While the fight over health care was being waged, key members of Congress were also waging a battle with the Navy on another front—funding for ATSDR studies at Camp Lejeune. In December 2009, the Navy agreed to spend $2 million on a new review of cancer and birth defects in babies conceived or born at the base while some water systems were contaminated. The 1998 study on so-called "birth outcomes" had been inconclusive, but it had indicated that there could have been more than the expected number of health problems among children whose mothers had drunk tainted water. The decision to fund the study did not come easily, though. Congressman Miller of North Carolina and the two members of the House Energy and Commerce Committee who were investigating the pollution problems at Lejeune, Congressmen John Dingell and Bart Stupak of Michigan, had to threaten Navy Secretary Ray Mabus with harsh action if the Pentagon kept delaying funds for ATSDR studies. "It would be great if the Navy did the right thing for the right reason, but fortunately the law requires any polluter, including the Navy, to pay for the studies necessary to find out just how much harm they've done to innocent people," Miller, Dingell, and Stupak wrote to Mabus. "The law doesn't make victims of toxic exposure beg and plead a polluter for justice; the law gives them rights."[43]

Two months later, citing the National Research Council report saying that further investigation of health problems at Lejeune would be fruitless, the Navy refused to pay $1.6 million for a mortality study of former residents at the base. The timing of the Navy's funding refusal couldn't have been worse, though. Barbara Barrett, a Washington-based reporter for the McClatchy Newspapers in North Carolina, dug up documents in February 2010 showing that over the years, storage tanks and underground pipes at Lejeune probably had leaked as much as 800,000 gallons of fuel near wells providing water to the Hadnot Point system. One memo Barrett uncovered said that a contractor had told base officials in 1996 that about half a million gallons of the fuel had been recovered. "The other 300,000 gallons? I know what happened to it," Mike Partain told Barrett. "We drank it."[44]

Then, just a few days after Barrett's story was published, the Associated Press reported that a Navy contractor, the Michael Baker Corporation, based in Pennsylvania, had grossly understated the benzene levels found in one well serving the Hadnot Point water system in a report to the ATSDR in 1992, just as the federal health agency was beginning its research at the base. The AP found documents showing that benzene in the well had measured 380 parts per billion in 1984, but the 1992 report by the consultants showed the level to be 38 ppb. Then, in a final report on the well that was sent to the ATSDR in 1994, the Navy's consultant failed to mention benzene at all. "It was probably a mistake on the part of the contractor, but I can't tell you for certain why it happened," the Marine Corps spokesman, Captain Brian Block, told the AP's Kevin Maurer. A former enforcement officer for the Environmental Protection Agency, Kyla Bennett, offered a different assessment. "It is weird that it went from 380 to 38 and then it disappeared entirely," she said. "It does support the contention that they did do it deliberately."[45]

Miller, chairman of the Investigations and Oversight Subcommittee of the House Science and Technology Committee, was livid. He said he would demand that the Navy turn over all relevant documents and data on Camp Lejeune. "We want to know what did [the Navy and the Marine Corps] know about the water, when did they know[,] and what did they do about it?" Miller told McClatchy's Barrett. "Did they know about it during the 30 years when Marines and families were exposed to the water? Did they know about it and not do anything to stop it?" Navy Secretary

Mabus responded that the ATSDR had "full access" to documents on benzene levels at Lejeune—they had been available in a county library in North Carolina since 1992. This just made Miller angrier. "I cannot imagine that this was inadvertent, that this was the result of inadvertence, that there were not officials at the Navy who didn't look at the levels of benzene contamination that came back from tests of water supply wells and did not understand just what that meant," he said.[46]

More bad news for the Navy came after William Levesque, whose paper had been renamed the *Tampa Times*, kept digging for information about Lejeune after reporting about the breast cancer problems in 2009. Levesque discovered in March 2010 that the Navy and Marine Corps had failed to provide the ATSDR with databases containing more than 700,000 documents, including one estimating that leaks from the Hadnot Point fuel farm exceeded a million gallons. "This is catch me if you can," Jerry Ensminger told Levesque for his story. "The Marine Corps just wants to delay ATSDR's work as long as they possibly can." The Marine Corps spokesman, Captain Block, again issued what had become the service's standard response. "We are very interested in ATSDR completing their work, and the Marine Corps has made every effort to ensure that all information in our possession is available to ATSDR researchers," Block said in a written statement. "We will continue to do so because we are committed to using the best science to get our Marines and sailors, their family members and former residents the answers they deserve."[47]

Miller had had enough. He began organizing for a House Committee on Science and Technology hearing on Camp Lejeune that would once again put all the players on the same stage, as the Energy and Commerce subcommittee hearing had done in 2007. The session was set for September 16, 2010, under the title "Camp Lejeune: Contamination and Compensation, Looking Back,

Moving Forward." And the star witness this time around was Mike Partain, the first to provide testimony. "'You have male breast cancer' were the words which greeted me and my wife on our 18th wedding anniversary," he began. Partain told of his struggles with the disease nearly forty years after he was born at Lejeune in 1968. A retired Navy medical officer, James Watters, who had been stationed at Lejeune from 1977 to 1979, told of his Stage III kidney cancer. Former Marine Peter Devereaux told of the death sentence he was handed after his breast cancer spread through his bones. "I have a great wife and we have a 12-year-old daughter," Devereaux said. "This disease has not only ravaged me, it has ravaged my entire family. It has impacted my daughter severely. She is not confident of her future with me and I am not confident of my future with her. I have no idea if I will see my daughter graduate high school, go to college or get married. Before my diagnosis I had been a very productive person. I feel like such a burden to everyone especially my wife and daughter. I am no longer able to work due to the devastating side effects and physical limitations from my treatments and surgeries."[48]

Then the panel heard from Major General Eugene G. Payne Jr., assistant deputy commandant at Marine Corps headquarters. "The Corps is and always has been a large family, and we all knew people who were stationed or worked at Camp Lejeune during their military careers," Payne said. "My first tour of duty was at Camp Lejeune in 1970. Many of my friends and most of the senior leadership of the Corps, both officers and enlisted, were at Camp Lejeune during the period when this water was contaminated. We have a personal and professional interest in finding answers to questions about the health of our Marine families."

This heartfelt statement was followed by a more surprising one, when Payne was asked by Congressman Paul Broun, a Republican from Georgia, if, "looking back over the past 30 years," there was "any action or inaction" he "would have changed." "Sir, there are a number of actions that I would have changed," responded Payne:

> I would—I can't tell you how many times over the last three years in working with this issue on behalf of the Marine Corps, I would have given anything to have rolled back the clock and to have known and to have been able to influence during that era what we know today to be the case. It is astounding some of the things that happened, and I think that they happened for a number of reasons. I think part of it was mentioned earlier. I think we were ignorant, quite frankly, of some of the implications. I think we were lulled into a sense of complacency or at least a lack of urgency by the fact that we were not out of compliance. And I am not trying to excuse what happened. I think that there were many, many errors made on behalf of the Marine Corps. But it is difficult to look back through the lens of 2010 at what we did or did not know, or should or should not have done in the sixties, seventies, and early eighties, but there are many things that I would have done differently. There are things I would have done differently five and ten years ago. I have only been working this for about three years and it is—one normally shakes their head and wonders at some of the things that did or did not occur.

The hearing closed with testimony from Christopher Portier, who had been installed earlier that year as director of the ATSDR. Portier also made some news, when asked by Broun about the 2009 report by the National Academies of Sciences saying that illnesses could not be definitively linked to water contamination at Lejeune, and that further research would not be any more conclusive. "We are going to go forward and evaluate this population because we believe it is scientifically credible," Portier responded. "We believe it is the right public health move, and we believe it is what needs to be done. And so we will do it. And I think that is our answer to the report from the academy."

Portier added: "In terms of their finding that there is limited information relating TCE and PCE to disease, I simply need to look at the disease of cancer and point out to them that virtually every national authority or international authority that has looked at TCE and PCE has labeled it 'reasonably anticipated to be a human carcinogen' or a 'probable human carcinogen.' And so the linkage there is extremely strong. There is no doubt in my mind that these are toxins that you do not want in your water."

The following month, October 2010, there were two key announcements from the ATSDR that backed up Portier's statements at the hearing. A 300-page report on the contamination of the Hadnot Point water system confirmed that more than a million gallons of fuel had probably leaked into the base groundwater in the decades before 1987, and that the Marine Corps had known about it years before it had shut down contaminated wells. "The fact that the Hadnot Point WTP [water treatment plant] was substantially contaminated with PCE and TCE was well known to USMCB Camp Lejeune by May 1982; however the Base did not initiate sampling of raw and finished water at the Hadnot Point WTP until early December 1984," the report said.[49]

Portier also put his views about the National Research Council report on paper in a letter to top Navy and Marine Corps officials. "The review of cancer risks by the NRC was incomplete and only partially addressed concerns at Camp Lejeune," Portier wrote. "Let me be perfectly clear; there was undoubtedly a hazard associated with drinking the contaminated water at Camp Lejeune. The epidemiological studies and the associated exposure modeling will hopefully help us to decide on the level of risk associated with this hazard."

North Carolina Senator Kay Hagan told the *Jacksonville Daily News* that she had discussed the National Academies report with

Portier at a meeting earlier in October 2010 and was pleased to see that his agency was now going on record discrediting it. "The 2009 National Research Council . . . report on Camp Lejeune had significant shortcomings, and failed to identify all contaminants present in Camp Lejeune's drinking water such as benzene and vinyl chloride," Hagan said in a statement to the newspaper. "The report also failed to provide an accurate picture of the adverse health effects associated with exposure. The report has become a major stumbling block for veterans attempting to receive VA benefits associated with their exposures at Camp Lejeune. This faulty report should not be used to determine benefits for our veterans."[50]

In fact, the Marine Corps had put the report to exactly that use. Earlier in 2010, it had issued a brochure citing the NRC report as evidence that the water contamination at Lejeune did not cause illnesses, and the Veterans Affairs Department was using the brochure and the report to deny disability claims for diseases said to be caused by the base water. Portier told Jerry Ensminger that he would send a letter discrediting the NRC report to the VA. Ensminger asked the Navy to do the same thing for all former residents of Camp Lejeune.

"It's only fair to ask, now that the federal agency that was created and mandated by Congress to investigate human health exposures at superfund sites has pointed out errors in the NRC report, that the Marine Corps would send a copy of this letter out to registrants," Ensminger said, referring to the tens of thousands of people who had signed up for information updates on the Marine Corps website. The Marine Corps never responded to the request, however, and information about the flawed NRC report was never distributed to those most concerned about the contamination.[51]

14

VICTIMS UNITE

At what point will there be an end to the reports,
and meetings, and all the washing of the facts?
—JODY MACPHERSON, WIFE OF
MARINE COLIN MACPHERSON (1957–2004)

After wrestling with the Department of Veterans Affairs for
two years, Bob Kahaly, in 2010, became one of the first former Marines to be awarded disability benefits because of exposure
to the toxic water at Camp Lejeune. He had been diagnosed with
a rare form of lymphoma, and the VA had ruled that his cancer
could be linked to the tainted water. "I had just had my fifty-
fourth treatment," he said. "I was in trouble. I had to borrow
$10,000 from my dad. I was about to lose everything; I was on the
verge of foreclosure."[1]

Kahaly was one of six young men from Jacksonville, Florida,
who had joined the Marines together shortly after graduating from
Terry Parker High School in 1977. Five of the six ended up at

Camp Lejeune; one did not. Three of the five who went to Lejeune would die of rare diseases before any of them reached the age of fifty; the other two—Kahaly and Frank Oshman—suffered crippling illnesses. Kahaly, now living outside of Jacksonville in Ponte Vedra, Florida, was at Lejeune in 1979 and 1980, working mostly in the French Creek area served by the Hadnot Point water system. "We were sweating all the time," he said in an interview in 2013, "and we didn't have bottled water. I remember the water had a sweet odor but it tasted nasty. I was a mechanic, so I was also exposed to TCE."[2]

Kahaly's lymphoma diagnosis came in 2001, when he was forty-two years old. Seven years later he received a letter from the Marine Corps notifying him about the base water contamination. "When I started doing my homework, basically everything was like puzzle pieces coming together—my buddies dying and all that," he said. That's when he began applying for full disability benefits in addition to the health care he was provided by the VA.[3]

Convincing the VA that his illness was related to his service at Lejeune was no easy matter. The federal agency had been insisting for a decade that none of the scientific studies that had been done on the situation at the base proved a connection between the water and the health problems people had encountered, and the National Academies of Sciences report in 2009 further entrenched the VA's position. But as criticism of the NAS report mounted, both from independent scientists and those at the Agency for Toxic Substances and Disease Registry, a slow shift began to occur inside the VA. In September 2009, John Hartung, of Waukesha, Wisconsin, was awarded a 30 percent disability benefit after he presented a letter to a veterans' compensation board saying that the large cysts on his back and his chronic fatigue were "more likely than not" caused by exposure to toxic chemicals. Hartung, a Marine at Lejeune for six months in 1977, was one of the first to persuade the VA that his ailments were likely linked to the base contamination.

"Every case is different," Jerry Ensminger said at the time of the award. "You're not going to find a doctor who's going to sign a letter for everybody for every type of ailment they have." What was needed, he said, was a clear statement from the government—meaning Congress, if the military was not going to make the declaration—that veterans who had lived at Camp Lejeune during the time of the contamination would be entitled to full disability payments if they incurred specific illnesses known to be caused by the chemicals in the water. "What we're trying to do with this legislation is to try to take these hoops and hurdles away from the people so they don't have to deal with this stuff," Ensminger said in 2009. "The only hurdle these people will have to clear is to prove they were at Camp Lejeune during the years of contamination."[4]

Until that happened, veterans seeking disability benefits for their exposure to toxins at Camp Lejeune faced a mountain of frustration from the VA. Six months after applying in 2008, in the same month he learned that his breast cancer had spread through his bones, Peter Devereaux was denied compensation. He and his wife set about preparing a new application for VA benefits, this time with a binder filled with information about his disease, his exposure to contaminants at Camp Lejeune, and a letter from his doctor establishing a clear link between the two. The whole process required about eighty hours of work, including sitting through a one-hour hearing with a decision review officer for the VA, all while Devereaux was going through time-consuming and debilitating treatments for his cancer. "Finally everything fell into place," Devereaux said. The letter from the VA approving a full package of benefits arrived in June 2010, two and a half years after he had been diagnosed with breast cancer and more than a year after he had been told he might only have two to three years to live. The key, he said, was a so-called "nexus letter," signed by a doctor, stating that his disability was "more likely than not" caused by something that happened to him during his military service.

Tom Gervasi, a Florida retiree who had served at Lejeune in the 1950s, had to fight the same battle as Devereaux. Gervasi spent two years in Easy Company, 2nd Battalion, 8th Marines, spending much of his time in North Carolina working and training in the heat and drinking tainted water from a canteen. He left Lejeune in 1956 with a wife and a baby on the way and spent the next forty-five years in his hometown of Rochester, New York, working mainly as a police officer and later as an investigator for the district attorney's office. Two years after moving to Florida in 2001, Gervasi was diagnosed with breast cancer. His doctor told Gervasi that he was only the second man he had treated for the disease in his career.

A mastectomy was followed by chemotherapy in 2004 and 2005, and Gervasi felt like he was getting better. "My hair came back," he said. "And in 2009 I had a CT scan and they said I was cancer-free." His joy was short-lived. Two weeks later he was back at the hospital with a fever. The doctor came in after more tests were done and reported that Gervasi had bone cancer throughout his body. It wasn't until 2011 that Gervasi learned about the water contamination at Camp Lejeune. A cousin told him she had read an article about environmental issues at the base, and Gervasi's wife went online and found out about Mike Partain. "I ended up going to a meeting in Tampa later with him and Jerry Ensminger," Gervasi said.

Once he learned about the long history of water contamination at Lejeune, Gervasi was a man possessed, despite the weakness caused by the cancer spreading through his body. "I read an article in the paper about an Army guy with cancer trying to get VA help, so I called his wife and she referred me to a reporter, Donna Koehn, at the *Sarasota Herald-Tribune,* and she was fantastic," Gervasi said in an interview in June 2013. "She spent three hours here and we made the front page and the whole page 8. This was back in October just before my birthday. Donna wrote other articles. Every time I got a denial letter I let her know. Jerry [Ensminger] and Mike [Partain] said contact your senators—so I called Rubio and Nelson," he said, referring to the two senators from Florida, Republican Marco Rubio and Democrat Bill Nelson. "Rubio gave me to Terry Finger on his staff, and she called me two or three times a week. She worked very diligently on my case. It took thirteen months and finally . . . after three rejections, the director of the VA agreed to honor my claim, I think to shut me up."[5]

Gervasi said the process with Veterans Affairs can be grueling. "You need to make a lot of noise," he said. "The VA is going to shut you down. You're just a piss pot to them. They generate papers and paperwork and you submit and then they want it done again."

It was the same story over and over for former Marines seeking disability benefits for the harm they believed had been done to them by Lejeune's drinking water. The process almost always involved rejections followed by time-consuming appeals for those who didn't give up, and sometimes even required help from friends in high places in Washington. Tom McLaughlin of Hampden, Massachusetts, was diagnosed with kidney cancer in 2007, more than four decades after the two-year stint that he and his wife, Sally, did at Lejeune. They had a child who had died shortly after she was born with part of her brain missing. After learning about the tainted water at the base, Sally McLaughlin immediately wondered if it was connected to her daughter's death, and when her husband came down with kidney cancer, her suspicions became certainty. Tom had been a mechanic at Camp Lejeune and had been exposed to the toxic solvent trichloroethylene at work. He and his wife had also been exposed to both TCE and its sister cleaning solvent, PCE, in their drinking water at home. It took three full years, and help from the two senators from Massachusetts at the time, Edward Kennedy and John Kerry, for the VA to approve Tom McLaughlin's application for disability benefits. The decision finally came through in June 2010. Six months before that, Sally McLaughlin had died from stomach cancer. "I give her most of the credit," McLaughlin told the local newspaper after he got the news about his benefits. "She was the one who pushed it, who did most of the legwork. I just threw up my hands and said this will never happen. But she was very tenacious. She wouldn't give up on this."[6]

By September 2010, a top official of the VA, Thomas Pamperin, told a congressional committee that about two hundred veterans had sought benefits for disabilities connected to Lejeune's tainted water, but only about twenty had been approved. In most cases, Pamperin said, the requests were denied because the veterans did not establish a clear "medical nexus" between exposure to toxic chemicals and their diseases. A few months after the hearing, under pressure to be more responsive, the VA opened an office in Louisville, Kentucky, just to handle claims from veterans who had spent time at Camp Lejeune. More than a year later, in April 2012, the VA reported that more than 1,200 claims had been submitted to the office, but still only about a quarter of them had been approved.[7]

The frustration among victims was reaching a boiling point. A doctor from South Carolina named Paul Akers had lived at Lejeune as a young boy in the 1950s when his father was a Marine stationed there. Once he learned about the chemicals in the water in 2009, he started to make sense of his mother's death from cancer in 1960, his sister's death from cancer in 2009, and his own diagnosis of non-Hodgkin's lymphoma not long before that. Akers decided to volunteer for the ATSDR's Community Assistance Panel to offer his medical expertise, and after just a few meetings he vented to the agency's scientists. "There are only three cases of cancer in my family: my mother and my sister and myself," he said at a CAP meeting in April 2012. "They're both deceased, okay? When is bench work going to be done to prove that we were victims of contamination? We do water models, and I appreciate statistics, but I want to know when somebody's going to sit down at the bench and do some hard science to determine can these agents cause what we're being diagnosed with. I mean, we can do large trends, of course. I want—I would like for someone to sit down and say yes, PCE can produce non-Hodgkin's lymphoma. Hard science."[8] Akers would never know if his plea was heard—the cancer took his life in February 2013.

One former Marine, Colin MacPherson, who had been born at Camp Lejeune and had later served there for a decade, couldn't even get a proper diagnosis from VA doctors of an aggressive form of prostate cancer that took his life in 2004. "He died never knowing what poisoned him," his widow, Jody MacPherson, told the *St. Petersburg Times* in 2009. In a blog post she wrote the year before the *Times* story was published, Jody MacPherson told how her late husband had been misdiagnosed until two years before his death and had been denied benefits from the VA. She had lost her home to foreclosure when her husband's life insurance didn't pay out either. "I miss my husband," Jody MacPherson. "He died a horrible death. He died a quiet hero. Colin lost his battle with the VA, and with life. I feel it is too late for my family, our lives are already shattered. I can't get Colin back. My kids can't get their father back. We can't get Colin's father back, who had also died young of leukemia. I want to know how many more will die before the Marine Corps and Congress decide enough is enough? At what point will there be an end to the reports, and meetings, and all the washing of the facts? When can our heroes rest in peace?"[9]

The way that Marines and their families learned about the water contamination was almost as painful as the illnesses it caused, with the information coming decades after the fact and in language couched in euphemisms by the military. Lou Freshwater, whose mother Mary had lost two babies at Lejeune and later died of cancer, recounted how she had learned about the cause of those problems in a personal 2012 blog post entitled "Poisoned by Your Own Government: My Camp Lejeune Story." "In what is a world-class bureaucratic insult, the Marine Corps calls what happened 'Historic Drinking Water' instead of the largest water contamination incident in our nation's history," Freshwater wrote. "Almost certainly because of exposure to my government's historic water, last March my mother was diagnosed with two types of acute leukemia. The genetic testing came back with the cause being Benzene exposure."[10]

Internet postings of blogs and news stories did more than anything else to bring Lejeune victims together and help them blow up the endless denials and obfuscations by the military. After the Florida media reported Kahaly's success in getting VA disability benefits in 2010, he began hearing from other veterans with similar difficulties. "So many were calling it was crazy," he said. "I thought I'd try to get others to help." So in 2012 Kahaly founded the Poisoned Patriots Fund of America, a nonprofit that raises money to assist veterans affected by military contamination. "We're helping more than a hundred families now," he said in the spring of 2013.

Mike Partain might never have uncovered the apparent cluster of breast cancer cases among men exposed to the Lejeune water without the networking made possible by search engines such as Google and Yahoo. By the middle of 2013, Partain had tracked down eighty-four other men besides himself who had spent time at the base and were later diagnosed with breast cancer, an astonishingly high number for a type of cancer that occurs in men only about 2,000 times per year, compared to 200,000 annual cases among women. Some of the men Partain had found by 2010 decided to make a statement and raise some money for the cause by posing with their shirts off for a calendar. They gathered for the photo shoot at the Liberty Hotel in Boston, where Peter Devereaux was undergoing treatment for breast cancer. "When we took our shirts off, we were all checking each other out," Devereaux told a reporter later, doing his best to put a positive light on a dire situation. The 2011 calendar, entitled "Men, Breast Cancer and the Environment," sold several hundred copies within a month after it became available in October 2010, further raising public awareness about the problems at Camp Lejeune.[11]

Credit for the first website devoted to the health problems caused by Lejeune's water went to the two sisters, Terry Dyer and Karen Strand, whose father was the school principal who died in 1973 after fifteen years on the base. Their Water Survivors site, launched in 2002, had people connecting for a common cause years before social media exploded with Facebook and Twitter. Ironically, though, the way the site was managed ended up dividing victims into two camps rather than uniting them in battle with the Marine Corps. Dyer and Strand invited former Lejeune residents to share stories about what had happened to them, but only under certain conditions. People were required to register with the sisters before posting comments on the website, and they could only do so under pseudonyms and without providing any personal information, such as their phone numbers or hometowns. Violators of the rules, which the site managers said would allow people to speak out while preserving their privacy, would be banned from future access.

Ensminger joined the Water Survivors group early in his quest to uncover information about his daughter's death from leukemia, but he quickly found himself in trouble with Dyer. After Ensminger was quoted in a news story, Dyer told him he should not do any press interviews without her permission. The scolding did not sit well with the former Marine drill instructor, fast emerging as a forceful and outspoken advocate for victims of Lejeune's pollution. No one was going to get him to pull the reins on his charge against the Marine Corps.

Jeff Byron, too, said he joined Water Survivors for a time, but soon left. "They wanted to control every aspect of it," he said. "They also were afraid civilian employees like their father wouldn't get justice. They didn't trust the Marines." Byron shared his frustrations with Ensminger, and the two decided to start their own site with no holds barred. They brashly borrowed the well-known Marine Corps recruiting slogan—"The Few, the Proud, the Marines"—and tweaked it into an online statement about how they felt they had been treated: "The Few, the Proud, the Forgotten." Byron's web-savvy daughter Andrea helped set it up, and www.tftptf.com was born in 2003.

Ensminger and Byron were determined to make their site as open as possible. Visitors were encouraged to use their real names, tell their stories, and post comments on the blog. They filled the site with news articles, with links to studies and reports, and, most important, with many of the documents they and retired Marine Tom Townsend had uncovered through Freedom of Information Act requests, web searches, and other digging for data. After Partain came on board in 2007 and added the detailed timeline of events that had transpired since Camp Lejeune had opened in 1941, "The Few, the Proud, the Forgotten" became the most authoritative place to go for information about the Lejeune saga. "We're all over the place," Partain said in 2013.

The site connected people in deeply personal ways without them ever speaking directly or even seeing each other's faces. One of the first to join was Denita McCall, a former Marine from Colorado who had spoken eloquently and emotionally about her parathyroid cancer before the ATSDR's expert panel of scientists in 2005. McCall became an active member of the federal agency's Community Assistance Panel, at least until surgery, chemotherapy, and radiation treatments in 2008 forced her to abandon trips to Atlanta for the meetings. But she kept in touch through the website, right up until she died at age forty-four in July 2009. Prior to her final round of chemo in October 2008, McCall posted a defiant message on the tftptf.com blog: "I don't know what my future holds, but I can tell you that I am coming out SWINGING!! I am so angry with the way the USMC, VA, Navy and DOD have treated us. I am angry for the hell that they have put our families through. . . . To every victim whose life has been destroyed/damaged, you are not forgotten.—Denita."[12]

The real rift between "The Few, the Proud, the Forgotten" and Water Survivors came later, after Ensminger heard from an attorney that Dyer and Strand had approached him with an offer to sell the undisclosed names of people who had registered on their website for use in future litigation against the Navy and Marine Corps. When that proposal was rejected, the attorney said, Dyer asked if she could be guaranteed part of any future settlement if she provided the names and contact information for hundreds of potential plaintiffs, according to Ensminger. That offer, too, was turned down, he said. And he was livid. "I told her, 'You're victimizing the victims,'" Ensminger said.

Dyer admitted in an hour-long interview in early 2013 that she had offered to sell her website to an attorney, Richard Hibey, after he and his team visited her house to consider taking her case against the military for exposure to toxic chemicals at Camp Lejeune. "Then they called later and said they couldn't do it," she said. "I asked if they'd buy the website with all the names and I can give the money to my sister," who Dyer said was destined to spend her life in assisted living. But after consulting with another attorney later about the ethics of her proposal, Dyer said, she withdrew the offer to Hibey because of how it might have looked. "I don't know if Hibey told Jerry, but he started spreading it around that I was trying to sell my website," she said. "He's made my life a living hell."

A few weeks after the interview, Dyer said she would have no further comments about her past activities involving Camp Lejeune. She also said none of the members of her group would provide any information for a book that included Ensminger.

The friction between Dyer and her website members and Ensminger and his followers exploded in a public forum in 2011. A website called Veterans News Now had published a story about a planned ATSDR study of health problems at Lejeune, and one of the members of the Community Assistance Panel that had pushed for the study posted a comment urging anyone with concerns about the contamination to attend an upcoming meeting of the CAP in Wilmington, North Carolina. Dyer posted a comment in response saying she had been a member of the CAP "for many, many years" and quit because "I for one am tired of these 'meetings' that do no more then get people's names in the press and more pictures in the paper."[13]

Ensminger, who had been a member of the CAP since it was set up by the ATSDR in 2006, couldn't help but correct the record, pointing out that Dyer had resigned after being a member for only eighteen months. "Those of us who remained on the CAP and worked with ATSDR to hammer out the studies that are currently under way are now subject to the 'sniping' of individuals such as Ms. Dyer and her cronies. It is easy to sit back and let everyone else do the work and then once it is done they can sit back and find fault with it!" He urged Dyer to attend the next CAP meeting, saying he would be happy to engage in a face-to-face debate on the issues.[14]

Ensminger later followed with another post directed at Dyer:

> I would challenge any/everyone who is involved in this issue to join Terry Dyer's web-site, http://www.watersurvivors.com and attempt to post your personal contact information or to dispute any of the rhetoric being spewed by her selected cronies on their discussion board. First of all, your posting will be deleted, secondly, you will receive an email chastising your post, and thirdly if you persist, you will be banned from her web-site! I spent a quarter of a century defending the constitution of this nation and I do recall something in it that refers to the issue of "freedom of speech!" I will be damned if I will ever give up that right to someone whose's [*sic*] only goal is to receive a government check![15]

Dyer shot back: "I was going to DC and meeting with members of Congress before you ever even thought about gracing the halls on the Hill and we made a real difference at that time too and it was a good one! We just do not call everyone we can think of at 11 pm to tell them everything we have done and how much others haven't!"[16]

More animosity was directed at Ensminger after he was prominently featured in a seventy-six-minute film about the Lejeune contamination, *Semper Fi: Always Faithful*, released in 2011. Ensminger said his sister, a public relations specialist in Pennsylvania, had met in Philadelphia several years earlier with New York filmmaker Rachel Libert. She knew Libert from previous projects and showed her some documents about the decades of tainted drinking water at Camp Lejeune. Libert, according to Ensminger, responded, "Oh my God!" The result was a documentary produced by Libert and colleague Tony Hardmon that focused largely on Ensminger's efforts to push Congress to provide health care for Lejeune victims and on Partain's efforts to track down male breast cancer cases among former base residents. The film's release became a watershed event in the struggle for a government acknowledgment that the military had potentially harmed thousands of people through its failure to provide clean, safe drinking water. It was shown on Capitol Hill soon after it was released in the spring of 2011, won numerous awards at documentary film festivals around the country, and nearly made the final list of Academy Award nominations for Best Documentary in 2012. The cable news network MSNBC showed *Semper Fi* to a national audience in February 2012, just when members of Congress were considering legislation to provide health care for victims.

It would not be easy to convince the gridlocked legislative branch to do anything in an election year, let alone pass a measure that could cost the government billions of dollars at a time when it was approaching a "fiscal cliff." But it was also clear that the story of Ensminger's daughter, told in heartbreaking fashion in *Semper Fi*, was having an impact. Congressman Brad Miller (D-NC) sponsored a bill to assist Lejeune victims, naming it "the Janey Ensminger Act."

15

THE WAY TO THE OVAL OFFICE

Much of the human suffering caused by
this problem could have been avoided if, years ago,
some educated soul had picked up the phone and requested
a water analysis, if only to err on the side of caution.
—FORMER SENATOR ELIZABETH DOLE (R-NC)

Veterans who were denied disability benefits from the Department of Veterans Affairs faced a significant roadblock if they wanted to file claims against the government that military wastes had made them sick. It was called the Feres Doctrine, and Mike Gros, the Navy obstetrician who worked at Camp Lejeune for three years in the early 1980s and was diagnosed with a rare form of leukemia in 1997, ran smack into it in 2005 after he filed a federal lawsuit seeking damages. Most of Gros's medical bills were covered by the VA and later Medicare, but some of his estimated $12 million in health-care costs—which mounted as Gros faced complications from a bone-marrow transplant that included "graft versus host" disease and numerous side effects from treatments—had come out of his own pocket. Not to mention the losses he sustained after being unable to continue his practice as an Ob/Gyn in Texas.

The Feres Doctrine refers to a US Supreme Court ruling after World War II that said military personnel could not sue the government for injuries sustained while on active duty. "They keep extending it to cover every occasion," Gros said. "When I filed a claim, they ran me out of the courtroom. I then went to the Fifth Circuit, and they dumped me out, too." His attorney had argued that Gros's illnesses were not "incident to service," because they had resulted from consumption of water in his home. But the US District Court in Houston cited a ruling under the Feres Doctrine that said a serviceman's injury in a fire in his barracks while he was sleeping was in fact "incident to service." Since Gros's alleged injury occurred in his home, on military property during off-duty hours, it was a similar situation, so he was blocked from seeking damages.[1]

Family members of Marines had no such limitation on their ability to seek damages from the government for exposing them to toxic chemicals in water provided by the military. Victims could not just rush into federal court, though, and demand millions of dollars for pain and suffering from health problems, lost income, or the deaths of loved ones. Under the Federal Tort Claims Act of 1948, anyone who wants to sue a federal agency for causing harm must first file a claim with the agency seeking compensation. Only if the claim is denied or if there has been no response in six months can the applicant go to court as a plaintiff against the government.

Hundreds of former residents at Camp Lejeune filed claims against the Navy after the water contamination became public in the late 1990s. The Navy's Office of the Judge Advocate General

(JAG) reported in 2010 that in the previous decade, 2,182 claims had been filed seeking more than $37.7 billion in damages from toxic exposure at Lejeune. But not a single claim had a response: the Navy steadfastly insisted it could not appropriately rule on the validity of any claims until all the studies of Lejeune's pollution were done. "It is the Navy's intention to wait for the ATSDR study to be completed in order to insure that we have the best scientific research available so we may thoroughly evaluate each and every claim on its own merits," Pat Leonard of the JAG Office told a congressional subcommittee in 2007. "We truly believe this approach is in the best interests of both the claimants and the Department of the Navy."[2]

Nearly all who have filed claims—mostly family members of Marines who were at Lejeune when the water was contaminated, along with some civilian employees and former Marines, such as Jerry Ensminger, who filed claims on behalf of injured or deceased children and spouses—are waiting for the Navy to respond after the ATSDR finishes all its health studies in 2014 or 2015. But citing the section of the Federal Tort Claims Act that allows lawsuits to be filed if a federal agency has not responded to a claim after six months, nearly a dozen individuals have gone to court charging the government with negligence at Camp Lejeune, and in most cases seeking to recover millions of dollars in health-care costs, lost wages, and damages for pain and suffering.

A long road lay ahead for victims taking the path of litigation. In June 2009, the US Supreme Court rejected an appeal by a former Marine whose lawsuit had been dismissed in federal district court. Donal McLean Snyder Jr. had argued that his son, who had been born at the base in 1971, had a congenital heart defect because his pregnant wife had drunk the base's tainted water. The boy had undergone two open-heart surgeries because of the defect. The district court had ruled that the Marine Corps was not liable, because there were no regulations for the chemicals found in Lejeune's drinking water until the late 1970s.[3]

Then, in July 2009, a lawsuit was filed in federal court in North Carolina alleging that the government knowingly exposed thousands of Marines and their families as well as civilian employees at Camp Lejeune to highly contaminated drinking water. The suit was filed by a law firm that Ensminger had contacted three years earlier, Anderson Pangia & Associates, and a Pennsylvania firm, Smorto, Persio, Webb & McGill. Named as the lead plaintiff was an Iowa woman, Laura Jones, who had been diagnosed with non-Hodgkin's lymphoma twenty years after she and her Marine husband had lived at Lejeune. He had been stationed there from 1980 to 1983.

"The lawsuit alleges that the United States Government, through agents within the Department of Defense, knowingly exposed hundreds of thousands of Marines, sailors, their family members, and civilian employees to highly contaminated drinking water on the base at Camp Lejeune, while at the same time actively disseminating disinformation to those exposed in an effort to minimize the significance of the exposure," the two law firms said in a joint news release on July 1, 2009. Jones, a former nurse, had to quit working in her midforties because of all her medical problems subsequent to the lymphoma, said the fourteen-page complaint that was filed along with supporting documents. "She continues to suffer, among other problems, resulting fibromyalgia requiring high dosages of narcotics to address the pain, an adrenaline insufficiency, immune system difficulties requiring her to take high dosages of immunoglobulin and other medications to address these ongoing problems and suffers confusion and loss of memory as a result of chemotherapy," the lawsuit said.[4]

The government moved for dismissal of the lawsuit on the grounds that the statute of limitations required damage claims against a federal agency to be filed within two years of a health problem occurring. The government also argued that the chemicals found in the base water had not been regulated at the time of Laura Jones's exposure. But in February 2010, US District Judge Terrence Boyle in North Carolina denied the request for dismissal. The judge's ruling was damning. "To summarily bar such claims from entering the courthouse would be a profound miscarriage of justice," Boyle declared. "To apply the statute of repose in this case would bar all potential claims from the over 500,000 Marines and their families affected. Indeed, it would bar the overwhelming majority of claims involving any cancer," he said.[5]

"The Government is correct to note that blameless ignorance of available facts is not sufficient to delay the onset of the limitations period," the judge wrote in his decision. "But the Department of the Navy's unwillingness to release information regarding contamination at Camp Lejeune or to provide notice to former residents remains relevant in that such conduct limited the information available to potential claimants."

Boyle also blew away the Navy's contention that because toxic chemicals found at Lejeune in the 1980s were not yet regulated by the EPA, the government could not be accused of negligence for failing to remove the tainted water supply. "The December 1972 Bureau of Medicine and Surgery (BUMED) Instructions for Camp Lejeune [that] mandate regular testing of the water supply state that 'Drinking water shall not contain impurities in concentrations which may be hazardous to the health of the consumers,' and specifically limit acceptable levels of chlorinated hydrocarbons," Boyle wrote:

Reports on tests of the water supply at Camp Lejeune in October and December of 1980 and March of 1981 indicate contamination by halogenated hydrocarbons, chlorinated hydrocarbons, and organics. The Government argues that TCE and PCE were not the types of hydrocarbons regulated in the early 1980s and that no standard method existed for testing for concentrations of these specific chlorinated hydrocarbons. But a 1982 report to the Commanding General of Camp Lejeune specifically describes the presence of TCE and PCE in amounts exceeding the BUMED Instructions acceptable levels for all chlorinated hydrocarbons. Moreover, DCE, TCE, PCE, vinyl chloride, and benzene were regulated as "toxic pollutants" under the Clean Water Act beginning in 1978. And although the EPA did not regulate these chemicals under the Safe Drinking Water Act until January 1989 (for benzene, TCE, and vinyl chloride), and July 1992 (for DCE and PCE), the EPA estimated a suggested no adverse response level for TCE in November of 1979.

"In sum," the judge wrote, "during at least part of Plaintiff's residence at Camp Lejeune, the Department of the Navy had notice of the presence and toxicity of the chemicals at issue in the water supply of Camp Lejeune. And specific instructions were in place regarding the types of chemicals that Plaintiff alleges were responsible for her injuries."

Laura Jones's case against the government had survived two dismissal motions and seemed to be headed toward argument in a federal courtroom. But while waiting for the suit to proceed, Jones—unable to work because of her cancer—went broke from medical bills and other expenses. She made a critical mistake when filing for bankruptcy, though: Jones failed to disclose to the bankruptcy court that she had a $10 million claim pending against the government in US district court. She also failed to tell the district court about her bankruptcy, even though she was required in the discovery process to disclose all "legal proceedings to which she was a party." When government attorneys learned about her bankruptcy through her medical records, Jones admitted under oath that she had not been forthcoming; she said she had not told the bankruptcy court about her $10 million lawsuit because her attorney had said her chances of winning were slim. Jones's case in district court was dismissed, and the ruling was upheld by a three-judge panel from the US Court of Appeals for the Eleventh Circuit. "Most litigation is somewhat speculative," the appellate court said in rejecting Jones's argument that she didn't disclose her district court suit to the bankruptcy court because she did not think she would win. "Jones's case may be difficult to prove, but if she did not believe she had at least some chance at recovering $10 million, she would not be actively prosecuting it."[6]

The law firm that was handling Jones's lawsuit over the Camp Lejeune contamination, Anderson Pangia & Associates, was dealt a huge setback, but it had at least thirty or forty similar claims ready to be pursued against the Navy, said Michael Pangia, an attorney in the firm's Washington, DC, office. The firm filed a new case under the Federal Tort Claims Act on behalf of Sharon Kay Boling, an Ohio woman who had lived at Lejeune with her Marine husband for eight months in 1977 and 1978 and was later diagnosed with leukemia. Her suit, still pending in late 2013, seeks damages for pain and suffering, "loss of mobility and enjoyment of life," lost income, and medical expenses related to her leukemia and to other problems resulting from her exposure to toxic chemicals at Lejeune, including nerve damage, a weakened immune system, anxiety, and depression.[7]

Other cases against the Marine Corps in federal court began to pile up. An Alabama couple, John and Connie Edwards, filed suit in federal court in 2010 charging that their exposure to toxic water at Lejeune had caused brain cancer to develop in two of their children, including a girl who died in 2000 at the age of fourteen. A former Marine, Joel Shriberg, filed a federal complaint in 2011 alleging that the water he drank at the base from 1957 to 1959 had led to a diagnosis of breast cancer in 2004; Shriberg was asking for $16.2 million for medical expenses, "past and future pain and suffering, loss of enjoyment of life, and diminished life expectancy." Also in 2011, a woman who had worked in food service on the base for twenty-two years, Linda Jones of Jacksonville, North Carolina, argued in another federal case that she had developed an aggressive form of non-Hodgkin's lymphoma in 2007 at the age of sixty-two.[8]

With so many similar cases being filed, the federal courts consolidated the discovery process for Camp Lejeune lawsuits into "multidistrict litigation" in the Atlanta court of US District Judge J. Owen Forrester. The legal maneuvering began almost immediately, including a motion for dismissal filed by the government citing the Feres Doctrine. One attorney representing plaintiffs in the consolidated case called the government's effort a disgrace. "The Feres Doctrine was never intended to protect the US Government from lawsuits that have nothing to do with military actions," said William Dubanevich, an environmental attorney with the New York firm of Parker Waichman. "It most certainly was not intended to protect it from basic duties owed by every US municipality to provide all citizens and residents of the nation with life-sustaining services, including clean water. The US Government should be disgraced at their attempt to hide from their alleged wrongdoings, knowingly exposing service men and women, their spouses and children and civilians to chemical-laden water, by invoking the Feres Doctrine in this case."[9]

It would likely be years before all the preliminary motions were dealt with in the consolidated cases, especially if individual rulings were appealed, but attorneys for the plaintiffs could see some benefit in waiting while the ATSDR completed its studies of the effects of Camp Lejeune's contamination. Chances seemed good in 2013 that at least some of the findings from several ongoing studies would produce evidence that would be helpful in damage claims against the government.

In 2013, the ATSDR was two years into the largest health survey ever conducted by the agency—an effort to reach more than 300,000 people who had lived or worked at either Camp Lejeune or Marine Base Camp Pendleton in California prior to 1986. The goal was to compile and compare health data on similar populations that had one key difference: the people who lived at Lejeune had been exposed to toxic drinking water, and the ones at Pendleton had not. With the modeling studies estimating exposure levels at various times and places on Camp Lejeune, the ATSDR would have a pretty good idea how much tainted water past residents of the base had consumed, depending on where they had lived and when they had lived there. "We'll be able to give each person at Camp Lejeune a different amount of exposure based on what they drank, how much they drank," the agency's director, Christopher Portier, told a reporter as the massive survey began in June 2011. "And then we'll break them into different groups as a function of their level of exposure," to see if there are connections between those exposures and health problems. The survey would take at least three years to complete, until 2014 or later, Portier said.[10]

The health agency's announcement was followed in the fall of 2011 by a long-awaited report from the Environmental Protection Agency—a full decade in the making—finally assessing the risks of human exposure to trichloroethylene, the most ubiquitous contaminant in the nation's environment. In a 1,200-page report, the agency said extensive research showed that TCE is far more toxic than previously believed, "a potential human health hazard for noncancer toxicity to the central nervous system, kidney, liver, immune system, male reproductive system, and the developing fetus" and a compound that is "carcinogenic in humans by all routes of exposure."[11]

It was a far stronger warning on TCE exposure than the EPA had issued in its draft assessment in 2001, a report that had triggered protests from the Defense Department that risks posed by the chemical were being overstated. The Pentagon had mostly been concerned that its cleanup costs at contaminated sites, including Camp Lejeune, would skyrocket if the 2001 EPA assessment was adopted as scientific fact, and now it was faced with exactly that situation. The stage was set for the EPA to tighten its national exposure limits for the chemical, currently set at 5 parts per billion in water and 1 microgram per cubic meter in air.

"This risk assessment is a big deal because it will strengthen protections for people who live and work above TCE plumes—and there are a lot of them—and could force serious rethinking about the extent of cleanup efforts," Lenny Siegel, executive director of the Center for Public Environmental Oversight in Mountain View, California, told the *Los Angeles Times*. Siegel's group, which closely monitors contaminated industrial and military sites around the country, had just posted an open letter signed by environmental activists demanding that the EPA release its assessment of TCE immediately. Two days later it was published. Jennifer Sass, a senior scientist at the Natural Resources Defense Council (NRDC), told the *Times* that the assessment "launches new arguments about what the safety standards should be. In the meantime, people impacted by this pollution can now link their disease to it in litigation with more confidence because the science is no longer in dispute. TCE causes cancer."[12]

After twenty years of investigation, the ATSDR finally had some momentum behind its studies at Camp Lejeune, though it still had to weather more storms stirred up by the Department of Defense. The Marine Corps continued to question publicly whether the water contamination at the base had actually harmed people. In a pamphlet on the base's environmental issues that was posted on the DOD website and distributed to members of Congress in 2010—and thus before the fall 2011 release of the EPA's report—it had been flatly stated that past contamination had never been established as a health threat. "At this time, scientific studies have not linked exposure to the impacted drinking water at Camp Lejeune to any illnesses," the brochure said, citing the 2009 report by the National Research Council, since discredited, that said it was impossible to directly connect illnesses to the base contamination.

There were complaints about the brochure even before the EPA's fall 2011 report appeared. "It suggests there is no problem," the ATSDR's Thomas Sinks said in a January 2011 letter to the Marine Corps protesting its continued use of the brochure. "It understates the potential hazards from the contaminated drinking water and may discourage individuals from participating in planned research studies." It took six more months of pressure, from both federal health officials and key members of Congress, before the Marine Corps pulled the document off its website in July 2011. But a Marine spokeswoman, Captain Kendra Hardesty, insisted the move was only temporary. "As soon as it is vetted and approved, it will be put back up," she said. "The secretary of the Navy has seen it, and the commandant will see it soon."[13]

An even bigger dustup between the ATSDR and the Marine Corps took place in early 2012, at the same time that Congress was considering the legislation to provide health care for victims of Lejeune's pollution. Major General J. A. Kessler sent a letter to the ATSDR on January 5, 2012, requesting that information about active water wells at the base be redacted from upcoming studies as a security precaution. "The Marine Corps understands the need to share information with the scientific community," wrote Kessler, assistant deputy commandant for installations and logistics. "Prudence requires, however, that information sharing be within the rubric of responsible force protection." The request was met with derision from Jerry Ensminger, who called it another attempt to suppress damning information. "This is exactly what happens when you have one federal agency investigating another," Ensminger told the *Huffington Post*, which published an online story about the Marine Corps request.[14]

The cries of foul play grew louder a month later, when the ATSDR released another chapter of its continuing water-modeling studies. This time, detailed information about active wells at the base was redacted, as the Marines had requested. "As you know, we provide ATSDR with access to the information they need to conduct these studies," Captain Hardesty told the *Jacksonville Daily News* in North Carolina. "The request to redact was only with regards to public release. It is important for the Marine Corps and ATSDR to cooperate, not only in the search for science-based answers regarding the Camp Lejeune Historic Drinking Water issue, but also in the safekeeping of critical infrastructure information." ATSDR officials defended the redactions, saying the failure to disclose specific data about well locations did not compromise the integrity of the water-modeling studies. Thomas Frieden, director of the CDC, which has responsibility for the ATSDR, wrote members of Congress to assure them that the new report included only "limited redactions," which had been allowed "because the longitude and latitude coordinates of active drinking water infrastructure was scientifically unnecessary for the purpose of the document."[15]

As soon as Frieden's letter to members of Congress became public, the chief hydrologist for the water-modeling study, contract engineer Robert Faye of the Eastern Research Group, wrote a strong letter of protest to ATSDR Director Christopher Portier. Faye said Frieden's statement that precise well locations were not important to the study was "patently false on its face and, from a scientific point of view, borders on the inane and silly." In fact, the only way a scientific study has integrity is if all information is public so that peer reviewers can replicate the results in independent laboratories, Faye said. "I want to state for the record herein that, as a matter of professional ethics and common sense, I did and do totally disagree with ATSDR's policy decision to redact data," Faye told Portier.[16]

Faye said in an interview later that Frieden's letter to Congress implied that he and the ATSDR engineer in charge of the modeling studies, Morris Maslia, were willing to compromise on scientific integrity, which would be seen by their peers as unethical behavior. Not only did he want to clear his own reputation, but he felt he needed to defend Maslia, who was prohibited by the ATSDR from commenting publicly on the ongoing studies. "I have absolute personal knowledge of this," Faye said in the interview in June 2013. "Morris Maslia is one of the most ethical, upstanding individuals I ever worked with. He fought tooth and nail to maintain the integrity of the program."

The letter from Faye made its way to Capitol Hill and prompted a request by Senator Richard Burr, a Republican from North Carolina, for an investigation by the inspector general at the Department of Health and Human Services, the parent agency of the CDC and the ATSDR. "The hundreds of thousands of veterans and their families who lived at Camp Lejeune are anticipating that the ATSDR reports will provide them with the information they need to become informed about the scope and severity of the water contamination and educate them on the possible association between their exposures and current and future health effects," Burr wrote to Inspector General Daniel Levinson.[17]

Ensminger also raised the issue of the Marine Corps' redactions at a March 2012 hearing of the Senate Judiciary Committee. The federal agency investigating the contamination "estimates that as many as one million people were exposed to horrendous levels of carcinogenic chemicals through their drinking water at Camp

Lejeune," Ensminger told the committee. "These people need the uncensored truth concerning their exposures so they can be more vigilant about their and their family's health." Other members of Congress joined the chorus of protests, but their efforts fell short. When the final modeling study for the Hadnot Point water system at Camp Lejeune was published in March 2013, much of the information about the wells was redacted.[18]

Against the backdrop of Marine Corps stonewalling, Congress slowly worked its way toward action on Lejeune's contamination and its effects. Legislation enacted in 2011 called for a report by the end of the year on the processing of claims by enlisted personnel and veterans seeking health benefits and compensation for environmental exposures on military bases. In the House, Democratic congressmen Brad Miller of North Carolina and John Dingell of Michigan were pushing a bill to provide health care for victims of Camp Lejeune's contamination and were facing minimal resistance.[19]

The Senate was a different story. In early 2011, at the start of the 112th Congress, North Carolina's Senator Burr reintroduced the same bill he had sponsored in the previous Congress, the Caring for Camp Lejeune Veterans Act. Cosponsored by his Democratic colleague from North Carolina, Senator Kay Hagan, the bill would require the Department of Veterans Affairs to provide health care for any current service member, veteran, or family member who had been exposed to water contamination at Camp Lejeune before tainted wells were shut down in 1985. "We now have another shot at doing the right thing for the thousands of Navy and Marine veterans and their families who were harmed during their service to our country," Burr said. "While we continue to seek more answers, we can minimize further suffering by allowing Lejeune veterans and their families to receive the care they need and deserve."[20]

Members of the Senate Committee on Veterans Affairs, including its new chairman in 2011, Democratic senator Patty Murray of Washington, had a different idea than Burr and Hagan, however. They argued that since the Defense Department had been responsible for the pollution at Camp Lejeune, the Pentagon—not the VA—should pay for the victims' health care. There were several problems with that approach, though. First, the Defense Department's health-care program, known as TRICARE, operated a little differently in every state, depending on which insurance providers and medical services had been contracted. There were concerns among veterans, who were enrolled in the VA's health program, that if they went to a DOD provider and mentioned their exposure to contaminants at Camp Lejeune, they would be met with blank stares. At least the VA had a national program and its employees could be trained to be aware of potential health problems caused by Lejeune's drinking water. More important, veterans such as Ensminger who had been fighting the military over the Lejeune pollution no longer trusted the DOD to be sympathetic to their health problems. They could foresee enormous difficulties getting care if the Defense Department was responsible for providing it. And finally, there was resistance to having the DOD fund veterans' care in the Senate Armed Services Committee, which was responsible for the Pentagon's budget. Senators on the committee were aware of all the litigation pending against the military over the Lejeune pollution, and they knew that any law stating that the Defense Department must be held responsible for the damages it had caused would open the door for thousands of claims for compensation.

Of course, there were concerns about Burr's bill coming from the Veterans Affairs Department. VA Administrator Eric Shinseki made clear in statements to Congress that if everyone who spent time at Camp Lejeune was eligible for health-care coverage from his agency, as many as a million new people could be added to its rolls at a cost exceeding $4 billion over ten years. Veterans' groups heard this and called it a travesty if family members were put ahead of veterans for health care at the VA. Number crunchers at the Congressional Budget Office (CBO) did the required analysis of Burr's bill and found the VA's cost figure to be inflated because it assumed that all of the estimated million people who spent time at Lejeune before 1985 were still alive in 2011. The CBO cut that estimate down to around 650,000 people who potentially had been exposed and had not yet passed away, cutting the cost estimate for VA coverage nearly in half. Then Burr and his cosponsor agreed to limit the eligibility for coverage to people who had spent a minimum of thirty days at Camp Lejeune between 1957 and 1987; in addition, only specific types of diseases that were linked to the base contaminants would be covered. Those were the fourteen specific health problems that had been listed in the 2009 National Research Council report as potentially linked to the Lejeune pollution—esophageal cancer, lung cancer, breast cancer, bladder cancer, kidney cancer, leukemia, multiple myeloma, myleodysplasic syndromes, renal toxicity, hepatic steatosis, female infertility, miscarriage, scleroderma, and neurobehavioral effects—plus one more added by Burr's staff at the request of victims, non-Hodgkin's lymphoma. The limitations helped to reduce the projected cost of VA health care for Lejeune victims to less than $350 million over five years.

In the middle of 2011, the Department of Veterans Affairs reported that its office in Louisville, Kentucky, that was handling all Camp Lejeune water cases had so far received more than 2,300 claims, but had approved only about a quarter of them. Victims of the contamination stepped up their pressure on Congress. Nearly forty of the men with breast cancer who believed their cancer had been caused by Lejeune's water sent a letter to President Obama urging him to support Burr's legislation. "We, the undersigned, are constituents of the largest male breast cancer cluster ever identified—73 men," the letter said. "What happened to us is no coincidence."[21]

Former senator Elizabeth Dole, who had lost to Hagan in North Carolina's Senate election in 2008, weighed in with an op-ed piece that was published in a number of newspapers in January 2012. "The contamination of Camp Lejeune's water supply, which involves several hundred thousand Marines, sailors, their families and civilian employees who were posted to the installation from the mid-1950s to the mid-1980s, is a sad chapter in the Marine Corps' otherwise superlative history," Dole wrote. "Much of the human suffering caused by this problem could have been avoided if, years ago, some educated soul had picked up the phone and requested a water analysis, if only to err on the side of caution." Dole said it was now up to Congress to address the problems by providing medical care for victims of the contamination. "The cost of that care may eventually be high in terms of dollars," she said. "We must, nevertheless, meet our nation's ethical and moral responsibilities."[22]

In the spring of 2012, Ensminger enlisted an online group, Change.org, to start a petition drive demanding that Congress assist Lejeune's victims. Within a few weeks it had more than 100,000 signatures. "I hear from people who are suffering from the water every day," Ensminger said. "We need action, and we can't wait any longer." Finally, Congress responded. After passionate pleas for support on the Senate floor by Burr, Hagan, and Veterans Affairs Committee Chairman Murray, the Senate passed the bill by unanimous consent (with no roll-call vote needed because no objections were raised) on July 18, 2012. Two weeks later the bill sailed through the House on a voice vote and was headed to the White House for President Obama's signature.[23]

When Obama signed the bill on August 6, 2012, standing beside him in the Oval Office were Jerry Ensminger and Mike Partain; the two producers of the *Semper Fi* documentary, Rachel Libert and Tony Hardmon; and two members of Congress, Democrat Brad Miller of North Carolina and House Veterans Affairs Committee Chairman Jeff Miller, a Republican from Florida. It was a heady moment for Ensminger. "I never expected to be in the Oval Office, and I never expected to get a bill passed by the House and the Senate," he said. The signing ceremony lasted only a few minutes, but it was an experience Ensminger and Partain would never forget. As they walked out of the White House on a hot summer day, Ensminger recalled that he could hear the sound of the presidential helicopter rising from the South Lawn. Obama was on his way to an event for his 2012 reelection campaign, knowing he had just gone a long way toward securing the support of thousands of former Marines.

—m—

In January 2013, the ATSDR released another water-modeling report that said the contamination at Lejeune had begun as far back as August 1953, four years earlier than previously believed. A follow-up report two months later pushed the start date for the drinking-water contamination back even further, to around 1948, with the peak levels recorded in the years just before the tainted wells were shut down in 1985. "This reinforces what I always viewed as being the major point here, and that is the levels that existed in the drinking water were astoundingly high, and I'd be very concerned for the health of people who were exposed," said Gerald LeBlanc, the head of environmental toxicology studies at North Carolina State University. Added Jerry Ensminger: "This is vindication and verification of what I've been saying for nearly 16 years. I've had to be aggressive to make sure this happened. A lot of people have called me bullheaded and some other choice words. I'm under no illusion that had I not taken such a strong stance on this in the 1990s that we would not be anywhere close to where we are now."[24]

In the spring of 2013, the Associated Press moved a three-part series on the Lejeune contamination that started with a story about the cleanup efforts at the base, nearly thirty years after the tainted wells had been shut down. "We probably have the most aggressive sampling regime for our drinking water than anybody else in the nation," Bob Lowder, head of environmental quality for the base, said during a tour with an AP reporter. "Maybe in the world." Lowder said the final remedy for toxic pollution at Lejeune would be in place by 2014. "So, for the most part, we're on the down-swing," he said.[25]

The final story in the series focused on the tragic legacy of the contamination even as it was being cleaned up. AP reporter Allen Breed talked with Ron Poirier, who had been a Marine technician at Camp Lejeune in the mid-1970s. Poirier told Breed that he had dumped hundreds of gallons of toxic solvents onto the ground while working as an electronics technician at the base. He described how he and his fellow Marines had poured TCE that had been used to clean components into the woods by the Hadnot Point Industrial Area, where water wells were later found to be contaminated with the toxic solvent and other hazardous compounds.[26]

"Over the two years, how much did I dispose of?" Poirier asked. "Christ. We used to go through 55 gallons in less than a month. So, you know, if I had to say a rough guess would be 100 gallons a month. . . . It was probably more. That's a conservative figure."[27]

At the time of the conversation in March 2013, Poirier was

battling esophageal cancer—one of the diseases that had been clearly linked to TCE. He died two months later at the age of fifty-eight. But while he was battling the cancer, Poirier had seen a report on NBC featuring Mike Partain and other former Lejeune residents who had been diagnosed with male breast cancer. The report aired in February 2013, and Poirier went online afterward and posted a rough apology.

"It is very difficult living with the tought that i took part in this ground polution and facing death from this cancer," he wrote without going back to correct his typos. "I joined the USMC to serve and protect, not to harm."[28]

In the interview with the AP reporter, Allen Breed, Poirier elaborated on his feelings. "I'm a religious person," he said. "I believe in the universe. I don't think it's a direct thing. But I have guilt, let's put it that way. I have guilt." Breed wrote that while Poirier knew he couldn't change the past, he had a final wish. "When judgment day comes, you know, I hope those people that suffered . . . realize that I didn't know what I was doing."[29]

16

CHANGING THE CULTURE

They think . . . because what they're doing is important
they can do any damn thing they want.
—REPRESENTATIVE JOHN D. DINGELL (D-MI)

No doubt the commandant of the Marine Corps, General
James Amos, had plenty on his plate in the spring of 2013.
Congress had made deep cuts in the Pentagon's budget, President
Obama had a firm plan for disengaging from the war in Afghanistan, new threats to national security were emerging from continued political turmoil in the Middle East, and, closer to home,
reports of sexual assault and abuse by members of the military continued popping up in the headlines, putting all the service commanders on the defensive about their enforcement of codes of
conduct. Still, it seemed at least remotely plausible that Amos, who
was expected to step down soon as commandant after more than
forty years in the Navy and Marines, might be able to spare twenty
or thirty minutes to discuss the decades-old saga of environmental

health issues at Camp Lejeune, which seemed finally to be moving into its closing chapters. Wrong. "I'm afraid the Commandant's schedule is booked up for the foreseeable future. Sorry about that," wrote Lieutenant Colonel Wesley Hayes in an e-mail on June 10, 2013, responding to a long-standing request for an interview with Amos about Camp Lejeune.[1]

Then again, the response from Hayes, the press secretary for the commandant, wasn't surprising. Whenever there has been any significant development in the investigations and studies of Camp Lejeune's toxic water, the Marine Corps inevitably has declined to comment—even when the *Washington Post* asked for a response to the report by the commandant's own panel essentially exonerating the Navy and Marines of any wrongdoing in addressing the pollution problems when they were first discovered. Occasionally, on specific issues, the Marines would issue a statement, but usually only in response to written questions. It was clear, too, that every official comment to the media had been carefully crafted and fully vetted by top brass, especially the Navy lawyers.

The military's discussions of Camp Lejeune on Capitol Hill were much the same—mostly characterized as a one-way street. Brooks Tucker, senior policy adviser for national security and veterans' affairs to the senior senator from North Carolina, Richard Burr, has been present at more than a dozen meetings between his boss and Marine Corps officials. Tucker, a former Marine officer, described one meeting on the Lejeune contamination that was opened by one of the Marine Corps attorneys—later identified as Robert Hogue, counsel to the commandant—with a firm pronouncement: "This is not a negotiation."

"They've been lawyered up for decades," Tucker said. "It's very hard once you have layers and layers of obfuscation—and more so for an institution that has integrity as its core—to come out and say we've been lying for forty years." During the decades that hazardous wastes were building up in some of the base water supplies, it was evident that environmental officials either at Camp Lejeune or in the Navy Facilities Engineering Command at Norfolk, Virginia, were not paying much attention to the problems, Tucker said. "I don't think anyone really wanted to acknowledge the elephant that was getting bigger," he said. "There was some turning a blind eye. The talking points were that they were very much concerned about the health issues, but they needed to wait for the science on this."

At the same time, Tucker said, "there was a fair amount of bullying going on," mainly directed at the federal scientists assigned to investigate the effects of Lejeune's pollution. And among those researchers at the Agency for Toxic Substances and Disease Registry, "there was a systemic governmental desire to not want to be confrontational with another government branch," he said. "Plus they're relying on the agency that caused the pollution to fund the studies."

Of course, concerns about potential liabilities, conservatively estimated to be at least several billion dollars, had a lot to do with the military's hard-line stance. Tucker said that at one meeting with Burr and others on Capitol Hill, the Marine Corps commandant asked rhetorically, "Do we want to open the treasury?" Lawyers at the Justice Department and the Defense Department were all on the same page with their legal strategy, Tucker said: "Delay, delay, delay." But as a former Marine, Tucker said he was disappointed by the institution's deep-rooted refusal to respond to the concerns of those who felt they had been harmed by Lejeune's pollution. "At some point at the mid-level, some of them could have pushed back on the way things were being done," he said. "I would hesitate to even call them Marines."

Brad Miller, the former Democratic congressman from North Carolina who had led investigations of the Lejeune pollution, also expressed dismay at the military's posture. "I was disappointed in the Marines and the Navy," Miller said:

There's a natural human tendency to try to minimize the harm your agency has done even if it was done before you were there. But they were not pursuing this with the eagerness and enthusiasm they should have. It was not so much covering up. But the liabilities seem so small in comparison to the loyalty they should have felt for their own people. They didn't come to Congress and say we have a problem and we need to compensate people. The push had to come from people like Jerry [Ensminger] and then Congress, and it was against the resistance of the Marine Corps and the Navy.

The Capitol Hill veteran, Democratic congressman John Dingell of Michigan, wasn't just disappointed in the military's response to its pollution problems—he was downright angry. "Those people down there [at Lejeune] are entitled to be safe when they serve their country and are entitled to have their family safe," Dingell said. "Lejeune isn't the only place. There's hardly a military base in this country that isn't effectively a Superfund site. Frankly we tore 'em up on it. And they were recalcitrant as hell and still are. We're gonna make them stop. There just has to be enough pain there."

Dingell added that he had been dealing with the military for decades on issues ranging from toxic waste to contract fraud. "They think . . . that because what they're doing is important they can do any damn thing they want. And that's not the case."

Sherri Goodman, who was deputy undersecretary of defense for environmental security during the Clinton administration, spent most of her eight years at the Pentagon in the 1990s pushing the military to address its contaminated sites. Goodman went on to become senior vice president and general counsel at CNA, a think tank in Alexandria, Virginia, that runs the Center for Naval Analyses and the Institute for Public Research. She said one of the most difficult challenges she faced at the Pentagon was changing old environmental standards that were deeply ingrained in the military's culture. "The practices of the twenties and forties and sixties were no longer appropriate," she said. It took the Navy time to understand that. Plus, Goodman said, "the Marine Corps at the time was not as accustomed as other services to getting complaints from their own. So the Lejeune case probably put the Marine Corps a little on the defensive."

Goodman pointed out that the military has now been moving in the right direction on environmental issues. It has even agreed to set aside land at some of its bases, including Camp Lejeune, to provide a buffer between its operations and nearby residents. "It helps build trust with communities," she said.

Still, nearly nine hundred Superfund sites are abandoned military facilities or industrial sites where defense materials have been produced, according to a recent federal report on environmental hazards in America. The threats from military sites range from toxic chemicals in groundwater to radioactive wastes buried at former nuclear weapons plants.[2]

Some communities near the sites have been dealing with increased health problems, premature deaths, and deep anxieties for years and years. Kelly Air Force Base in San Antonio was shut down in 2001, not long after it was labeled by the EPA as the "top priority" for cleanup in the state of Texas. To this day, neighborhoods surrounding the former base are dotted with purple crosses in front yards, signifying homes where someone has cancer. "We are dying day by day," longtime community resident Robert Alvarado Sr. told the *Los Angeles Times* in 2006. "I have kidney failure, my wife has thyroid cancer, my neighbor just died of breast cancer." Illnesses such as liver cancer, which has been confirmed by the Texas Health Department as occurring at twice the normal rate in several San Antonio neighborhoods, are the legacy of sixty years of solvents and wastes, such as TCE and battery acids, being dumped directly onto the ground. Kelly became the nation's first Air Force base in 1940 and at its peak was performing half the maintenance work on Air Force planes and equipment. By the time it was closed, TCE levels as high as 49,000 parts per billion were found on the base, and levels of between 10 and 100 ppb in the groundwater beneath 22,000 nearby homes.[3]

In some communities near military toxic sites, residents have used tactics like those of the Lejeune victims to try to force the government to address their problems. "I created this website to document what happened to me at George Air Force Base, and my 39-year quest to find out what I was exposed to," wrote a website manager in Jamestown, California, Frank Vera III:

> I now know that I am not the only one to suffer adverse health effects because of an exposure to environmental contaminants at George AFB.
>
> Over one hundred people have contacted me through GeorgeAFB.Info regarding health problems that these people, and their friends and family developed during and shortly after being stationed at George AFB. In some families, every child who was born at George AFB died before the age of twenty-four years, with some families experiencing the loss of up to four children. In other families, all but one of up to five family members, including adults, died at or shortly after leaving George AFB.[4]

The efforts by the Lejeune victims to demand justice seem to have had impacts nationwide. Lenny Siegel, head of the California-based Center for Public Environmental Oversight that has been monitoring cleanups at military and industrial sites since 1992, said he has seen a culture change among scientists addressing contamination issues like those at Camp Lejeune. "I know this from [National Academies of Sciences] panels I'm on—everybody's aware of Camp Lejeune," Siegel said. "There's a feeling of let's do this right. That means something has gotten across. . . . Maybe there's a new sensitivity."

Christopher Portier, who left as director of the ATSDR in the spring of 2013, acknowledged that he had been asked to move from the National Institute of Environmental Health Sciences in 2010 to help turn things around at the agency, which was facing heavy criticism during the George W. Bush administration for bowing to pressures from the military and from the industries in its studies. "In my three years at ATSDR the culture has undoubtedly changed," Portier said. "We've put in a large number of changes to force greater accountability, to speed up processes, and to ensure quality of the work that's going on."

Portier defended the agency's research on Camp Lejeune and other contaminated sites. "The people who work at ATSDR, regardless of what you might hear about them from outside, these people are very dedicated and very hard-working in every situation they work in," he said. "They really work very hard because it tears them up to see these communities going through struggles they're going through from some of the exposures they're looking at. So they've always tried to do their absolute best to address issues in every single community. I've worked with them day in, day out on hundreds of sites and I have never seen people so concerned and hard-working to get things out the door so communities can understand what's going on."

A new Public Health Assessment for Camp Lejeune, a new study of male breast cancer cases, and a study of the causes of death among Marines who were at the base while the water was contaminated were all expected to be completed by the end of 2013 or early in 2014, said Portier. In addition, the massive survey of health issues among hundreds of thousands of Marines stationed at both Camp Lejeune and Camp Pendleton would be done in 2014 or 2015.

None of the health studies ever would have advanced this far without the relentless pressure on the government from the victims of the contamination. "They are an amazing group of people," Portier said. "Their efforts have been remarkable. For lay public, for people who are not scientists, to have developed an understanding of what's going on to the degree that these folks have, to participate to the degree they have participated, and to challenge both ATSDR and the Marine Corps and the Navy to do their job appropriately the way they have is astonishing. I have never seen it before."

Portier added that the agency might never have realized the potential concerns about male breast cancer cases connected to Lejeune had it not been for Mike Partain's search for fellow victims. "The health study might have found the relationship," Portier said. "But I think the push by them to do a formal study to look at this issue, it clearly came from them and we would not be doing that type of study without their efforts."

"They're incredibly effective advocates and forceful individuals," agreed Richard Clapp, the veteran epidemiologist in Boston who worked with Jerry Ensminger and others on the ATSDR's Community Assistance Panel for years. "Jerry in particular is like a force of nature," Clapp said. "I have seen people like that in other communities. But this is an unusually effective group and the CAP is one of the most effective I've ever seen."

The Marine Corps—an institution revered in America for more than two centuries—may be indelibly stained by its response to the Lejeune contamination. "As more people learn the facts, the Marine Corps leadership will be left defending an untenable position," said former senator Elizabeth Dole of North Carolina. "Denying what happened at Camp Lejeune is a blemish on the Corps' unmatched reputation."

"There are former and retired Marines today who will tell you of how, when they served at the installation, they used to run the tap for five or ten minutes in the morning before the smell of gasoline would dissipate so they could draw what they thought was safe water to make coffee. That tells you something," she said. "It appears that no one in a position of leadership took any meaningful action." Dole noted that the Navy had its own standards for safe drinking water in the 1960s and 1970s, and they were ignored. "The extensive array of Marine Corps documents that Jerry Ensminger and his colleagues present on their website tells this story convincingly—and in the Corps' own words and on their own letterhead," she said, adding:

> The water contamination problem evolved—and got worse—over time. It was a local issue in the mid-1960s. Years later, once the issue found its way to Washington, DC, and the Pentagon, it became a problem for the Corps. And as the scope and potential cost of the problem—that the water had been contaminated for decades and involved hundreds of thousands of Marines and their families—became known, it then had to compete for space in an always-inadequate Marine Corps budget, to say nothing of the profound embarrassment it would cause the Corps.

Most damaging of all to the Corps was the sense of betrayal felt by many victims who had been promised that they were part of a family and that whatever happened to them, "the Marines take care of their own." The sense that the Marine Corps leadership had turned its back on their problems and, even worse, flat-out denied it was to blame was especially painful for men and women who had devoted big chunks of their lives to the service.

Sadly, the abandonment of service members has been a repeated theme in recent years throughout the US military. There was the 2005 Army cover-up of the fact that former National Football League star Pat Tillman was killed by friendly fire in Afghanistan. There was the 2007 scandal of shabby treatment for wounded war veterans at the Walter Reed Army Medical Center in Washington, DC. There were the myriad problems of mis-marked graves and lost remains at Arlington National Cemetery uncovered in 2010.

Nor was the Pentagon alone in its mistreatment of veterans and active-duty personnel. The Department of Veterans Affairs had a backlog of nearly 900,000 claims for disability benefits in 2012, according to the VA, and 19,500 of the veterans awaiting benefits died while their claims were pending, a study by the independent Center for Investigative Reporting found. The situation for Camp Lejeune victims was even worse. Senator Richard Burr was told by the VA in March 2013 that the law signed by President Obama the previous August, providing health coverage for veterans and family members made sick by the base pollution, would not be fully implemented until at least March 2014, and possibly not until 2015, because rules needed to be written for providing benefits to family members, or nonveterans. Burr threatened to try to freeze pay bonuses for VA leaders until the rules were in place.[5]

Among the Lejeune victims themselves in 2013, there was anger at leaders of the Marine Corps, frustration that studies of the contamination had gone on for so long, and occasionally a message of hopefulness amid so much pain and anguish.

"I'm not mad at the Marine Corps," said Jeff Byron, who is convinced that both of his daughters were harmed by the pollution at Lejeune. "I'm mad at the leaders of the Department of Defense who have known this since 1980." Byron expressed pride that his son joined the Marines even after what happened to his family. "We love the Corps," he said. "But then you find out the leadership did what they did. I feel like Jonah. I've been swallowed up and they've spit us out. Tell the Marine Corps leaders, they're damn lucky this wasn't two hundred years earlier," Byron said. "I wouldn't be talking to lawyers; I'd be getting my six-shooter. They allowed tens of thousands of children to become sick and had no moral fortitude to do anything about it."

"Once a Marine, always a Marine," said Tom Gervasi, who was based at Lejeune in the 1950s and diagnosed with breast cancer in 2003. "I have no problem with the Marine Corps other than the politics—the generals, the colonels, and others who lied. I was proud to serve. If I was eighteen or twenty years old again I would have no problem serving." Gervasi noted that he was granted full disability for his cancer in April 2013. "In the end I have won, to a degree," he said. "But I don't know how much time I have left. Each day is a struggle." Gervasi's days were truly numbered; he died on December 3, 2013, at age 77.

Mike Partain said in June 2013 that even though he had survived breast cancer to that point, the disease and the battle with the Marine Corps had taken a heavy toll. "By 2011 I felt like I was dying, was having panic attacks, from all the stress," he said. "I told Margaret the stress was killing me and asked for a divorce."

Tom Townsend, who believes that both his son and his wife died from exposure to the Lejeune contamination, also said he suffered bouts of depression, though for the most part his health was good for a man in his eighties. "I'd like to see the Marine Corps admit they covered up an environmental disaster and the Navy be required to compensate people, pay our claims," Townsend said. "I don't know why they did the cover-up. I guess maybe they were ashamed of what they did."

For Jerry Ensminger, the fight was far from over in mid-2013. He was keeping the pressure on Congress to demand a better response from the VA and to amend the new law named after his daughter so that it would declare a "presumptive disability" for all veterans who had suffered from health problems after spending time at Camp Lejeune, making them eligible for disability benefits without having to beg for help.

Ensminger, too, has strong feelings for the rank and file in the service. "Our motto is Semper Fi and the slogan 'We take care of our own' is still very much alive at the operating levels of the Marine Corps," he said. "But those very words only have meaning for the leadership of the Corps when they can benefit from it. They have done everything in their power not to do what was right."

Peter Devereaux, despite living with a death sentence after his breast cancer spread through his bones in 2009, maintained a remarkably upbeat attitude considering all that had happened to him. In 2012, he told his hometown newspaper, the *North Andover Citizen* outside of Boston, that he was already a year past the life expectancy his doctor had given him three and a half years earlier, and was doing everything he could to try to stay alive. "When you're first diagnosed, you feel like you've lost control," Devereaux said. "The one thing you can control is your attitude toward fighting the disease. I try anything that might work."[6]

On an early summer Saturday in 2013, Devereaux proudly proclaimed that he had just walked a mile and a half for the first time in years. "I constantly do treatment," he said. "Physically my body has taken a beating. I'm fifty-one now, but some days I feel like eighty."

There was still a flash of resentment and fury in Devereaux, though. "I would never recommend to anyone that they go into the Marine Corps, especially at Camp Lejeune, knowing how contaminated the bases are," he said. "I'm beyond pissed. The Marines are like a mafia."

He added, "I would like them to tell my daughter that her dad may not see her graduate."

EPILOGUE

The history of the Marine Corps is rich with stories of heroism, going all the way back to the American Revolution when John Paul Jones led brash attacks on British warships off the coasts of Ireland and England. At the beginning of the twentieth century, Major Smedley Butler earned two Medals of Honor fighting in Mexico and Haiti. During World War I, First Sergeant Dan Daly led his troops into battle under heavy fire at Belleau Wood in France, shouting "Come on, you sons-o'-bitches! Do you want to live forever?" In World War II, John Basilone, a machine gunner, was credited with taking out hundreds of Japanese at Guadalcanal before being killed by a mortar shell during the attack on Iwo Jima.

Such acts of valor would not be possible without total faith and trust in the military branches and their leaders. In the Marine Corps, especially, the institutional vows to leave no one behind and to care for each other as family remain the ideal, and loyalty

seems to be undiminished among the rank and file today. Love for
the service would have to be deep for so many to volunteer for
three or four or more tours of duty, most recently in Iraq and
Afghanistan.

After active duty ends, however, it is not clear how strong these
bonds remain, even for those who had stellar and lengthy careers.
Following World War II, returning troops were rewarded in part
with a fully paid education under the GI Bill, and the health care
and pensions that veterans receive seem to be the least the country
can do for those who have served. But for many, much more is
needed, and lately, in times of fiscal stress, the government has
been failing to respond.

The most dramatic signs of disregard for struggling veterans
came in 2007 when the *Washington Post* revealed shoddy and inadequate care for wounded warriors from Iraq and Afghanistan at
the Walter Reed Army Medical Center. Years later, despite prom-
ises by the Obama administration to do better, out of a backlog of
900,000 pending claims, more than half a million filed with the
Department of Veterans Affairs had seen no action for four
months or more. In August 2013, a petition signed by 26,000 veterans was sent to President Obama asking him to fire VA Secretary
Eric Shinseki for failing to eliminate the backlog.[1]

In the case of Camp Lejeune, the government hasn't just been
slow to respond to the victims of pollution at the base; it has stifled
and bullied and outright ignored them. Initially it was a story of
negligence: the Navy violating its own standards for drinking water, ignoring evidence of toxic contamination all over the Marine
base, and waiting for years before shutting down tainted wells after
lab tests showed there were problems. Then the Navy and Marine
Corps turned to dissembling, stonewalling, and obfuscation: failing to cooperate with ATSDR studies, refusing to notify people who
had been exposed to contaminants at Lejeune, coaching its people

on how to answer questions by investigators, and fighting hard against claims from victims seeking compensation.

Many of the victims of Lejeune's pollution have been as heroic in these instances as any warriors wounded in battle. In some cases, they have given up far more for their country than battle-scarred fighters—they have lost loved ones or seen them stricken with debilitating illnesses, or have had their own quality of life destroyed by cancer and other diseases. All they have asked in return is fair compensation for their losses or disabilities—suffering they would never have undergone had they not had the misfortune of being stationed at Lejeune when the water was contaminated. Yet they have had to fight for years to force their government to acknowledge that the military's mismanagement sickened or killed many people, and they have waited two decades for studies to be completed that would help determine the full extent of the damages.

In exposing the harm caused by the pollution at Camp Lejeune, the victims also helped thwart the military's reckless effort to obtain exemptions from environmental laws. Had that scheme succeeded, there is no telling how many more in the service would have been sickened by toxic wastes. There are hundreds of sites contaminated by the US military around the nation and the world, and much more investigation and cleanup—not less—are needed to ensure that people living and working on or near those installations are safe.

The Camp Lejeune contamination constitutes the largest and worst incidence of a poisoned water supply in history. Had a corporation been responsible, there would almost certainly have been a massive criminal complaint filed by the federal government, as the Justice Department did against Occidental Chemical Corporation after the Love Canal disaster in New York in the late 1970s, and as it did again against BP and its partners in the Gulf of Mexico after the 2010 explosion on the Deepwater Horizon drilling rig caused the biggest offshore oil spill in US history. In contrast, there have been only a few inconclusive investigations of the Marine Corps' misconduct at Camp Lejeune, and a push by Congress to require that some surviving victims of the pollution at least be provided with health insurance.

As this book was being completed in late 2013, a report was circulating through the ranks of Lejeune victims that the Marine Corps was seeking an "endgame" for the long-running saga of the base pollution and its effects. Presumably the military was hoping for something less than the conclusions already in sight—completion of all ATSDR studies and full implementation of the 2012 law guaranteeing health care for veterans and family members with illnesses linked to the base water. But twenty years after it began its studies at Lejeune, the ATSDR still had not released three promised studies on health problems caused by the pollution, and the VA still had not issued rules for providing health coverage to all Lejeune victims. If the "endgame" to the Camp Lejeune story falls short of complete health assessments and full compensation for victims, the result may become one of the most egregious betrayals of its citizens in American history.

NOTES

All quoted material not cited in the endnotes is from personal interviews conducted by the author.

1: THE MARINE CORPS FAMILY

1. This chapter is based on author interviews with Tom Townsend, 2013, and a written statement by Anne Townsend (in author's files).

2: LEJEUNE

1. Chapter 4, "Encroachment: MCB Camp Lejeune," in *Conserving Biodiversity on Military Lands: A Guide for Natural Resources Managers*, Conserving Biodiversity on Military Lands website, NatureServe, funded by the US Department of Defense Legacy Resource Management Program, 2008, www.dodbiodiversity.org/index.html; "North Carolina Natural Resources Inventory," North Carolina Heritage Program, North Carolina Department of Environment and Natural Resources, April 2013.

2. "Post of the Corps: Camp Lejeune, N.C.," *The Leatherneck*, October 1981.

3. J. Robert Moskin, *The U.S. Marine Corps Story* (New York: McGraw Hill, 1977), 682.

4. Allan R. Millett, *Semper Fidelis: The History of the United States Marine Corps* (New York: Macmillan, 1980), 276–285; Moskin, *U.S. Marine Corps Story*, 26–27.

5. Moskin, *U.S. Marine Corps Story*, 36–37.

6. Ibid., 54.

7. Ibid., 61–67.

8. Ibid., 89–90.

9. Millett, *Semper Fidelis*, 267–272.

10. Ibid., 271–277.

11. Major General John A. Lejeune, *The Reminiscences of a Marine* (Philadelphia: Dorrance and Company, 1930), 68–80.

12. Millett, *Semper Fidelis*, 322–324.

13. Chuck Lawliss, *The Marine Book: A Portrait of America's Military Elite* (New York: Thames and Hudson, 1988), 23.

14. Lejeune, *Reminiscences*, 321.

15. Moskin, *U.S. Marine Corps Story*, 207; Millett, *Semper Fidelis*, 322.

16. Millett, *Semper Fidelis*, 322–324.

17. Lawliss, *Marine Book*, 23; Millett, *Semper Fidelis*, 326–327.

18. Millett, *Semper Fidelis*, 328.

19. "Origins of Marine Corps Base Camp Lejeune," Cultural Resources Management: Marine Corps Base Camp Lejeune, Marines: The Official Website of the United States Marine Corps, www.lejeune.marines.mil/OfficesStaff/EnvironmentalMgmt/CulturalResources/HistoryLive/HistoryofCampLejeune.aspx.

20. Millett, *Semper Fidelis*, 348; Moskin, *U.S. Marine Corps Story*, 224–225.

21. "Origins of Marine Corps Base Camp Lejeune," US Marine Corps website.

22. "History," Marine Corps Base Camp Lejeune, Marines: The Official Website of the United States Marine Corps, www.lejeune.usmc.mil/visitors/history/.

23. David G. Thompson, "Memorandum in Regard to Ground-Water Supplies in the Vicinity of Jacksonville, North Carolina," United States Geological Survey, May 20, 1941; Harry E. LeGrand, consulting geologist, "Interim Report of Groundwater Conditions at Tarawa Terrace, Camp Lejeune, N.C.," April 2, 1959.

24. "Facts About Camp Lejeune," brochure, Public Affairs Office, Camp Lejeune, North Carolina, January 2000.

25. "Report to the Department of Justice on Disposal Practices at Camp Lejeune," Davis L. Ford and Associates, Austin, Texas, September 2009.

26. Interview with Danny Sharpe, Camp Lejeune Environmental Fact-Finding Group, June 2, 2004. All interviews cited as "Camp Lejeune Environmental Fact-Finding Group" interviews were conducted in 2003 and 2004 by a contractor for the United States Marine Corps for the Marine Corps Fact-Finding Panel, which released a report entitled "Drinking Water Fact-Finding Panel for Camp Lejeune: Report to the Commandant, U.S.M.C.," dated October 6, 2004.

27. Interview with Julian Wooten, Camp Lejeune Environmental Fact-Finding Group, May 30, 2004.

28. Sharpe interview.

29. Wooten interview.

3: "Baby Heaven"

1. Some of the quotations from the McLaughlins and other details of their story in this chapter are from Jo-Ann Moriarty, "N.C. Base Left Deadly Legacy," *Springfield (Mass.) Republican*, July 22, 2007.

2. The Stasiaks are quoted in Jo-Ann Moriarty, "Senators Seek to Alert Marines," *Springfield (Mass.) Republican*, August 12, 2007.

3. Maggie Gagnoni, letter to President George W. Bush, June 15, 2001, obtained through Freedom of Information Act request by Tom Townsend.

4. Quotations from Mary Freshwater in this chapter are from Cynthia McFadden, "Sick Families of N.C. Military Base Water Contamination May Finally Get Help, 30 Years Later," ABC News Nightline, June 28, 2012, http://abcnews.go.com/US/sick-families-nc-military-base-water-contamination-finally/story?id=16670758&singlePage=true.

5. Joan Lewis is quoted in Amanda Greene, "Family Attributed Health Problems to Bad Luck, But Now Think Lejeune's Water the Source," *Wilmington (N.C.) Star-News*, August 27, 2007, www.starnewsonline.com/article/20070827/NEWS/708270314.

6. "Statement of Sandra Carbone," Camp Lejeune Toxic Water: The Few, the Proud, the Forgotten, http://tftptf.com/CLW_Docs/Carbone_Story.pdf. For other statements, see www.tftptf.com/9401.html.

7. Terry Dyer, daughter of John Fristoe, is quoted in Richard Currey, "Troubled Waters: The Toxic Legacy of Camp Lejeune's Contaminated Water Supply," *The Veteran*, August/September 2004, www.vva.org/archive/TheVeteran/2004_08/feature_TroubledWaters.htm.

4: SOLVENTS!

1. Letter from Donald J. Guinyard, chief of water supply branch, Environmental Protection Agency, Region IV, to Commanding General, September 8, 1980.

2. Trihalomethane (THM) surveillance reports, William C. Neal, chief of laboratory services, Army Environmental Hygiene Lab, October 1980 to February 1981.

3. Interview with William C. Neal, Camp Lejeune Environmental Fact-Finding Group, July 7, 2004.

4. Results of water samples at Camp Lejeune, Jennings Laboratories, Virginia Beach, Virginia, October 31, 1980; interview with Wallace Carter, Camp Lejeune Environmental Fact-Finding Group, July 12, 2004.

5. Interview with Steve Azar, Camp Lejeune Environmental Fact-Finding Group, July 8 and 21, 2004; Government Accountability Office (GAO), "Activities Related to Past Drinking Water Contamination at Marine Corps Base Camp Lejeune," May 11, 2007, 23.

6. Interview with Elizabeth Betz, Camp Lejeune Environmental Fact-Finding Group, June 18 and 29, 2004.

7. Ibid.

8. Interview with Julian Wooten, Camp Lejeune Environmental Fact-Finding Group, May 30, 2004.

9. Interview with Danny Sharpe, Camp Lejeune Environmental Fact-Finding Group, June 2, 2004.

10. Memorandum by J. R. Bailey, Naval Facilities Engineering Command, "Suspected Chemical Dump, Rifle Range Area," May 8, 1981.

11. Memorandum by Elizabeth Betz, supervisory chemist, Camp Lejeune Quality Control Lab, Environmental Section, "Suspected Chemical Dump, Rifle Range Area," May 12, 1981.

12. GAO, "Activities Related to Past Drinking Water Contamination," 21.

13. US Department of the Navy, "A Primer on the Navy Installation Restoration Program," June 6, 1982.

14. Memorandum for the Record by Elizabeth Betz, supervisory chemist, Camp Lejeune Quality Control Lab, Environmental Section, "Phone Conversation with Mike Hargett on 6 May 1982," May 25, 1982, online at US Senate, Committee on the Judiciary, www.judiciary.senate.gov/judiciarydocs/CLHDW%20CDR%20Docs/Docs%20(PDFs)/2–1197/CLW/CLW%205176.pdf.

15. Memorandum for the Record by Elizabeth Betz, supervisory chemist, Camp Lejeune Quality Control Lab, Environmental Section, "Briefing Col Millice on April's Trihalomethane Analysis," May 25, 1982.

16. Bruce A. Babson, Grainger Laboratories, to "Commanding General," Camp Lejeune, "Analyses of Samples 206 and 207 from Site Coded 'TT' and Samples 208 and 209 from Site Coded 'HP'," August 10, 1982.

17. Interview with Bruce Babson, Camp Lejeune Environmental Fact-Finding Group, August 19, 2004.

18. Testimony of Michael C. Hargett, Hearing Before the House Committee on Science and Technology, Subcommittee on Investigations and Oversight, "Camp Lejeune: Contamination and Compensation, Looking Back, Moving Forward," September 16, 2010, transcript at US Government Printing Office, Federal Digital System, www.gpo.gov/fdsys/pkg/CHRG-111hhrg58485/html/CHRG-111hhrg58485.htm.

19. Memorandum from Elizabeth Betz, supervisory chemist, Camp Lejeune Quality Control Lab, Environmental Section, to Danny Sharpe, supervisory ecologist, Environmental Section, "Grainger Laboratories Letter of 10 August 1982," August 19, 1982; Betz interview.

20. Hearing Before the House Committee on Energy and Commerce, Subcommittee on Oversight and Investigations, "Poisoned Patriots: Contaminated Drinking Water at Camp Lejeune," June 12, 2007, transcript at US Government Printing Office, Federal Digital System, www.gpo.gov/fdsys/pkg/CHRG-110hhrg37793/html/CHRG-110hhrg37793.htm.

21. US Department of the Navy, Bureau of Medicine and Surgery, BUMED Instruction 6240.3B, September 30, 1963.

22. William R. Levesque, "No Evidence Marine Corps Conducted Critical Water Test at Camp Lejeune," *Tampa Bay Times*, February 3, 2013, www.tampabay.com/news/military/no-evidence-marine-corps-conducted-critical-water-test-at-camp-lejeune/1273599.

23. Captain Kendra N. Motz, media officer, Division of Public Affairs, US Marine Corps, "Marine Corps' Full Response to NBC News Regarding Water Contamination at Camp Lejeune," February 21, 2013.

24. Memorandum for the Record by Elizabeth Betz, supervisory chemist, Camp Lejeune Quality Control Lab, Environmental Section, "Results of 18 March 1982 Sampling of Suspected Chemical Dump," September 8, 1982.

25. Memorandum by Bruce Babson, Grainger Laboratories, "Analysis of Samples Received 12/2/82," December 9, 1982.

26. SCS Engineers, Reston, Virginia, "Final Report, Oil Pollution Survey for Marine Corps Base Camp Lejeune," March 31, 1977 (only the cover sheet is available).

27. Memorandum by J. G. Leech, Naval Facilities Engineering Command, "Recommended Corrective Actions for Remaining Known Wastewater/Oil Environmental Deficiencies," February 8, 1979.

28. Memorandum by J. G. Leech, Naval Facilities Engineering Command, "Monitoring of Leachate from Solid Waste and Chemical Landfills," September 7, 1978.

29. O'Brien and Gere, report to Naval Facilities Engineering Command, "Product Recovery System Design, Hadnot Point Fuel Farm, Marine Corps Base Camp Lejeune," October 1989.

30. Report by Cal Ingram, Naval Facilities Engineering Command, "Condition Survey, POL [Petroleum, Oil, Lubricants] Facilities, Camp Lejeune, North Carolina," June 27, 1980.

31. Wallace Eakes, Naval Facilities Engineering Command, "Trip Report for Water and Air Research at Camp Lejeune," March 7–21, 1982; Memorandum by J. R. Bailey, Naval Facilities Engineering Command, "Pesticide Analysis of Soil Samples, MCB Camp Lejeune," June 4, 1982.

32. Initial Assessment Study, NACIP Program, Camp Lejeune, Water and Air Research, Inc., for Naval Facilities Engineering Command, June 1982.

33. Memorandum by L. L. Scudder, Environmental Law Counsel, Office of Staff Judge Advocate, Camp Lejeune, "Hazardous Wastes," October 6, 1982.

34. Memorandum by J. G. Wallmeyer, Naval Facilities Engineering Command, "Official Telephone Call (outgoing)," November 22, 1982.

35. Environmental Protection Agency, National Priorities List Fact Sheet, Wurtsmith Air Force Base, February 2012; Environmental Protection Agency, Current Site Information,

Naval Air Development Center Warminster, January 2013; Agency for Toxic Substances and Disease Registry, Public Health Assessment, Willow Grove Naval Air Station, May 2002.

36. GAO, "Activities Related to Past Drinking Water Contamination," 64; Letter from Colonel M. G. Lilley, assistant chief of staff, Facilities, Camp Lejeune, to Charles Rundgren, chief of Water Supply Branch, North Carolina Department of Human Resources, Division of Health Services, December 12, 1983.

37. Memorandum from W. R. Price, Utilities System Operator General Foreman, to Director of the Utilities Branch, "Inadequate Raw Water Supply at Tarawa Terrace and Camp Johnson," March 30, 1983.

5: TROUBLE AT TARAWA TERRACE

1. Quotations from Jeff Byron and other details of his family's story in this chapter are from interviews with the author, 2013; "Statement of Jeff Byron," Camp Lejeune Toxic Water: The Few, the Proud, the Forgotten, http://tftptf.com/CLW_Docs/JeffByronStory.pdf; Jen Roppel, "Marine Seeks Answers in Lejeune Pollution Case," Cox News Service, October 2, 2002; Testimony of Jeff Byron, Hearing Before the House Committee on Energy and Commerce, Subcommittee on Oversight and Investigations, "Poisoned Patriots: Contaminated Drinking Water at Camp Lejeune," June 12, 2007, transcript at US Government Printing Office, Federal Digital System, www.gpo.gov/fdsys/pkg/CHRG-110hhrg37793/html/CHRG-110hhrg37793.htm.

2. The Ensmingers' story and quotations are from numerous author interviews; Lloyd Grove, "Semper Fi: Always Faithful: A Father's Searing Take on a Marine Corps Coverup," *Daily Beast*, April 24, 2011, www.thedailybeast.com/articles/2011/04/24/semper-fi-always-faithful-ensmingers-tribeca-film-on-a-marine-corps-cover-up.html; Testimony of Jerry Ensminger, Hearing Before the House Committee on Energy and Commerce, Subcommittee on Oversight and Investigations, "Poisoned Patriots: Contaminated Drinking Water at Camp Lejeune," June 12, 2007, transcript at US Government Printing Office, Federal Digital System, www.gpo.gov/fdsys/pkg/CHRG-110hhrg37793/html/CHRG-110hhrg37793.htm.

3. Interview with Rick Shiver, Camp Lejeune Environmental Fact-Finding Group, May 28 and June 25, 2004.

4. Environmental Science and Engineering, Inc., "Confirmation Study to Determine Existence and Possible Migration of Specific Chemicals in Situ," Marine Corps Base Camp Lejeune, May 1984.

5. "Environmental Study Kicks-Off," *The Globe*, Camp Lejeune, June 1984.

6. Shiver interview.

7. Memorandum by Elizabeth Betz, supervisory chemist, Camp Lejeune Quality Control Lab, Environmental Section, "Water Monitoring Related to the Installation Restoration Program," April 11, 1989.

8. Ibid.

9. Action Brief by M. G. Lilley, assistant chief of staff for facilities, Camp Lejeune, "Alternatives for Providing Water to the Tarawa Terrace Area," March 1, 1985.

10. Memorandum by Julian Wooten, director of environmental affairs, to assistant chief of staff, "Standards for Certain Types of Volatile Organic Compounds Found in Drinking Water Wells," March 11, 1985.

11. "Environmental Study Kicks-Off"; Florida Division of State Fire Marshal Report, Case No. 99–0110, January 8, 1999.

12. Major General L. H. Buehl, Camp Lejeune commanding general, "Notice to Residents of Tarawa Terrace," April 30, 1985.

13. Richard F. Smith, "Chemicals Discovered in Lejeune Water Wells," *Jacksonville Daily News*, May 10, 1985.

14. Donna Long and Shannon Brennan, "Base Closes Ten Wells; Wastes Found," *Wil mington (N.C.) Morning Star*, May 11, 1985.

15. Byron House Testimony.

16. Grove, "Semper Fi."

17. Ensminger House Testimony; Ensminger interview.

6: A PERILOUS MESS

1. New York State Department of Health, Office of Public Health, "Love Canal, Public Health Time Bomb," Special Report to the Governor and Legislature, September 1978, www.health.ny.gov/environmental/investigations/love_canal/lctimbmb.htm.

2. Government Accountability Office, "Superfund: Interagency Agreements and Improved Project Management Needed to Achieve Cleanup Progress at Key Defense Installations," GAO-10–348, July 15, 2010, www.gao.gov/new.items/d10348.pdf.

3. William Powell, "Remember Times Beach: The Dioxin Disaster, 30 Years Later," *St. Louis Magazine*, December 2012, www.stlmag.com/St-Louis-Magazine/December -2012/Remember-Times-Beach-The-Dioxin-Disaster-30-Years-Later/.

4. Memorandum from R. A. Tiebout, assistant chief of staff for facilities, Camp Lejeune, to commanding general, "Graphic Description of the Aquifer for Camp Lejeune and the City of Jacksonville," June 5, 1985.

5. Memo to File by Gold Johnson, utilities director, Camp Lejeune, June 21, 1985.

6. Memo from Bob Alexander, environmental engineer, Camp Lejeune, to Marine Corps headquarters, "Analyses of Camp Lejeune Water Supply," May 31, 1985.

7. Testimony of Thomas Sinks, Agency for Toxic Substances and Disease Registry, Hearing Before the House Committee on Energy and Commerce, Subcommittee on Oversight and Investigations, "Poisoned Patriots: Contaminated Drinking Water at Camp Lejeune," June 12, 2007, transcript at US Government Printing Office, Federal Digital System, www.gpo .gov/fdsys/pkg/CHRG-110hhrg37793/html/CHRG-110hhrg37793.htm.

8. US Geological Survey, Raleigh, North Carolina, "An Appraisal of the Ground-Water Resources of Camp Lejeune Marine Corps Base," August 14, 1985.

9. Letter from Charles Wakild, regional supervisor, North Carolina Department of Natural Resources and Community Development, to Major General L. H. Buehl, commanding general of Camp Lejeune, "Notice of Violation, Groundwater Classification and Standards," May 15, 1985.

10. Letter from Major General L. H. Buehl, commanding general of Camp Lejeune, to Charles Wakild, regional supervisor, North Carolina Department of Natural Resources and Community Development, "Notice of Violation, Groundwater Classification and Standards," July 19, 1985.

11. Jerry Allegood, "Civilians, Military Investigating Waste Dumps at Camp Lejeune," *Raleigh (N.C.) News and Observer*, September 15, 1985.

12. Memorandum from Chuck Wakild, regional supervisor, North Carolina Department of Natural Resources and Community Development, to Perry Nelson, chief of the groundwater section, "Mr. Larry Fitzpatrick's Inquiry, Groundwater Quality Problems, Camp Lejeune," October 8, 1985.

13. Rick Shiver, hydrogeologist, Wilmington Regional Office, North Carolina Division of Environmental Management, "An Assessment of Groundwater Pollution Sources at the Marine Corps Base Camp Lejeune," October 1985.

14. Memorandum from R. A. Tiebout, assistant chief of staff for facilities, Camp Lejeune, to commanding general, "State of North Carolina Data on Tarawa Terrace Water Supply Wells," November 6, 1985; Memorandum from Julian Wooten, director of environmental af-

fairs, Camp Lejeune, to Bob Alexander, environmental engineer, "Analysis of Drinking Water Systems Aboard Camp Lejeune," January 24, 1986.

15. Memorandum by Rear Admiral J. B. Finkelstein, US Navy chief of information, "Public Affairs Guidance—Hazardous Waste Site Cleanup," July 1, 1986.

16. Rick Shiver, notes on meeting at Camp Lejeune, July 31, 1986.

17. O'Brien & Gere, "Contaminated Ground Water Study, Hadnot Point Area, Marine Corps Base Camp Lejeune," December 1988; Minutes of Technical Review Committee meeting at Camp Lejeune, February 20, 1992; EPA Superfund Record of Decision, Camp Lejeune, EPA ID: NC6170022580, September 24, 1993; Site Management Plan for Camp Lejeune, prepared for the US Navy by Baker Environmental, Coraopolis, Pennsylvania, September 29, 1993; letter from L. L. Scudder, environmental law counsel, to the US Navy Judge Advocate General's office, Camp Lejeune, October 6, 1982; Environmental Science and Engineering, Inc., "Confirmation Study to Determine Existence and Possible Migration of Specific Chemicals In Situ," Camp Lejeune, May 1984.

18. Cheryl McMorris, North Carolina Solid Waste and Hazardous Waste Management Branch, "Site Inspection Report," ABC One-Hour Cleaners, May 27, 1987.

19. Letter from A. P. Tokarz, US Navy Judge Advocate General's office, to Lee Crosby, North Carolina Office of Attorney General, February 8, 1988; Environmental Protection Agency, Site Summary Profile, NCD024644494, ABC One-Hour Cleaners, updated April 2013.

20. Action brief by C. H. Baker, director of utilities branch, Camp Lejeune, "Environmental Concerns of Utilities Branch, Base Maintenance Division," March 15, 1988.

21. Environmental Science and Engineering, Inc., Feasibility Study for Hadnot Point Industrial Area, Camp Lejeune, "Description of Interim Alternatives," May 1988.

22. Memorandum by A. P. Tokarz, US Navy Judge Advocate General's office, to assistant chief of staff for facilities, Camp Lejeune, "Leaking Underground Storage Tanks; Gasoline Contamination in Hadnot Point Fuel Farm Area," March 29, 1988.

23. Memorandum from H. P. Scott, director, Naval Hospital at Camp Lejeune, to commanding general, "Installation Restoration Program," August 25, 1988; William R. Levesque, "Marine Corps Can't Find Records of Critical Tests," *St. Petersburg Times*, May 20, 2011, www.tampabay.com/news/military/marine-corps-cant-find-records-of-critical-tests/1170791.

24. Levesque, "Marine Corps Can't Find Records."

25. Letter from H. Kirk Lucius, chief of site investigation and support branch, Environmental Protection Agency, to assistant chief of staff, Camp Lejeune, "Characterization Step Report, Feasibility Study for Hadnot Point Industrial Area," September 29, 1988.

26. Environmental Protection Agency, Briefing Notes, Camp Lejeune Military Reservation, North Carolina, May 1988.

27. Colonel Dave Mundy, "Base Taps Into Drinking Water Concerns," *The Globe*, August 31, 1989.

28. Colonel Dave Mundy, "Measures Taken to Prevent Future Water Contamination," *The Globe*, September 14, 1989.

29. Environmental Protection Agency, National Priorities List (NPL), Site Narrative for Camp Lejeune Military Reservation, October 4, 1989.

7: THE STRUGGLE FOR DATA

1. Committee on Environmental Epidemiology, Board on Environmental Studies and Toxicology, and National Research Council, *Environmental Epidemiology*, vol. 1, *Public Health and Hazardous Wastes* (Washington, DC: National Academy Press, 1991), 92.

2. Sanford Lewis, Brian Keating, and Dick Russell for the Environmental Health Network

and National Toxics Campaign Fund, "Inconclusive by Design: Waste, Fraud and Abuse in Federal Environmental Health Research," May 1992, online at www.ejnet.org/toxics/incon clusive.html.

3. Testimony of Thomas Frieden, director, Centers for Disease Control, Hearing Before the House Committee on Science and Technology, Subcommittee on Investigations and Oversight, "Camp Lejeune: Contamination and Compensation, Looking Back, Moving Forward," September 16, 2010, transcript at US Government Printing Office, Federal Digital System, www.gpo.gov/fdsys/pkg/CHRG-111hhrg58485/html/CHRG-111hhrg58485.htm.

4. Letter from Nancy Sonnenfeld, epidemiologist, Agency for Toxic Substances and Disease Registry, to Neal Paul, Camp Lejeune, February 23, 1993.

5. Letter from Stephen Aoyama, environmental engineer, Agency for Toxic Substances and Disease Registry, to Neal Paul, Camp Lejeune, March 5, 1993; letter from Carol Aloisio, Office of Assistant Administrator, Agency for Toxic Substances and Disease Registry, to Yvonne Walker, Navy Environmental Health Center, September 2, 1994.

6. Letter from W. P. Thomas, commanding officer, Navy Environmental Health Center, to Commander, Naval Facilities Engineering Command, September 13, 1994.

7. Andrea Lunsford, head, Health Risk Assessment Department, Navy Environmental Health Center, "Medical Review of Initial Release of Public Health Assessment for U.S. Marine Corps Base Camp Lejeune," October 28, 1994.

8. Hearing Charter, Hearing Before the House Committee on Science and Technology, Subcommittee on Investigations and Oversight, "Camp Lejeune: Contamination and Compensation, Looking Back, Moving Forward," September 16, 2010, transcript at US Government Printing Office, Federal Digital System, www.gpo.gov/fdsys/pkg/CHRG-111hhrg58485 /html/CHRG-111hhrg58485.htm.

9. Agency for Toxic Substances and Disease Registry, "Public Health Assessment for U.S. Marine Corps Base Camp Lejeune," August 4, 1997.

10. Memorandum by Kelly Dreyer, public affairs manager, Marine Corps headquarters, "Study of Drinking Water Contamination and Childhood Cancer at MCB Camp Lejeune," August 29, 1997.

11. Mark Bashor's quotations throughout this section are from Letter and Report from Mark Bashor, associate administrator for federal programs, Agency for Toxic Substances and Disease Registry, to Elsie Munsell, deputy assistant secretary of the Navy, environment and safety, July 16, 1997.

12. Jeanetta Churchill, epidemiologist, Division of Health Studies, Agency for Toxic Substances and Disease Registry, "Request for OMB Review and Approval: Exposure to Volatile Organic Compounds and Childhood Leukemia Incidence at Marine Corps Base Camp Lejeune," July 1997.

13. Ibid.

14. Letter from Elsie Munsell, deputy assistant secretary of the Navy, environment and safety, to Mark Bashor, associate administrator for federal programs, Agency for Toxic Substances and Disease Registry, October 10, 1997.

15. Quotations throughout this section from epidemiologist Jeffrey Hyman at the Navy Environmental Health Center are from his "Review of Camp Lejeune—Childhood Leukemia Study Proposal," August 1997.

16. Government Accountability Office, "Activities Related to Past Drinking Water Contamination at Marine Corps Base Camp Lejeune," May 11, 2007, 7.

17. Agency for Toxic Substances and Disease Registry, "Volatile Organic Compounds in Drinking Water and Adverse Pregnancy Outcomes, United States Marine Corps Base Camp Lejeune," August 1998.

18. E-mail from Neal Paul, Camp Lejeune information officer, to Kelly Dreyer, Marine Corps public affairs manager, Washington, DC, October 23, 1998.

19. E-mail exchanges between Kelly Dreyer, Marine Corps public affairs manager in Washington, DC, and Kathy Skipper, chief of public affairs, Agency for Toxic Substances and Disease Registry, April 1999.

20. Department of Defense News Briefing, Colonel Michael Lehnert, November 1, 2000.

21. Robert Burns, "Marine Corps Warns of Camp Lejeune's Bad Water," Associated Press, November 2, 2000.

8: SLOW AWAKENING FOR THE VICTIMS

1. Quotations and details for Mike Gros in this chapter are from an author telephone interview with him in May 2013; Testimony of Mike Gros, Hearing Before the House Committee on Energy and Commerce, Subcommittee on Oversight and Investigations, "Poisoned Patriots: Contaminated Drinking Water at Camp Lejeune," June 12, 2007, transcript at US Government Printing Office, Federal Digital System, www.gpo.gov/fdsys/pkg/CHRG-110hhrg 37793/html/CHRG-110hhrg37793.htm; Lise Olsen, "Doctor Blames Marines for Illness; Base's Water May Be Tied to Cancer," *Houston Chronicle*, April 4, 2004.

2. Joan Lewis, telephone interview with author, April 2013; Amanda Greene, "Family Attributed Health Problems to Bad Luck, But Now Think Lejeune's Water the Source," *Wilmington (N.C.) Star-News*, August 27, 2007.

3. Louella Holliday, telephone interview with author, April 2013; "Statement of Louella D. Holliday," Camp Lejeune Toxic Water: The Few, the Proud, the Forgotten, http://tftptf.com/CLW_Docs/LouellaHollidayStory.pdf.

4. Quotations and details for Terry Dyer and Karen Strand in this chapter are from Terry Dyer, telephone interview with author, February 2013; Richard Currey, "Troubled Waters: The Toxic Legacy of Camp Lejeune's Contaminated Water Supply," *The Veteran*, August/September 2004, www.vva.org/archive/TheVeteran/2004_08/feature_TroubledWaters.htm.

5. Quotations and other details in this chapter for Sandra Carbone and Anita Roach are from telephone interviews in April and May 2013; "Statement of Sandra Carbone," Camp Lejeune Toxic Water: The Few, the Proud, the Forgotten, http://tftptf.com/CLW_Docs /Carbone_Story.pdf.

6. Jeff Byron's quotations and other details are from telephone interview with author, April 2013; Testimony of Jeff Byron, Hearing Before the House Committee on Energy and Commerce, Subcommittee on Oversight and Investigations, "Poisoned Patriots: Contaminated Drinking Water at Camp Lejeune," June 12, 2007, transcript at US Government Printing Office, Federal Digital System, www.gpo.gov/fdsys/pkg/CHRG-110hhrg37793/html/CHRG -110hhrg37793.htm; "Statement of Jeff Byron," Camp Lejeune Toxic Water: The Few, the Proud, the Forgotten, http://tftptf.com/CLW_Docs/JeffByronStory.pdf; Anna Griffin, "Camp Lejeune Veterans Haunted by Illnesses," Knight Ridder Newspapers, January 2, 2003, http://billingsgazette.com/lifestyles/health-med-fit/camp-lejeune-veterans-haunted-by-ill nesses/article_590a3878–4a86–5fae-8764-c2c32a2c0ebf.html; Jen Roppel, "Marine Fights for Answers," Cox News Service, October 2, 2002, www.yourlawyer.com/articles/title/marine -fights-for-answers.

7. Quotations from the Townsends are from Tom Townsend, telephone interviews with author in 2013; Anne Townsend, written statement (in author's files); Griffin, "Camp Lejeune Veterans Haunted."

8. Quotations from Jerry Ensminger in this chapter are from numerous author interviews; Lloyd Grove, "Semper Fi: Always Faithful: A Father's Searing Take on a Marine Corps Coverup," *The Daily Beast*, April 24, 2011, www.thedailybeast.com/articles/2011/04/24 /semper-fi-always-faithful-ensmingers-tribeca-film-on-a-marine-corps-cover-up.html; Testimony of Jerry Ensminger, Hearing Before the House Committee on Energy and Commerce, Subcommittee on Oversight and Investigations, "Poisoned Patriots: Contaminated

Drinking Water at Camp Lejeune," June 12, 2007, transcript at US Government Printing Office, Federal Digital System, www.gpo.gov/fdsys/pkg/CHRG-110hhrg37793/html/CHRG -110hhrg37793.htm.

9. "Survey of Childhood Cancers and Birth Defects at USMC Camp Lejeune, NC, 1968– 1985," July 16, 2003, Agency for Toxic Substances and Disease Registry, www.atsdr .cdc.gov/news/displaynews.asp?PRid=2068.

10. Testimony of Frank Bove, Hearing Before the House Committee on Energy and Commerce, Subcommittee on Oversight and Investigations, "Poisoned Patriots: Contaminated Drinking Water at Camp Lejeune," June 12, 2007, transcript at US Government Printing Office, Federal Digital System, www.gpo.gov/fdsys/pkg/CHRG-110hhrg37793/html/CHRG -110hhrg37793.htm.

9: EPA vs. DOD

1. M. Sittig, *Handbook of Toxic and Hazardous Chemicals* (Saddle River, NJ: Noyes, 1981); J. Fagliano, M. Berry, F. Bove, and T. Burke, "Drinking Water Contamination and the Incidence of Leukemia: An Ecologic Study," *American Journal of Public Health* 80, no. 10 (1990): 1209–1212.

2. Fagliano et al., "Drinking Water Contamination," 1209–1212.

3. Environmental Protection Agency, "Trichloroethylene Health Risk Assessment: Synthesis and Characterization," August 2001.

4. Ralph Vartabedian, "How Environmentalists Lost the Battle over TCE," *Los Angeles Times*, Part 1, March 29, 2006.

5. Ibid.

6. Ibid.

7. Environmental Protection Agency, "Review of Draft Trichloroethylene Health Risk Assessment: Synthesis and Characterization; An EPA Science Advisory Board Report," December 2002.

8. Vartabedian, "How Environmentalists Lost the Battle."

9. Paul Dugard, director of scientific programs, Halogenated Solvents Industry Alliance, commentary on White House Office of Management and Budget 2003 Draft Report to Congress on the Costs and Benefits of Federal Regulations, May 5, 2003.

10. E-mail from V. J. Cogliano to the author, June 9, 2005.

11. Paul Dugard, director of scientific programs, Halogenated Solvents Industry Alliance, memorandum to National Academy of Sciences panel on "Assessing the Human Health Risks of Trichloroethylene: Key Scientific Issues," November 16, 2005.

12. Shannon Cunniff, special assistant for emerging contaminants, US Department of Defense, "Summary of DoD, DOE, and NASA Science Issues Related to TCE," slides, February 10, 2006.

13. Jerry Ensminger, Statement to the National Academies of Sciences, April 20, 2005.

14. National Research Council, "Assessing the Human Health Risks of Trichloroethylene: Key Scientific Issues," June 2006.

15. Ralph Vartabedian, "Cancer Risk from Industrial Chemical Rises, Study Finds," *Los Angeles Times*, July 27, 2006, http://articles.latimes.com/2006/jul/27/nation/na-tce27.

10: THE PENTAGON TRIES FOR EXEMPTIONS

1. Memorandum from Paul Wolfowitz, deputy secretary of defense, to Secretaries of the Army, Navy and Air Force, "Consideration of Requests for Use of Existing Exemptions Under Federal Environmental Laws," March 7, 2003.

2. Ibid.

3. Hearing before the Senate Environment and Public Works Committee, "Environmental Laws: Encroachment on Military Training?" April 2, 2003, transcript at US Government Printing Office, Federal Digital System, www.gpo.gov/fdsys/pkg/CHRG-108shrg91745 /pdf/CHRG-108shrg91745.pdf.

4. Statement of Senator James Jeffords, "Camp Lejeune Survey of Childhood Cancers and Birth Defects," July 16, 2003.

5. Thomas Dail, "Water Study Review," *Jacksonville (N.C.) Daily News*, October 29, 2003.

6. Manuel Roig-Franzia and Catharine Skipp, "Tainted Water in the Land of Semper Fi; Marines Want to Know Why Base Did Not Close Wells When Toxins Were Found," *Washington Post*, January 28, 2004.

7. Thomas Dail, "Pentagon Delaying Notices," *Jacksonville (N.C.) Daily News*, February 16, 2004.

8. Press release, "Jeffords Seeks Expansion of Federal Study and Notification to Affected Marines About Camp Lejeune Drinking Water Contamination," February 10, 2004; Dail, "Pentagon Delaying Notices."

9. Manuel Roig-Franzia and Catharine Skipp, "Panel in Camp Lejeune Water Probe Criticized," *Washington Post*, March 12, 2004; United States Marine Corps, Division of Public Affairs, "Press Release: Commandant Appoints Independent Panel to Review Camp Lejeune Water Contamination Events," February 20, 2004, https://clnr.hqi.usmc.mil/clwater/Site/Articles/pr_2–20–04.html.

10. Roig-Franzia and Skipp, "Panel in Camp Lejeune Water Probe."

11. Testimony of Jerry Ensminger, Hearing Before the House Committee on Energy and Commerce, Subcommittee on Oversight and Investigations, "Poisoned Patriots: Contaminated Drinking Water at Camp Lejeune," June 12, 2007, transcript at US Government Printing Office, Federal Digital System, www.gpo.gov/fdsys/pkg/CHRG-110hhrg37793/html/CHRG -110hhrg37793.htm.

12. Ibid.

13. Richard Frandsen and Jerry Ensminger telephone interviews with author, May 2013.

14. Quotations through the end of this section are from Joint Hearing Before the House Committee on Energy and Commerce, Subcommittee on Commerce, Trade, and Consumer Protection and Subcommittee on Energy and Air Quality, "Current Environmental Issues Affecting the Readiness of the Department of Defense," April 21, 2004, transcript at US Government Printing Office, Federal Digital System, www.gpo.gov/fdsys/pkg/CHRG-108hhrg 93306/html/CHRG-108hhrg93306.htm; Richard Frandsen and Jerry Ensminger, telephone interviews with author, May 2013; Thomas Dail, "Military Dealt a Setback in Environmental Ruling by a House Committee," *Jacksonville (N.C.) Daily News*, April 30, 2004.

15. Eric Steinkopff, "Second Sewer Leak Elusive," *Jacksonville (N.C.) Daily News*, May 5, 2004.

16. Quotations from the June 24, 2004, hearing are from Eric Steinkopff, "Ex-Base Residents Want Wider Water Probe," *Jacksonville (N.C.) Daily News*, June 25, 2004, online at US Senate, Committee on the Judiciary, www.judiciary.senate.gov/judiciarydocs/CLHDW %20CDR%20Docs/Docs%20(PDFs)/1199–10257/9400_413%20AA%20USMC% 20250604.pdf.

17. Packard's meeting with Currey is recounted in Richard Currey, "Troubled Waters: The Toxic Legacy of Camp Lejeune's Contaminated Water Supply," *The Veteran*, August/September 2004.

18. All quotations from the panel's report are from "Drinking Water Fact-Finding Panel for Camp Lejeune, Report to the Commandant," US Marine Corps, October 6, 2004.

19. Manuel Roig-Franzia, "Water Probe Backs Marine Corps Defense," *Washington Post*, October 7, 2004.

20. Memorandum from Henry Falk, director, Agency for Toxic Substances and Disease

Registry, to Richard Frandsen, senior counsel, House Energy and Commerce Committee, September 30, 2004.

21. All quotations from this meeting are from Meeting Transcript, Expert Panel Meeting, February 17–18, 2005; Chris Mazzolini, "Experts Share Ideas for Bad-Water Study," *Jacksonville (N.C.) Daily News*, February 18, 2005.

22. Report of the Camp Lejeune Scientific Advisory Panel, Agency for Toxic Substances and Disease Registry, Atlanta, Georgia, February 17–18, 2005.

23. Martha Waggoner, "Panel: Lejeune Should Study Effects of Tainted Water on Thousands," Associated Press, July 1, 2005.

24. Chris Mazzolini, "Panel Eyeing Base Water Gets Plea to Expand Study," *Jacksonville (N.C.) Daily News*, February 2, 2006.

25. Chris Mazzolini, "Senate OKs Base Water Investigation," *Jacksonville (N.C.) Daily News*, June 24, 2006.

26. Ibid.

27. Both news releases are quoted in ibid.

28. Ibid.

11: Obstructed Justice?

1. The quotations in this chapter are from Transcript, Hearing Before the House Committee on Energy and Commerce, Subcommittee on Oversight and Investigations, "Poisoned Patriots: Contaminated Drinking Water at Camp Lejeune," June 12, 2007, US Government Printing Office, Federal Digital System, www.gpo.gov/fdsys/pkg/CHRG-110hhrg 37793/html/CHRG-110hhrg37793.htm.

12: "Florida Man Has Breast Cancer"

1. This chapter is based on Mike Partain, telephone interviews with author, 2012 and 2013; Robin Williams Adams, "Florida Man Has Breast Cancer," *Lakeland Ledger*, September 16, 2007, www.theledger.com/article/20070916/NEWS/709160466.

2. The stories by William R. Levesque eventually included "Camp Lejeune Vets Suffer from Drinking Water Contamination," *St. Petersburg Times*, May 29, 2009, www.tampabay.com /news/military/veterans/camp-lejeune-vets-suffer-from-drinking-water-contamination /1005564; "Male Breast Cancer and Camp Lejeune: Pollution or Coincidence?" *St. Petersburg Times*, June 27, 2009, www.tampabay.com/news/military/veterans/male-breast-cancer-and -camp-lejeune-pollution-or-coincidence/1013675; and "Hike in Camp Lejeune Male Breast Cancer Cases Expected, *St. Petersburg Times*, November 25, 2011, www.tampabay.com /news/military/veterans/hike-in-camp-lejeune-male-breast-cancer-cases-expected/1203436, among others. The *St. Petersburg Times* changed its name to the *Tampa Bay Times* in January 2012.

13: A Stone Wall Crumbles

1. Jo-Ann Moriarty and George Graham, "Sen. Kerry Pushes for Chemical Probe," *Springfield (Mass.) Republican*, August 1, 2007, www.masslive.com/chicopeeholyoke/republican /index.ssf?/base/news-10/1185955198167970.xml&coll=1.

2. Statement on the floor of the US Senate, Senator Elizabeth Dole (R-NC), July 17, 2007.

3. "Feds Gets Earful from Camp Lejeune Residents," WITN, Greenville, North Carolina, August 8, 2007, www.witn.com/home/headlines/9041482.html.

4. Ibid.

5. Ibid.

6. E-mail from Jerry Ensminger to Jennifer Walsh, media officer, National Academies of Sciences, November 30, 2007.

7. Gareth McGrath, "We Are Not Just Numbers in a Study," *Wilmington (N.C.) Star News*, November 18, 2007; Alyssa Litoff and Katie Hinman, "Sick Families of N.C. Military Base Water Contamination May Finally Get Help, 30 Years Later," ABC News Nightline, June 28, 2012.

8. Agency for Toxic Substances and Disease Registry, presentation to Camp Lejeune Community Assistance Panel, August 2007; Sarah Vos, "Chemical Linked to Parkinson's Disease," *Lexington (Ky.) Herald-Leader*, January 9, 2008.

9. Statement of John B. Stephenson, director, Natural Resources and Environment, Government Accountability Office, Before the House Committee on Energy and Commerce, Subcommittee on Oversight and Investigations, "New Assessment Process Further Limits the Credibility and Timeliness of EPA's Assessments of Toxic Chemicals," September 18, 2008, transcript at US Government Printing Office, Federal Digital System, www.gpo.gov/fdsys/pkg/GAORE PORTS-GAO-08-1168T/html/GAOREPORTS-GAO-08-1168T.htm.

10. Testimony of Lynn R. Goldman, professor of environmental health sciences, Johns Hopkins University, Bloomberg School of Public Health, Hearing Before the Senate Committee on Environment and Public Works, April 28, 2008, www.epw.senate.gov/public/index.cfm?FuseAction=Files.View&FileStore_id=61c327e8-77a4-4568-b4a3-9d34bc1d17ef.

11. Ibid.

12. Ibid.

13. Testimony of Jerry Ensminger, Hearing Before the House Committee on Science and Technology, Subcommittee on Investigations and Oversight, June 12, 2008.

14. Alison Young, "Exodus, Morale Shake CDC," *Atlanta Journal-Constitution*, September 10, 2006.

15. Rita Beamish, "Study on Camp Lejeune Toxic Water Continues with Navy Money," Associated Press, May 30, 2008; Jerry Ensminger, e-mail to Agency for Toxic Substances and Disease Registry and others, May 29, 2008.

16. Frank Bove and Perri Zeitz Ruckart, Agency for Toxic Substances and Disease Registry, "An Assessment of the Feasibility of Conducting Future Epidemiological Studies at USMC Base Camp Lejeune," June 23, 2008.

17. Ibid.

18. Presentation by Dr. Howard Frumkin, director, National Center for Environmental Health (NCEH) / Agency for Toxic Substances and Disease Registry (ATSDR), "Understanding the National Conversation Purpose and Process," n.d., copy attached to Jerry Ensminger, e-mail, April 8, 2009.

19. "Update to the 1997 Camp Lejeune Public Health Assessment," Agency for Toxic Substances and Disease Registry, May 8, 2009.

20. Ibid.

21. Ibid.

22. Letter from Agency for Toxic Substances and Disease Registry (ATSDR), sender's name redacted, to Rick Raines at Camp Lejeune, June 6, 1997.

23. Memorandum by Katherine Landman, Naval Facilities Engineering Command, Atlantic Division, to David McConaughy, Navy Environmental Health Center, July 21, 1997.

24. Ibid.

25. Letter from Robert C. Williams, director, Division of Health Assessment and Consultation, Agency for Toxic Substances and Disease Registry, to commanding general and brigadier general, Camp Lejeune, August 4, 1997.

26. Christopher Portier, former director of the Agency for Toxic Substances and Disease Registry, telephone interview with author, May 2013.

27. Ibid.

28. E-mails from Jerry Ensminger and Mike Partain to Thomas Sinks, deputy director, Agency for Toxic Substances and Disease Registry, May 7, 2009.

29. Rita Beamish, "False Comfort: US Pulls Report That Minimized Cancer Risk from Toxic Water at Marine Base," Associated Press, June 20, 2009.

30. The quotations from the National Research Council's study through the end of this section are from Committee on Contaminated Drinking Water at Camp Lejeune, National Research Council, "Contaminated Water Supplies at Camp Lejeune: Assessing Potential Health Effects," June 2009.

31. National Research Council, "Scientific Evidence of Health Problems from Past Contamination of Drinking Water at Camp Lejeune Is Limited and Unlikely to Be Resolved with Further Study," press release, June 13, 2009.

32. Senator Kay Hagan (D-NC), press release, June 16, 2009.

33. Senator Richard Burr (R-NC), press release, June 17, 2009.

34. Statement in response to National Research Council report, signed by Ann Aschengrau, Richard Clapp, and David Ozonoff of the Boston University School of Public Health; Daniel Wartenberg of the Robert Wood Johnson Medical School; and Sandra Steingraber of Ithaca College, June 17, 2009.

35. William R. Levesque, "Critics Say Marine Corps Contract on Camp Lejeune Is Conflict of Interest," *St. Petersburg Times*, November 6, 2009, www.tampabay.com/news/military /critics-say-marine-corps-contract-on-camp-lejeune-is-conflict-of-interest/1050032.

36. Ibid.

37. Quoted in ibid.

38. William R. Levesque, "Now 17 Veterans with Rare Cancer or Tumors with Camp Lejeune Ties," *St. Petersburg Times*, July 3, 2009, www.tampabay.com/news/military /veterans/now-17-veterans-with-rare-cancer-or-tumors-with-camp-lejeune-ties/1015699.

39. Ibid.

40. Abbie Boudreau and Scott Bronstein, "Male Breast Cancer Patients Blame Water at Marine Base," CNN, September 24, 2009, www.CNN.com/2009/HEALTH/09/24 /marines.breast.cancer/; Abbie Boudreau and Scott Bronstein, "Poisoned Patriots? Stricken Marines Seek Help with Illnesses," CNN, September 25, 2009, http://edition.CNN.com /2009/HEALTH/09/25/marines.breast.cancer.folo/.

41. Mireya Navarro, "Reversal Haunts Federal Health Agency," *New York Times*, November 30, 2009.

42. Senator Richard Burr (R-NC), press release, July 28, 2009; Barbara Barrett, "Toxins in Camp Lejeune Water 30 Years Ago Still a Problem," McClatchy Newspapers, January 28, 2010.

43. Kevin Maurer, "Navy Will Pay to Restudy Lejeune Water," Associated Press, December 5, 2009.

44. Barbara Barrett, "Lejeune Water Study Stalled," McClatchy Newspapers, February 14, 2010.

45. Kevin Maurer, "Report on Marines' Water Omitted Cancer Chemical," Associated Press, February 17, 2010.

46. Barbara Barrett, "Lejeune Water Probe: Did Marine Corps Hide Benzene Data?"

McClatchy Newspapers, March 9, 2010; Barbara Barrett, "Congress Seeks More Records on Camp Lejeune Tainted Water," McClatchy Newspapers, March 19, 2010.

47. William R. Levesque, "Marines Keeping Files Secret?" *St. Petersburg Times*, March 29, 2010.

48. All quotations from this hearing are from Transcript, Hearing Before the House Committee on Science and Technology, Subcommittee on Investigations and Oversight, "Camp Lejeune: Contamination and Compensation, Looking Back, Moving Forward," September 16, 2010, transcript at US Government Printing Office, Federal Digital System, www.gpo.gov/fdsys/pkg/CHRG-111hhrg58485/html/CHRG-111hhrg58485.htm.

49. Hope Hodge, "ATSDR Report Sheds Light on Extent of Lejeune Water Contamination," *Jacksonville (N.C) Daily News*, October 22, 2010.

50. Hope Hodge, "ATSDR: Lejeune Water 'Undoubtedly a Hazard,'" *Jacksonville (N.C) Daily News*, October 27, 2010.

51. Ibid.

14: Victims Unite

1. Roger Weeder, "Local Marines Die, Face Health Issues Years After Service at Camp Lejeune," *First Coast News*, Jacksonville, Florida, November 16, 2012.

2. Ibid.

3. Ibid.

4. Associated Press, "Ex-NC Marine's Disability from Tainted Water OK'd," October 29, 2009.

5. The story by Donna Koehn was "Tom Gervasi Drank, Cooked with and Cleaned with the Water at Camp LeJeune, and Now He Believes It Is Killing Him," *Sarasota Herald-Tribune*, November 25, 2012, www.heraldtribune.com/article/20121125/ARCHIVES/211251026.

6. Patrick Johnson, "Thomas McLaughlin of Hampden Got Cancer from Exposure to Contaminated Drinking Water While in Marines, VA Rules," *Springfield (Mass.) Republican*, June 12, 2010.

7. Testimony of Thomas Pamperin, Department of Veterans Affairs, Hearing Before the House Committee on Science and Technology, Subcommittee on Investigations and Oversight, "Camp Lejeune: Contamination and Compensation, Looking Back, Moving Forward," September 16, 2010, transcript at US Government Printing Office, Federal Digital System, www.gpo.gov/fdsys/pkg/CHRG-111hhrg58485/html/CHRG-111hhrg58485.htm; Transcript, Camp Lejeune Community Assistance Panel meeting, Agency for Toxic Substances and Disease Registry, Atlanta, Georgia, April 2, 2012.

8. Transcript, Camp Lejeune Community Assistance Panel meeting, April 2, 2012.

9. William R. Levesque, "Camp Lejeune Vets Suffer from Drinking Water Contamination," *St. Petersburg Times*, May 29, 2009, www.tampabay.com/news/military/veterans/camp-lejeune-vets-suffer-from-drinking-water-contamination/1005564; Jody MacPherson, post on chatboard, Taxlaw.com, November 29, 2008.

10. Lou Freshwater, blog post, Loufreshwater.com, August 17, 2012.

11. Barbara Barrett, "Message in Marines' Calendar: Breast Cancer Strikes Men, Too," McClatchy Newspapers, October 29, 2010.

12. Denita McCall, blog post, October 29, 2008, 7:08 a.m., www.tftptf.com/v-web/bulletin/bb/viewtopic.php?f=1&t=105&start=0.

13. Comments section from Veterans News Now website, under story by Robert O'Dowd, "Lejeune Health Survery Flawed," May 27, 2011, www.veteransnewsnow.com/2011/05/26/lejeune-health-survey-study-or-cover-up/.

14. Ibid.
15. Ibid.
16. Ibid.

15: The Way to the Oval Office

1. Opinion of Judge Keith Ellison, *Gros v. US*, United States District Court, Southern District of Texas, Houston Division, September 27, 2005.

2. Report of the US Navy Judge Advocate General to the American Bar Association, 2010 Annual Meeting, p. 9; Testimony of Pat Leonard, US Navy Judge Advocate General's office, Hearing Before the House Committee on Energy and Commerce, Subcommittee on Oversight and Investigations, "Poisoned Patriots: Contaminated Drinking Water at Camp Lejeune," June 12, 2007, transcript at US Government Printing Office, Federal Digital System, www.gpo.gov/fdsys/pkg/CHRG-110hhrg37793/html/CHRG-110hhrg37793.htm.

3. Associated Press, "Justices Won't Hear Camp Lejeune Water Case," June 8, 2009.

4. Anderson, Pangia & Associates, "Lawsuit to Be Filed Regarding Camp Lejeune Water Contamination," press release, July 1, 2009.

5. Quotations by Judge Boyle here and below are from Ruling by US District Judge Terrence W. Boyle, US District Court for the Eastern District of North Carolina, *Laura J. Jones v. United States of America*, February 23, 2010.

6. Ruling of the US Court of Appeals for the Eleventh Circuit, *Laura J. Jones v. United States of America*, March 14, 2012.

7. Complaint for personal injury under the Federal Tort Claims Act, *Sharon Kay Boling v. United States of America*, US District Court for the Eastern District of North Carolina, March 30, 2012.

8. Kent Faulk, "Trussville Parents Say Tainted Water at Camp Lejeune, N.C., Caused Children's Brain Cancer," *Birmingham (Ala.) News*, July 29, 2010; Complaint, *Joel Shriberg v. United States*, US District Court in the Eastern District of North Carolina, January 11, 2011; "Judge to Hear Lejeune Cancer Lawsuit," *Winston-Salem Journal*, April 16, 2011.

9. Laurie Villanueva, "Camp Lejeune Toxic Water Lawsuits Consolidated," February 15, 2011, News Inferno, www.newsinferno.com/camp-lejeune-toxic-water-lawsuits-consolidated/; Parker Waichman LLP, "Parker Waichman LLP Opposes U.S. Government Efforts to Have Camp Lejeune Water Contamination Lawsuits Filed by Former Marines Dismissed Under Feres Doctrine," news release, April 17, 2012.

10. Martha Waggoner, "Federal Agency Begins Survey About Lejeune Water," Associated Press, June 22, 2011.

11. Environmental Protection Agency, "Toxicological Review of Trichloroethylene," September 2011.

12. Louis Sahagun, "Industrial Solvent TCE Even More Dangerous to People," *Los Angeles Times*, September 30, 2011.

13. William R. Levesque, "Marines Won't Correct Booklet on Camp Lejeune's Tainted Water," *St. Petersburg Times*, February 9, 2011, www.tampabay.com/news/military/marines-wont-correct-booklet-on-camp-lejeunes-tainted-water/1150682; Hope Hodge, "USMC Pulls Controversial Water Contamination Booklet," *East North Carolina News*, July 23, 2011.

14. Letter from Major General J. A. Kessler, assistant deputy commandant for installations and logistics, Marine Corps headquarters, to Thomas Sinks, deputy director, Agency for Toxic Substances and Disease Registry, January 5, 2012; Lynne Peeples, "Camp Lejeune Water Contamination Cover-Up Hinted in Navy Letter," *Huffington Post*, January 13, 2012.

15. Hope Hodge, "New Lejeune Water Report Raises Watchdog Hackles," *Jacksonville (N.C.) Daily News*, January 20, 2012.

16. Letter from Robert E. Faye, Eastern Research Group, to Christopher Portier, director, Agency for Toxic Substances and Disease Registry, February 19, 2012.

17. Letter from Senator Richard Burr to Daniel Levinson, Office of the Inspector General, US Department of Health and Human Services, March 7, 2012.

18. Martha Waggoner, "US Senate Panel Hears About Camp Lejeune Water," Associated Press, March 13, 2012.

19. "In Defense Spending Bill, a Map Around Congressional Gridlock," *Washington Post*, January 4, 2011, www.washingtonpost.com/wp-dyn/content/article/2011/01/03/AR201101 0305667.html.

20. Barbara Barrett, "Hagan, Burr Push Anew to Help Camp Lejeune Water Victims," Mc-Clatchy Newspapers, February 3, 2011.

21. Martha Waggoner, "Vet's Plea for Help Ends Forum on NC Toxic Water," Associated Press, July 20, 2011; Environmental Working Group, "Cancer-Afflicted Marines Call on Obama for Support," news release, December 14, 2011.

22. Elizabeth Dole, "Congress and Camp Lejeune's Water," *Raleigh (N.C.) News & Observer*, January 10, 2012.

23. "Retired Marine Calls on Veterans Affairs to Help Poisoned Military Families," May 24, 2012, press release, Change.org.

24. Agency for Toxic Substances and Disease Registry, "Summary and Findings: Analyses and Historical Reconstruction of Drinking Water in the Hadnot Point and Holcomb Boulevard Water Treatment Plants Service Areas," January 2013; Franco Ordonez, "Scientists Confirm Marines' Poisonous Camp Lejeune Water Wells Date Back to Mid-Century," McClatchy Newspapers, March 15, 2013, www.mcclatchydc.com/2013/03/15/185993/scientists-confirm -marines-poisonous.html#.UjjMidKTguc.

25. Allen G. Breed, "After Nearly 30 Years, Camp Lejeune Coming Clean," Associated Press, May 18, 2013, http://bigstory.ap.org/article/after-nearly-30-years-camp-lejeune-com-ing-clean.

26. Allen G. Breed, "Marine Who Dumped Toxins Felt Illness Was Payback," Associated Press, May 18, 2013, http://bigstory.ap.org/article/marine-who-dumped-toxins-felt-illness -was-payback.

27. Ibid.

28. Quoted in ibid.

29. Ibid.

16: CHANGING THE CULTURE

1. Lieutenant Colonel Wesley Hayes, US Marine Corps headquarters, e-mail to author, June 10, 2013.

2. President's Cancer Panel, "Reducing Environmental Cancer Risk: What We Can Do Now," 2008–2009 Annual Report, US Department of Health and Human Services, April 2010, http://deainfo.nci.nih.gov/advisory/pcp/annualReports/pcp08–09rpt/PCP_Report_08–09_508.pdf.

3. Cat Lazaroff, "Contaminated Texas Air Base Blamed for Neighbors' Illnesses," Environmental News Service, May 4, 2000; Ralph Vartabedian, "Cancer Stalks a 'Toxic Triangle,'" *Los Angeles Times*, March 30, 2006; Steve Lerner, "San Antonio, Texas: Contamination from Kelly Air Force Base Is Suspected of Causing Sickness and Death Among Residents in Adjacent Latino Community," Collaborative on Health and the Environment, August 23, 2007.

4. "Frank Vera," in "Personal Accounts," George Air Force Base, CA: Hazardous Toxic and Radioactive Waste, www.georgeafb.info/personal-accounts/frank-vera.

5. Steve Vogel, "VA Struggling with Disability Claims," *Washington Post*, November 11,

2012; Aaron Glantz, "VA Number of Veterans Who Die Waiting for Benefits Claims Skyrockets," *Daily Beast*, December 20, 2012, www.thedailybeast.com/articles/2012/12/20/number-of
-veterans-who-die-waiting-for-benefits-claims-skyrockets.html; William R. Levesque, "VA
Blasted for Dragging Feet on Aiding Camp Lejeune Families," *Tampa Bay Times*, March 3,
2013, www.tampabay.com/news/military/veterans/VA-blasted-for-dragging-feet-on-aiding
-camp-lejeune-families/1277317.

6. Sally Applegate, "Living One Victory at a Time," *North Andover (Mass.) Citizen*, August
26, 2012, www.wickedlocal.com/northandover/news/x1733881279/Living-one-victory-at-a
-time.

Epilogue

1. Dana Priest and Anne Hull, "Soldiers Face Neglect, Frustration at Army's Top Medical
Facility," *Washington Post*, February 18, 2007, www.washingtonpost.com/wp-dyn/content/article/2007/02/17/AR2007021701172.html; Steve Vogel, "VA Struggling with Disability Claims,"
Washington Post, November 11, 2012; Steve Vogel, "Petition Calls for Obama to Fire VA Secretary Shinseki," *Washington Post*, August 21, 2013.

ACKNOWLEDGMENTS

Jerry Ensminger usually signs off on his e-mails with a quote from scholar James Bryant Conant: "Behold the turtle, he only makes progress when he sticks his neck out . . . " He and other former Marines, such as Tom Townsend, Jeff Byron, and Mike Gros—along with a true son of the Marine Corps, Mike Partain—have been sticking their necks out for years to demand justice and accountability from the Navy and the Marine Corps. Without their efforts, and their willingness to share their stories and information, this book would not have been possible.

Nor would it have come to fruition if not for the wise counsel and expert guidance of literary agent Ronald Goldfarb and editor Merloyd Lawrence, who both believed in this story from the beginning.

Finally, thanks to Denise, Sean, and Emma Rose for their patience, love, and understanding while I was focused on this book.

INDEX

ABOUT THE AUTHOR

MIKE MAGNER, author of *Poisoned Legacy: The Human Cost of BP's Rise to Power*, has been a journalist for nearly four decades. He is currently a managing editor at *National Journal* in Washington, DC. Magner first heard about Camp Lejeune's water contamination in 2004 and has been working on the story ever since. A native of South Bend, Indiana, and a graduate of Georgetown University, he and his wife, son, and daughter live in Arlington, Virginia.